THREE
SHREW PLAYS

THREE
SHREW PLAYS

The Taming of a Shrew
Anonymous

The Taming of the Shrew
William Shakespeare

The Woman's Prize, or
The Tamer Tamed
John Fletcher

Edited, with Introduction and Notes, by
Barry Gaines and Margaret Maurer

Hackett Publishing Company, Inc.
Indianapolis/Cambridge

For further information, please address
  Hackett Publishing Company, Inc.
  P.O. Box 44937
  Indianapolis, Indiana 46244-0937

  www.hackettpublishing.com

Cover design by Elizabeth L. Wilson and Brian Rak
Interior design by Mary Vasquez
Composition by William Hartman
Printed at Sheridan Books, Inc.

Library of Congress Cataloging-in-Publication Data
Three shrew plays / edited, with introduction and notes, by Barry Gaines and
Margaret Maurer.
       p. cm.
     ISBN 978-1-60384-184-9 (pbk.) — ISBN 978-1-60384-185-6 (cloth)
     1. English drama—Early modern and Elizabethan, 1500–1600.
   2. Husband and wife—Drama. 3. Scolds—Drama. I. Gaines, Barry,
   1942– II. Maurer, Margaret. III. Shakespeare, William, 1564–1616.
   Taming of the shrew. IV. Fletcher, John, 1579–1625. Woman's prize.
   V. Taming of a shrew.
   PR1263.T465 2010
   822'.30803543—dc22

                                                          2009040587

The paper used in this publication meets the minimum requirements of
American National Standard for Information Sciences—Permanence of paper
for Printed Library Materials, ANSI Z39.48–1984.

For Janet and Carl

CONTENTS

INTRODUCTION

The motive and method of this book

This book positions William Shakespeare's play *The Taming of the Shrew* (hereafter Shakespeare's *Shrew*) between two plays closely related to it, *A Pleasant Conceited History, Called the Taming of a Shrew* (hereafter *A Shrew*), a play printed anonymously in a 1594 quarto, and *The Woman's Prize, or The Tamer Tamed* (hereafter *The Tamer Tamed*), printed in the 1647 folio of plays by Francis Beaumont and John Fletcher and attributed to Fletcher. Whether or not this order corresponds to the order in which these plays were written and first played, it does reflect the order of their publication. Shakespeare's *Shrew* made its first appearance in print in the first folio (F1) of 1623. Since there is no clear evidence as to which play, *A Shrew* or Shakespeare's *Shrew,* is earlier,[1] we have chosen to follow the order of publication. Doing so also corresponds to the motive of this collection: Shakespeare's *Shrew* is at the center of the issue we have designed this book to address.

Shakespeare's *Shrew* has all the elements prized in his plays generally. It is intricately constructed and verbally rich. Its characters spring to life for readers and admit a wide range of interpretations on the stage. Yet the action from which its title derives, shrew-taming, is one that makes many readers and playgoers wince. It represents, with a level of emphasis that is Shakespeare at his dangerous best, a headstrong woman being subdued by the man she has been forced to marry. So compelling a representation of shrew-taming, like the anti-Semitic overtones of *The Merchant of Venice,* can be hard to applaud in a world where the oppressive attitude the play dramatizes is still prevalent and can have brutal consequences.[2]

This book offers readers a distinctive opportunity to engage with the ambivalence Shakespeare's play inspires. The anonymous *A Shrew* shares many elements with it but deploys them differently, and *The Tamer Tamed* is a sequel to it. These three plays engage in different ways

---

1. Contemporary references to either play may not have consistently distinguished "*a* shrew" from "*the* shrew" (Thompson 1–2).

2. See Boose, entirely, and Wayne (159–61) for evidence that references in shrew plays to controlling women by brutal means, including bridling, were not altogether figurative.

with the orthodoxy of Shakespeare's day that wives should be subject to their husbands. Having them together in a single volume, then, invites a comparison of Shakespeare's treatment of this orthodoxy to its handling in the other two plays. To further facilitate this comparison, we edit and annotate all three plays according to the same standards (so Shakespeare's play does not look more up-to-date than the other two), following the early texts of these plays in all places where we can understand them.[3] Many readers, who may scarcely notice any changes in *A Shrew* and *The Tamer Tamed*, will find this version of Shakespeare's *Shrew* somewhat different from the one they know, particularly in the scenes centered on Bianca and the complex intrigue whereby she is married to Lucentio.[4]

Three Shrew Plays poses a question that has been asked before—what makes Shakespeare's play so compelling? Is it more or less interesting, more or less palatable than other contemporary plays about shrew-taming? This book invites readers to reconsider the question on a (so to speak) level playing field.

A Shrew and Shakespeare's *Shrew*

For much of the time that editors considered the anonymous *A Shrew* as a play distinct from Shakespeare's, that is, since Edmond Malone's edition (1790),[5] they have focused on questions of authorship (did Shakespeare have a hand in writing it?) and the still unresolved dating question (which play is earlier?). Almost invariably, arguments about either issue have entailed judgments of the relative literary merit of the two plays, with the majority opinion since the early 1900s deeming *A*

3. These are usually the first printed versions of the plays, although an early manuscript of *The Tamer Tamed* offers readings we also use. See below, "The texts," and Livingston (xiii–xx).

4. The cover illustration of our book, William Holman Hunt's painting of Bianca as "the patroness of heavenly harmony" (3.1.5), focuses attention on her proficiency with the lute as a musical instrument, not the retaliatory weapon it is for the shrew.

5. In his edition of Shakespeare first published in 1723, Alexander Pope incorporated lines and whole Sly interludes from *A Shrew*, which he assumed was an earlier edition of Shakespeare's play. They remained parts of the standard text until Malone's edition.

Shrew inferior and not written by Shakespeare.[6] About twenty-five years ago, however, some commentators began to question that judgment, evaluating *A Shrew* "as a very early instance of the extraordinary theatrical complexity and dramatic multiplicity of the popular Elizabethan drama" (Holderness and Loughrey 17). This is also, of course, true of Shakespeare's *Shrew,* particularly in its F1 form. Indeed, with respect to two elements that the plays share, Shakespeare's *Shrew* is at least as provocatively untidy as *A Shrew.*

Besides the taming action, both plays include two other actions that intersect with the taming but unfold separately. One, the sister action, represents the courtship of the shrew's sister or sisters. The other is of a different kind—radically so, in that it represents both the taming and the sister actions as elements of a play, one performed as part of a trick perpetrated by a nobleman on a drunken tinker named Sly. Both the sister action and the Sly action appear less perfectly contrived in Shakespeare's *Shrew* than in the more fully integrated sequences of *A Shrew.*

In both plays, the shrew (Kate, Katherine, or Katherina) is courted and won in a single scene early in the play, wed in its middle scene, tamed by being denied such necessities as food and sleep, and finally wins a wager for her husband (Ferando in *A Shrew,* Petruchio in Shakespeare's *Shrew*) when she proves more obedient than the other brides. The playwright of *A Shrew* seems to have had his eye on this conclusion from the start, plotting an action involving the three women needed for the final scene's test. The shrew has two sisters, Phylena and Emelia, Phylena being more mild-mannered than the outspoken Emelia. In the wager scene in *A Shrew,* Kate's obedience is thus contrasted to two different examples of wifely defiance. Summoned to her husband, Phylena sends word that "She is something busy but she'll come anon" (14.60), whereas Emelia sends word "that she will not come, / An [if her husband has] any business, [he] must come to her" (14.74–75).

In contrast, the triadic test in Shakespeare's *Shrew* seems carelessly plotted. In Shakespeare's *Shrew,* the sister action is a complicated intrigue involving four men who might be supposed, in one way or another, to be rivals for Bianca. Eventually, one is persuaded to abandon his suit and goes off to find another bride, who becomes the shrewish woman in the final scene. In all, the sister action of Shakespeare's *Shrew* seems only belatedly adapted to set off the shrew's transformation.

6. Oliver (13–22); for a critique of arguments that Shakespeare's *Shrew* is superior, Marcus.

The Sly action of Shakespeare's *Shrew* seems even less involved with shrew-taming. Shakespeare's play opens with a nobleman who comes across the drunken Sly and orders his servants to dress Sly as a lord and tell him when he awakes that he has been asleep for many years and must have simply dreamt he was a tinker. The nobleman himself then assumes a role as one of Sly's servants and gets a servant boy to pretend to be Sly's wife. As these practices are set in motion, a company of players arrive and Sly is persuaded to defer taking his boy-wife off to bed and instead to watch the play. This scene then evolves into the beginning of the play performed for Sly, introducing Katherina and her sister Bianca, their father, and their suitors. The rest of Shakespeare's *Shrew* is this play-within-the-play. Sly and his entourage, having once interrupted the elaborate unfolding of the wooing intrigues (in our 1.2), never appear in the text again.

As with its handling of the sister action, the anonymous *A Shrew* connects the Sly action more explicitly to the taming. Sly interrupts the play four times to comment on it and even, at one point, tries to interfere with it. At last, he falls asleep, and when he awakes in the final scene, he reflects on what he thinks has been a dream by observing to the tapster who rouses him, "I know now how to tame a shrew" (15.15). It is an ending that offers obvious comic possibilities (the tapster who is eager to "go home" with him and "hear the rest that thou hast dreamt tonight" [15.19–20] may be looking forward to Sly's comeuppance as he tries to put his newfound knowledge to use), as well as one that might be played to suggest that only such a foolish sot could see any value in the kind of taming tactics the play demonstrates. In contrast, the Sly action in Shakespeare's play has no such narrative closure and no such potential for ironic reflection on the taming action. The nobleman's trick is established and then dropped. This element of Shakespeare's *Shrew* seems so odd that it has led some scholars to believe that Shakespeare's play originally included additional scenes that have been lost or deleted to simplify the staging of the play and reduce the number of players required to perform it (Wentersdorf; Hosley). The most vigorous arguments supporting the view that Shakespeare wrote additional Sly material for his play focus on the need for a final Sly scene or epilogue (Alexander). It is, in fact, the last scene of the anonymous *A Shrew* that is most often added to productions of Shakespeare's play. An advantage of having similarly edited texts of *A Shrew* and Shakespeare's *Shrew* together in this book is that readers have easy access to these scenes if they want to imagine any such possibility.

In this Introduction, however, we want to put forward another way to "read" or understand Sly in Shakespeare's *Shrew*. We suggest that Sly's connection to the play that is performed for him depends not on how he might react to it, but on how aspects of what the lord does to him are repeated, with variation, in the two actions that unfold around the shrew and her sister. For example, clothes and food are used to persuade Sly he is a lord, and the tamer uses both to control the shrew; and the lord's care of his hunting dogs is echoed in the imagery of falconry that the shrew-tamer uses to explain his method. An especially prominent connection of this kind involves changes of clothing: a boy becomes a lady by putting on a gown; the shrew-tamer comes to his wedding outrageously dressed; a traveler is outfitted as a duke or a rich merchant. Particularly notable is the change of clothing in the sister action, which closely parallels the trick the lord plays on Sly. Sly is costumed as a lord, while the lord assumes the guise of his servant; and one of the mild sister's suitors courts her in disguise as someone of lesser station while his servant assumes his identity.

The prominence of the word *gentle* in Shakespeare's *Shrew* reinforces the significance of the lord's trick to the two actions in the play performed for Sly.[7] As a verb (or verbal noun), *gentle* (*gentling*) might seem to refer to the same activity as *taming* in the sense of breaking the instinctive behavior of an animal to make it serve human needs. In fact, the *Oxford English Dictionary* (*OED*) does not acknowledge that usage until a century after the composition of Shakespeare's play. Rather, as noun, adjective, or verb, the word *gentle* in early modern English was applied more often and perhaps exclusively to the condition of being well-born or having the manners associated with the refinements of that condition. Just that degree of ambiguity in the word, however, made its usage potentially volatile in a society still hierarchically organized by birth. Originally applicable only to the distinction conveyed by heritage, the word by Shakespeare's day also described the behavior presumed in persons of that status, behavior that could conceivably be induced by training, or, with respect to instances most objected to by the gently born, impersonated by anyone (such as common players) with access to the clothing of their social betters. Instances of its use in Shakespeare's play are consequently provocatively slippery; and through this word, in these two different

---

7. *Gentle* or its variants (*gently*, *gentleman*) occurs only a handful of times in *A Shrew* but many more times in Shakespeare's *Shrew*, sometimes in contexts that toggle between its two senses, mild behavior and socially superior status (see 4.1.73–74, and compare *A Shrew*, 8.44). Submerged play on the word may be behind Petruchio's inappropriate dress in 3.2.104–105, which he justifies as "com[ing] to keep my word, / Though in some part enforcèd to digress." If the word he arrives to keep is *groom*, he digresses in dress from bridegroom to manservant, particularly one who cares for horses.

senses, the Sly action can be seen to have a relationship with both the sister action and shrew-taming.

In its apparently truncated form, the Shakespearean Sly action is like the overture to a musical performance, sounding themes on which the actions around the shrew and her sister will work variations. Like an overture, it concludes and does not recur, except in recollected passages in the movements that follow. Shakespeare's Sly action addresses not an issue about husbands and wives but one that focuses on assumptions about human behavior and human nature that are inherent in the two senses of gentling. The lord undertakes an action that, in one sense of the word, attempts to modify Sly's behavior; on another level, the lord's trick is suggestive of something that many in the early modern period would consider a threat to the order of things—a base-born person becoming the facsimile of a gentleman born.

Shrew-taming is an instance of gentling in the behavioral sense of the word, a sense that obviously echoes the Sly action. Katherina is forced to avoid certain foods and learns to speak in a way that pleases men, just as Sly is instructed in what to eat and drink and inquires of his boy-wife how to address her. But Shakespeare's play also considers gentling in the more daring sense of carrying out a complete imposture of the social status conferred by birth. The lord undertakes to make Sly believe he is gentle in this sense and that the life he remembers was a dream; and in the sister action of both plays a base-born man takes on the identity of one of his betters. Significantly, only in Shakespeare's *Shrew* does a base-born man court the sister.

When Lucentio and Tranio plot the masquerade in Shakespeare's *Shrew,* their exchange leaves ambiguous whose idea it is; but it is clear that Lucentio adds the element that Tranio "make one among these wooers" (1.2.384). Lucentio plans for his feigned self (Tranio) to marry Bianca with the consent of her father in order to prevent her marriage to someone else. Lucentio's refusal to spell out his "good and weighty" (1.2.385) reasons for adding this element to their plan directs attention to the unspoken consequences of Shakespeare's plot. Lucentio and Tranio project no ending to the ruse they undertake; and it is only the unexpected arrival of Lucentio's father that prevents Bianca's paternally sanctioned marriage to Tranio. But even after the masquerade is exposed, gentility would remain compromised. A married Bianca could be mistress in more than one sense in a household that includes both her husband and a man who has demonstrated his ability to take her husband's place.

In *A Shrew,* the change-of-status wooing occurs alongside a more straightforward wooing of the third sister; but in Shakespeare's *Shrew,* the complications of the switch are undiluted by any parallel wooing of another sister. The nuances and uncertainties that characterize this action[8] suggest that Shakespeare's play seems to consider the possibility that social distinction is not innate, that gentility can be made and unmade.[9] This implication in the sister action provides a considerable counterweight to shrew-taming, a feature of the play's design not to be undervalued. In Shakespeare's *Shrew* as printed in F1, an already somewhat gentled Sly seems reassured to learn that the play to be performed for him is deeper fare than tumbling tricks and "household stuff" (1.2.137).

Shakespeare's *Shrew* and *The Tamer Tamed*

Without doubt *The Tamer Tamed* is a sequel to Shakespeare's *Shrew* (though Fletcher may also have been influenced by *A Shrew*). Three characters reappear in *The Tamer Tamed* from Shakespeare's *Shrew*—Petruchio, Byanca, and Tranio. While *The Tamer Tamed* has nothing equivalent to the Sly action, it imitates the plot of Shakespeare's *Shrew* in having a double-action plot focusing on the marital fortunes of two sisters—Maria, who tames Petruchio, and Livia, the focus of a complicated courtship intrigue.

Despite these points of correspondence, treating *The Tamer Tamed* as a sequel to Shakespeare's play has been questioned because of two features of the later play: *The Tamer Tamed* is set in England, not Italy; and the characters who continue from Shakespeare's *Shrew* seem different from their counterparts in the earlier play (Ferguson 12). Since the late twentieth century, however, the relationship between the two plays has

---

8. Oliver detects evidence of Shakespeare's "change of mind" (10) in the sister action, noting how Hortensio's role as Bianca's suitor and Petruchio's friend seems to be taken over by Tranio. The effect, however imperfectly worked out, is that Tranio seems to be becoming what he is playing. Scene 4.3 involves another instance of this effect. Alone with Lucentio, Biondello addresses him as Cambio (his assumed-to-be-base-born name) and refers to Tranio as "my master" (4.3.1, 3). Lucentio concludes this scene alone, saying of Bianca, "It shall go hard if Cambio go without her" (4.3.132).

9. Of course, gentility may be undermined in a more easily conceivable and downright way: Tranio's assumed gentlemanly status admits him to moments of intimacy with Bianca with whom he, base-born, might father a gentleman who would be Lucentio's son.

been more frequently acknowledged, often to stress the degree to which
The Tamer Tamed exposes the misogyny of Shakespeare's play.[10]

How scholars frame the relationship of *The Tamer Tamed* to
Shakespeare's *Shrew* is, like many arguments for the connection between
A Shrew and Shakespeare's *Shrew,* affected by judgments about their relative merit; and the emphasis is generally on how the plays differ. Those
who consider Shakespeare's play superior to Fletcher's emphasize the differences in the setting and characters of the two plays. Those who judge
Fletcher's play to be superior stress how the later play answers or even
corrects the unenlightened attitudes of Shakespeare's play. Placed side by
side, however, and in edited texts that more closely follow the early texts
of each, these two plays appear related in a way that would be familiar
to early modern audiences and readers and that would render judgments
about relative merit less important than efforts to appreciate the wit of a
later artist who can imitate and vary the outstanding features of a work
by his predecessor. Many members of Fletcher's audience would have
been schooled on works like Ovid's *Metamorphoses* or, to name the ones
pointedly signaled in the two plays, Ovid's *Heroides* (Shakespeare's *Shrew*
3.1.28–35) or Vergil's *Aeneid* (*The Tamer Tamed* 2.2.36–48), poems that
took the material of an earlier master (Homer or Vergil) and used the
elements of his poems as a stimulus to invention.

In this light, the shifted setting of *The Tamer Tamed* seems a subtle
reminder of the Sly action of Shakespeare's *Shrew.* In Shakespeare's play,
after all, the players who perform for Sly are Englishmen traveling the
English countryside; and in the part of their play representing Petruchio's
taming of Katherina, they seem to revert to their English names and
manners. So it is more than merely formally true that both Shakespeare's
Shrew and *The Tamer Tamed* are set in England, with English manners as
their target. Nor is the absence of a Sly action in *The Tamer Tamed* any
proof that the play is not a sequel to Shakespeare's *Shrew.* Indeed, that
there is no Sly action in Fletcher's play may be evidence that he regarded
Shakespeare's Sly action as complete and constructed his own play as
its sequel. If *The Tamer Tamed* were imagined as a sequel performed for
Sly's entertainment the following night, it would have no more need of
scenes representing Sly than does Shakespeare's play after its play within
the play begins.

The Tamer Tamed develops Petruchio, Byanca, and Tranio out of elements in Shakespeare's *Shrew.* If Petruchio, who emerges in *The Tamer*

---

10. See Smith; Bergeron; Lidh; and Daileader and Taylor's Introduction
(15–25).

Tamed as a full-fledged tyrant, seems a simplification of his earlier self, it is a transformation the play explains as the consequence of his marriage to Katherina. With Byanca and Tranio, however, what may seem changes in their characters is a response to something more complicated, related to the issue of gentility that Tranio foregrounds in Shakespeare's *Shrew*.

A single line makes clear that Byanca in *The Tamer Tamed* is married (4.1.126), though her husband never appears. Byanca, restrained by neither husband nor father, instigates both of the play's actions, counseling Maria to resist and masterminding the device that dupes Livia's father and her old-man suitor. In this latter action, Byanca's agent is Tranio, with whom she has some unspecified relationship. It seems, however, to be taken for granted that Tranio has achieved something like the status to which he pretended in Shakespeare's *Shrew*. He is as much a gentleman as Petruchio, though he also seems to acknowledge Byanca as a mistress whose commands he obeys. These differences in Byanca and Tranio develop elements of their characters in Shakespeare's *Shrew*, particularly as F1 presents the play.

Two scenes in Shakespeare's *Shrew* focus on Bianca with her suitors: 3.1 and 3.4 (3.1 and 4.2 in the standard numbering). In both, speeches of Bianca and her suitors (in all texts of the play since the early eighteenth century) are assigned differently from F1's disposition of them.[11] The text of Shakespeare's *Shrew* printed here, following F1, invites readers to consider Bianca in these scenes in relation to the paradigmatic character on whom Shakespeare modeled her—Ulysses' wife Penelope, married but with no husband in sight, the woman whose chastity, silence, and obedience are the stuff of legend in two senses of the word: legend as exemplary tale, and legend as a story with no warrant beyond being often repeated. In Shakespeare's *Shrew*, the "philosophy" Bianca is learning "as [she] please[s herself]" (3.1.20) is Ovid's letter of Penelope to an absent Ulysses. Fletcher's play acknowledges the significance of this. *The Tamer Tamed* has Petruchio's new wife Maria accede to his threat to leave her by assuring him she will await his return as his "glad Penelope" (4.5.204), a promise he understands as a threat to have many lovers, undoing by night with one what she does in the day with another (4.5.205–207).

In representing Byanca and Tranio as collaborators in the intricate scheme to betroth Livia to the young man she loves, *The Tamer Tamed* seems alert to the liability inherent in the household that Lucentio in Shakespeare's *Shrew* will set up, one that includes his manservant Tranio, who once, in his role as Lucentio, suggested that Bianca "practice how to

11. Maurer, "The Rowe Editions" and "Constering Bianca."

bride it" (3.2.248) with himself. The Bianca of Shakespeare's *Shrew* has "never yet beheld that special face / Which [she] could fancy more than any other" (2.1.11–12); and no one, not even Tranio, in *The Tamer Tamed* is any more sure of her than her absent husband. She has a Penelope-esque ability to flirt with and frustrate men. Byanca is "the spirit that inspires 'em all" (4.1.87)—all of the women who withhold from men their rights as husbands until they concede the impropriety of brutality in marriage.

Spousal taming as spectator sport: A brief stage history of these plays

Philip Henslowe's account book records the performance of "the taming of A shrowe" on June 11, 1594, in the Newington Butts theater. Despite the indefinite article and evidence that at that time the Newington Butts was used by other playing companies besides Shakespeare's company the Chamberlain's Men, theater historians are inclined to think that this is a reference to Shakespeare's *Shrew,* not *A Shrew* (Miller, Cambridge edition 40). There is evidence that Shakespeare's play was a popular commodity or that it was performed at court in the late sixteenth or early seventeenth century in a letter (c. 1600) transcribed into a manuscript now in the Leicestershire Public Record Office. Its witty writer quotes a piece of advice he attributes to "That Earl of Arundel that last died" and then observes, "I am as far from following his counsel as he was from Petruccio's."[12] If "Petruccio's" is a reference to Shakespeare's play, it suggests that Petruchio, not Ferando, was the household word for the household activity about which men liked to joke. That *The Tamer Tamed* is so explicitly a response to Shakespeare's *Shrew* also supports the early popularity of Shakespeare's *Shrew*. A 1631 quarto of Shakespeare's *Shrew* advertises that it had been performed at both the Globe and Blackfriars (the indoor theater of Shakespeare's company), and there is a record of a performance for the court of Charles I in 1633.

There is also evidence in this early period, however, that both *A Shrew* and *The Tamer Tamed* were attracting attention. This suggests not only that the general idea of taming one's spouse was of continual

12. Evelyn Simpson (313) and others have thought the letter-writer may be John Donne. Arundel ultimately embraced the Roman religion of his wife Anne Dacre. The writer may have considered that evidence of Arundel's submission in marriage.

interest but also that there were audiences and readers who appreciated a variety of perspectives on the matter. The text of *A Shrew* was reprinted in 1596 and 1609. This level of publishing activity might reflect interest generated by performance of that play or of Shakespeare's play, of both plays, or of a conflation of the two. *The Tamer Tamed* was probably first performed in 1609 or 1610 by a boy's company at the indoor theater Whitefriars; and it was revised (in response to the censorship of the Master of the Revels) and revived in 1633 in performance by the King's Men, Shakespeare's company, though, of course, without Shakespeare (Daileader and Taylor 25–28).

There are better theatrical records after the Restoration. These establish Shakespeare's *Shrew* as among the first of his plays to be revived. A version of Shakespeare's *Shrew* may have been performed at the Theatre Royal in 1663–1664; but by 1667, the King's Company was playing not Shakespeare's *Shrew,* but an adaptation of it by John Lacey, *Sauny the Scot, or The Taming of the Shrew* (Haring-Smith 174). Though *Sauny* is closer to Shakespeare's *Shrew* than to *A Shrew,* Holderness and Loughrey are right to suggest that it may well have been influenced by the anonymous play (28). Sauny, the shrew-tamer's servant (Lacey's role), seems inspired by Sander, Ferando's servant.

Beaumont and Fletcher's plays seem to have appealed to Restoration audiences more than Shakespeare's. Daileader and Taylor suggest that the popularity of *The Tamer Tamed* might have inspired Lacey to revise Shakespeare's *Shrew* the way he did (28). This suggestion has merit. Lacey's adaptation echoes and outdoes the taming tactics in *The Tamer Tamed.* When Lacey's shrew Margaret decides to resist by not speaking, Petruchio attributes her silence to a toothache and summons a tooth-drawer. Subsequently, she pretends to be dead, a piece of business that recalls Maria's giving out that Petruchio has the plague and his retaliatory strategy of pretending to be dead. Lacey considerably simplifies the sister action, arranging it (like the sister action of *A Shrew*) to highlight a contrast between the shrew and her sister. He also includes a dialogue between the sisters in which Margaret begins to tutor Biancha in the ways of shrewishness, perhaps inspired by the dialogue between Byanca and Maria in *The Tamer Tamed.*

Further simplification of the multiple-action *Shrew* motivates adaptations after *Sauny.* The Sly business is developed into a short play of its own (*The Cobler of Preston*), and relatively undiluted shrew-taming becomes the focus of subsequent adaptations of Shakespeare's play. In *A Cure for a Scold,* the suitor of the shrew's sister has only one rival and none at all in the equally-if-not-more taming-obsessed *Catharine and Petruchio.* It is not until the late nineteenth century that Shakespeare's

Shrew is revived.[13] By then the text of Shakespeare's play itself had been influenced by adaptations that had themselves been influenced by *Sauny* (Maurer, "The Rowe Editions") and thus indirectly by *A Shrew* and *The Tamer Tamed*.

In the twentieth and twenty-first centuries, productions of Shakespeare's *Shrew* usually incorporate additional Sly material from *A Shrew* or eliminate Sly altogether.[14] Directors also stage the play in general and the final scene in particular to convey interpretive possibilities that seem inspired by *A Shrew, The Tamer Tamed,* and subsequent adaptations. Katherina is played to suggest she is like *A Shrew*'s Kate, who "turns aside and speaks," saying directly that she "will consent and marry [Ferando] / For I methinks have lived too long a maid, / And match him too, or else his manhood's good" (3.168–71); she is also played as recognizing the appeal of the mutual agreement of Maria and Petruchio in *The Tamer Tamed;* and some productions go in the direction of the increased brutality of *Sauny,* though generally not without signaling that the audience should not approve. In 2003 the Royal Shakespeare Company mounted a production of *The Tamer Tamed* in repertory with Shakespeare's *Shrew,* using casting and even renaming of characters across the two productions to enhance the sense of *The Tamer Tamed* as a needed response to Shakespeare's play (Daileader and Taylor 35).

Conclusion: Full disclosure

It must be obvious that we, the editors of this volume, both longtime teachers of Shakespeare's plays, consider Shakespeare's *Shrew* to be a wonderful play by all measures of quality, exclusive of the one (deemed spurious by some) that requires plays to hold a mirror up to society in order to improve it. Shakespeare's *Shrew* surpasses, in its poetry and intricacy of plot, the two other plays included here. Seeing all three together is an opportunity to take the measure of this judgment. Especially in its bold F1 design, Shakespeare's *Shrew* play is a formidable salvo in the always fascinating and ongoing debate surrounding the relationship between husbands and wives.

13. Two versions of *The Cobler* played in 1716, Charles Johnson's and Christopher Bullock's; James Worsdale's *A Cure for a Scold* opened in 1735; David Garrick's *Catharine and Petruchio,* in 1754 (Haring-Smith 12–22).

14. One of us was once asked to compose additional lines for Shakespeare's Sly (and refused).

The complexity of its language and structure (more visible in relation to the anonymous *Shrew* that it so much resembles or that so much resembles it) and the patriarchal orthodoxy it appears to endorse (to which *The Tamer Tamed* replies) are a powerful combination. Four centuries after its composition, it is still the basis of popular, often exhilarating theater. The rationale of this book is the realization that the anonymous *A Shrew* and Fletcher's *The Tamer Tamed* set it off (contextualize it, ignite it) in significant ways.

The texts

(1) *The Taming of a Shrew* (1594): The text of this anonymous play is based on the surviving quarto copy, now in the Huntington Library (Q1). A photocopy of that text is available in the 1998 Malone Society Reprint prepared by Stephen Roy Miller. Miller has also edited the quarto for The New Cambridge Shakespeare Early Quartos series. Two other quartos, based on Q1, were also published. We have modernized the spelling and punctuation of Q1.

(?) *The Taming of the Shrew* (c. 1592–1594): The text of Shakespeare's play has been edited continuously since the early eighteenth century. Our text is based on the 1623 first folio (F1), the first appearance of the play in print. We have used the Hinman Folio as our copy text and reconsidered and retained much of the folio text that has been emended by later editors. Our edition is in modern spelling with modern punctuation.

(3) *The Woman's Prize, or The Tamer Tamed* (c. 1609–1610): John Fletcher's response to Shakespeare's play was first published in the Beaumont and Fletcher first folio (F1) of 1647. A second folio (F2) was printed in 1679 and provides the text of the song at 2.6. The play also exists in a manuscript copy (MS) based upon an early prompt-book, the book of the play that was consulted by the theatrical company's bookkeeper. The manuscript appears to provide some words and phrases that were censored by the Master of the Revels for their religious or sexual content. The manuscript is also a Malone Society Reprint edited by Meg Powers Livingston.

George B. Ferguson published a critical old-spelling edition in 1966 that incorporates readings from the manuscript into the folio text. It remains the fullest treatment of the play. Fredson Bowers repeated Ferguson's work when he included the play in his multivolume *The Dramatic Works in the Beaumont and Fletcher Canon. The Woman's Prize* is printed in volume 4 of *The Dramatic Works*. Celia R. Daileader and Gary Taylor have edited the play for the Revels Student Editions, following the manuscript and demoting several scenes not in the manuscript to an appendix. Our edition stays closer to the folio text, although we incorporate some manuscript readings where the folio is deficient. We have modernized the spelling and punctuation. A modern edition with a two-page glossary may be found in Fischlin and Fortier.

WORKS CITED OR OF INTEREST

Alexander, Peter. "The Original Ending of *The Taming of the Shrew*." *Shakespeare Quarterly* 20 (1969): 111–16.

Beaumont, Francis, and John Fletcher. *The Dramatic Works in the Beaumont and Fletcher Canon*. Ed. Fredson Bowers. 10 vols. Cambridge: Cambridge University Press, 1966–1996.

Berek, Peter. "*Tamburlaine*'s Weak Sons: Imitation as Interpretation before 1593." *Renaissance Drama* 13 (1982): 55–82.

Bergeron, David M. "Fletcher's *The Woman's Prize*: Transgression, and *Querelles des Femmes*." *Medieval and Renaissance Drama in England* 8 (1996): 146–64.

Boas, Frederick S., ed. *'The Taming of a Shrew' Being the Original of Shakespeare's 'Taming of the Shrew.'* The Shakespeare Classics. New York: Duffield and Company, 1908.

———, ed. *Tragedy of Caesar and Pompey, or Caesar's Revenge*. Malone Society. Reprints. London: Oxford University Press, 1911.

Boose, Lynda E. "Scolding Brides and Bridling Scolds: Taming the Woman's Unruly Member. *Shakespeare Quarterly* 42 (1991): 179–213.

Bowers, Fredson, ed. *The Woman's Prize,* by John Fletcher. In *The Dramatic Works in the Beaumont and Fletcher Canon*. 4:1–148. Cambridge: Cambridge University Press, 1979.

Brandon, Richard. *The Confession of Richard Brandon the Hangman*. London: n. p., 1649.

Brooke, Tucker, ed. *Locrine,* by William Shakespeare. In *The Shakespeare Apocrypha*. Oxford: Clarendon Press, 1908. 37–65.

Bullock, Christopher. *The Cobler of Preston*. London: R. Palmer, 1716.

Cotgrave, Randle. *A Dictionarie of the French and English Tongues*. London: Adam Islip, 1611.

Daileader, Celia R., and Gary Taylor, eds. *The Tamer Tamed, or, The Woman's Prize,* by John Fletcher. Revels Student Editions. Manchester: Manchester University Press, 2006.

Dent, R. W. *Shakespeare's Proverbial Language: An Index*. Berkeley: University of California Press, 1981.

Ferguson, George B., ed. *The Woman's Prize or The Tamer Tamed: A Critical Edition,* by John Fletcher. The Hague: Mouton, 1966.

Fischlin, Daniel, and Mark Fortier, eds. *The Woman's Prize; or The Tamer Tamed,* by John Fletcher. In *Adaptations of Shakespeare: A Critical Anthology of Plays from the Seventeenth Century to the Present.* London: Routledge, 2000. 23–65.

Fletcher, John. *See* Beaumont, Francis, and John Fletcher.

Garrick, David. *Catharine and Petruchio.* London: J. and R. Tonson and S. Draper, 1756.

Gascoigne, George. *Supposes and Jocasta.* Ed. John W. Cunliffe. Boston: Heath, 1906.

Glapthorne, Henry. *Albertus Wallenstein.* In *The Plays and Poems of Henry Glapthorne,* edited by R. H. Shepherd. 2 vols. London: John Pearson, 1874. 2:1–80.

Grimal, Pierre. *The Dictionary of Classical Mythology.* Translated by A. R. Maxwell-Hyslop. Oxford: Basil Blackwood, 1986.

Haring-Smith, Tori. *From Farce to Metadrama: The Stage History of* The Taming of the Shrew, *1594–1983.* Westport, CT: Greenwood Press, 1985.

Hibbard, G. R., ed. *The Taming of the Shrew,* by William Shakespeare. New Penguin Edition. Harmondsworth: Penguin Books, 1968.

Hinman, Charlton, ed. *The First Folio of Shakespeare,* by William Shakespeare. New York: Norton, 1968.

Holderness, Graham, and Bryan Loughrey, eds. *A Pleasant Conceited Historie, Called The Taming of A Shrew.* Shakespearean Originals: First Editions. Hemel Hempstead, England: Harvester Wheatsheaf, 1992.

Hosley, Richard. "Was There a 'Dramatic Epilogue' to *The Taming of the Shrew?*" *Studies in English Literature, 1500–1900* 1 (1961): 17–34.

Houk, Raymond A. "*Doctor Faustus* and *A Shrew.*" *PMLA* 62 (1947): 950–57.

Johnson, Charles. *The Cobler of Preston.* London: W. Wilkins, 1716.

Jonson, Ben. *Epicoene, or The Silent Woman.* In *The Complete Plays of Ben Jonson,* edited by G. A. Wilkes. 4 vols. Oxford: Clarendon Press, 1981–1983. 3:121–222.

Lacey, John. *Sauny the Scott, or The Taming of the Shrew.* London: E. Whitlock, 1698.

Lidh, Todd. "John Fletcher's Taming of Shakespeare: *The Tamer Tam'd.*" *Journal of the Wooden O Symposium* 4 (2004): 66–80.

Livingston, Meg Powers, ed. *The Woman's Prize* by John Fletcher. Malone Society Reprints 172. Manchester: Manchester University Press, 2008.

———. "Henry Herbert's Censorship of Female Power in Fletcher's *The Woman's Prize.*" *Medieval and Renaissance Drama in England* 13 (2001): 213–32.

Malone, Edmond, ed. *The Plays and Poems of William Shakespeare.* 10 vols. London: H. Baldwin, 1790.

Marcus, Leah. "The Editor as Tamer: *A Shrew* and *The Shrew.*" In *Unediting the Renaissance: Shakespeare, Marlowe, and Milton.* London: Routledge: 1996. 101–31.

Marlowe, Christopher. *Complete Plays and Poems.* Ed. E. D. Pendry. London: Dent, 1976.

Maurer, Margaret. "The Rowe Editions of 1709/14 and 3.1 of *The Taming of the Shrew.*" In *Reading Readings: Essays on Shakespeare Editing in the Eighteenth Century,* edited by Joanna Gondris. Madison, NJ: Fairleigh Dickinson University Press, 1998. 244–67.

———. "Constering Bianca: *The Taming of the Shrew* and *The Woman's Prize, or The Tamer Tamed.*" *Medieval and Renaissance Drama in England* 14 (2001): 186–206.

———, and Barry Gaines. "Putting the Silent Woman Back into the Shakespearean *Shrew.*" In *Gender and Power in Shrew-Taming Narratives, 1500–1700,* edited by David Wootton and Graham Holderness. Basingstoke, England: Palgrave Macmillan, 2010. 101–22.

Maxwell, Baldwin. "*The Woman's Prize, or The Tamer Tamed.*" *Modern Philology* 32 (1935): 353–63.

McKeithan, Daniel Morley. *The Debt to Shakespeare in the Beaumont-and-Fletcher Plays.* New York: AMS Press, 1970.

Miller, Stephen Roy, ed. *The Taming of a Shrew.* Malone Society Reprints 160. Oxford: Oxford University Press, 1998.

———, ed. *The Taming of a Shrew: The 1594 Quarto.* New Cambridge Shakespeare. Cambridge: Cambridge University Press, 1998.

Moisan, Thomas. "Interlinear Trysting and 'Household Stuff': The Latin Lesson and the Domestication of Learning in *The Taming of the Shrew.*" *Shakespeare Studies* 23 (1995): 100–19.

Morris, Brian, ed. *The Taming of the Shrew,* by William Shakespeare. New Arden Edition. London: Methuen, 1981.

Nares, Robert. *A Glossary of Words, Phrases, Names, and Allusions in the Works of English Authors.* New Edition by J. O Halliwell and Thomas

Wright. Detroit: Gale Research, 1966. Originally published London: George Routledge, 1905.

Oliver, H. J., ed. *The Taming of the Shrew,* by William Shakespeare. Oxford Shakespeare. Oxford: Clarendon Press, 1982.

Onions, C. T. *A Shakespeare Glossary.* Enlarged and revised by Robert D. Eagleson. Oxford: Clarendon Press, 1986.

Ovid [Publius Ovidius Naso]. *Heroides, Amores.* Translated by Grant Showerman, revised by G. P. Gould. The Loeb Classical Library. Cambridge, MA: Harvard University Press, 2002.

Parker, Patricia. "Construing Gender: Mastering Bianca in *The Taming of the Shrew.*" In *The Impact of Feminism in English Renaissance Studies,* edited by Dympna Callaghan. Basingstoke, England: Palgrave, Macmillan, 2007. 193–209.

Peele, George. *The Arraignment of Paris.* Ed. Oliphant Smeaton. London: Dent, 1905.

Pope, Alexander, ed. *The Works of Shakespear.* 6 vols. London: Jacob Tonson, 1723–1725.

R., E., Gent. *The Experienced Farrier.* London: Richard Northcott, 1678.

Rowe, Nicholas, ed. *The Works of Mr. William Shakespear.* 6 vols. London: Jacob Tonson, 1709.

Royal Shakespeare Company. *The Tamer Tamed,* by John Fletcher. London: Nick Hern Books, 2003.

Rubinstein, Frankie. *A Dictionary of Shakespeare's Sexual Puns and Their Significance.* 2nd ed. New York: St. Martin's Press, 1995.

Shakespeare, William. *The Complete Works of Shakespeare.* Ed. David Bevington. 4th ed. New York: Longman, 1997.

Simpson, Claude M. *The British Broadside Ballad and Its Music.* New Brunswick, NJ: Rutgers University Press, 1966.

Simpson, Evelyn. *A Study of the Prose Works of John Donne.* 2nd ed. Oxford: Clarendon Press, 1962.

Smith, G. C. Moore, ed. *Tom Tyler and His Wife.* Malone Society Reprints. London: Chiswick Press, 1910.

Smith, Molly Easo. "John Fletcher's Response to the Gender Debate: *The Woman's Prize* and *The Taming of the Shrew.*" *Papers on Language and Literature* 31 (1995): 38–60.

Spenser, Edmund. *The Faerie Queene.* Ed. Thomas P. Roche, Jr. Penguin Classics. London: Penguin Books, 1978.

Stapylton, Robert. *The Slighted Maid.* London: Thomas Dring, 1663.

Sugden, Edward H. *A Topographical Dictionary to the Works of Shakespeare and His Fellow Dramatists.* Manchester: Manchester University Press, 1925.

Theobald, Lewis. *Shakepeare Restored.* New York: AMS Press, 1970. Originally published London: Francklin, Woodman, Lyon, and Davis, 1726.

Thompson, Ann, ed. *The Taming of the Shrew,* by William Shakespeare. New Cambridge Shakespeare. Cambridge: Cambridge University Press, 1984.

Tilley, Morris Palmer. *A Dictionary of the Proverbs in England in the Sixteenth and Seventeenth Centuries.* Ann Arbor: University of Michigan Press, 1950.

Wayne, Valerie. "Refashioning the Shrew." *Shakespeare Studies* 17 (1985): 159–87.

Wentersdorf, Karl P. "The Original Ending of *The Taming of the Shrew:* A Reconsideration." *Studies in English Literature* 18 (1978): 201–15.

Williams, Gordon. *A Dictionary of Sexual Language and Imagery in Shakespearean and Stuart Literature.* 3 vols. London: Athlone Press, 1994.

Worsdale, James. *A Cure for a Scold.* London: L. Gilliver, 1735.

THE TAMING
OF A SHREW

ANONYMOUS

[The Names of All the Characters

A tapster
A lord who disguises himself as the servant Simon or Sim
SLY, a drunken tinker
A boy who disguises himself as Sly's lady
A messenger
Players, others

In the play performed for Sly

ALFONSO, an Athenian merchant
KATE
PHYLENA } Alfonso's daughters
EMELIA
JEROBEL, Duke of Sestos
AURELIUS, his son, suitor to Phylena
VALERIA, his servant, who disguises himself as both a music teacher
    and the son of the Duke of Sestos
POLIDOR, a student in Athens, suitor to Emelia
CATAPIE, Polidor's boy
FERANDO, suitor to Kate
SANDER, his servant
PHYLOTUS, a merchant who disguises himself as Aurelius' father
A haberdasher, a tailor, servants including Will and Tom]

A PLEASANT CONCEITED HISTORY, CALLED THE TAMING OF A SHREW

[SCENE 1]

Enter a tapster, beating out of his doors Sly, drunken.

Tapster. You whoreson drunken slave, you had best be gone
    And empty your drunken paunch° somewhere else,   *belly*
    For in this house thou shalt not rest tonight. *Exit tapster.*
Sly. Tilly vally.° By crisee,° tapster, I'll   *nonsense / Christ*
    feeze° you anon.° Fill's t'other pot   *drive away, beat / immediately; soon*
    and all's paid for. Look you, I do drink it of mine own
    instigation. *Omne bene.*° Here I'll lie a while.   *"All good" (a toast?)*
    Why, Tapster, I say, fill's a fresh cushion° here.   *drinking-vessel*
    Heigh ho, here's good warm lying.

He falls asleep.

Enter a nobleman [Lord] and his men from hunting.

Lord. Now that the gloomy shadow of the night,   10
    Longing to view Orion's[1] drizzling looks,
    Leaps from th' antarctic world unto the sky
    And dims the welkin° with her pitchy° breath,[2]   *sky / darkening*
    And darksome night o'ershades the crystal heavens,
    Here break we off our hunting for tonight.
    Couple up° the hounds and let us   *leash together in pairs*
        hie° us home,   *hurry*
    And bid the huntsman see them meated° well,   *fed*
    For they have all deserved it well today.

---

1. Constellation of the hunter with belt and sword, associated with rain.
2. This is the first of more than a dozen examples of the playwright's direct borrowing from Christopher Marlowe, whose *Tamburlaine* and *Doctor Faustus* were wildly popular on the London stage. These lines are exactly those of the 1616 edition of *Doctor Faustus*. See Boas (Appendix 1) and Berek.

But soft,[3] what sleepy fellow is this lies here?
Or is he dead? See, one,° what he doth lack.   someone
Servant. My lord, 'tis nothing but a drunken sleep.   21
    His head is too heavy for his body,
    And he hath drunk so much that he can go no further.
Lord. Fie,[4] how the slavish villain stinks of drink.
    Ho, sirrah,[5] arise. What, so sound asleep?
    Go take him up and bear him to my house,
    And bear him easily for fear he wake,
    And in my fairest chamber make a fire,
    And set a sumptuous banquet on the board,°   table
    And put my richest garments on his back,   30
    Then set him at the table in a chair.
    When that is done, against° he shall awake,   anticipating the time
    Let heavenly music play about him still.
    Go, two of you, away and bear him hence,
    And then I'll tell you what I have devised,
    But see in any case you wake him not. *Exeunt two with Sly.*
    Now take my cloak and give me one of yours,
    All fellows now, and see you take me so,
    For we will wait upon this drunken man
    To see his count'nance° when he doth awake   face, expression
    And find himself clothed in such attire.   41
    With heavenly music sounding in his ears
    And such a banquet set before his eyes,
    The fellow sure will think he is in heaven.
    But we will be about him when he wakes.
    And see you call him "lord" at every word.
    [To one servant] And offer thou him his horse to ride abroad,
    [To another servant] And thou his hawks and hounds to hunt the
        deer,
    And I will ask what suits he means to wear.
    And whatsoe'er he saith, see you do not laugh,   50
    But still° persuade him that he is a lord.   continually

Enter one [Messenger].

---

3. This imperative exclamation is used throughout the play to indicate a pause
and shift of thought; "wait a moment."

4. Exclamation of disgust or reproach.

5. Form of address to male inferiors.

Messenger. And° it please your honor, your players be come   *if*
    And do attend your honor's pleasure here.
Lord. The fittest time they could have chosen out.
    Bid one or two of them come hither straight.°   *immediately*
           [Exit Messenger.]
    Now will I fit° myself accordingly,   *suit*
    For they shall play to him when he awakes.

      Enter two of the players [Sander and Tom] with
        packs at their backs, and a boy.

    Now, sirs, what store of plays have you?
Sander. Marry,[6] my lord, you may have a tragical or a   59
    commodity° or what you will.   *mistake for "comedy"*
The other.° A comedy, thou shouldst say. 'Souns,[7] thou'lt   *(i.e., Tom)*
    shame us all.
Lord. And what's the name of your comedy?
Sander. Marry, my lord, 'tis called *The Taming of a Shrew.* 'Tis a
    good lesson for us, my lord, for us that are married men.
Lord. The Taming of a Shrew, that's excellent sure.
    Go see that you make you ready straight,
    For you must play before a lord tonight.
    Say you are his men and I your fellow.
    He's something° foolish, but whatsoe'er he says,   *somewhat*
    See that you be not dashed out of countenance.   71
    And, sirrah, go you make you ready straight,°   *right away*
    And dress yourself like some lovely lady,
    And when I call, see that you come to me,
    For I will say to him thou art his wife.
    Dally° with him and hug him in thine arms,   *flirt*
    And if he desire to go to bed with thee,
    Then feign° some 'scuse° and say thou wilt   *pretend / excuse*
      anon.°   *soon*
    Be gone, I say, and see thou dost it well.
Boy. Fear not, my lord. I'll dandle° him well enough,   *tease*
    And make him think I love him mightily. *Exit boy.*
Lord. Now, sirs, go you and make you ready, too,   82
    For you must play as soon as he doth wake.

---

6. An interjection adding emphasis to the speaker's words.

7. A mild oath, an abbreviation of "by God's wounds." Also spelled "zounds."

Sander. O brave,° sirrah Tom, we must play before a foolish   excellent, fine
    lord. Come, let's go make us ready. Go get a dishcloth to make
    clean your shoes, and I'll speak for the properties.°   objects used in a play
    My lord, we must have a shoulder of mutton for a property,
    and a little vinegar to make our devil roar.[8]
Lord. Very well. Sirrah, see that they want° nothing.   lack

                              Exeunt omnes.

[SCENE 2]

*Enter two with a table and a banquet on it, and two other, with
Sly asleep in a chair, richly appareled, and the music playing.*

One. So, sirrah, now go call my lord, and tell him that all things
    is ready as he will'd it.
Another. Set thou some wine upon the board, and then I'll go fetch
    my lord presently.°   immediately
                              Exit.

Enter the Lord [as Simon] and his men [Will and Tom].

Lord. How now, what, is all things ready?
One. Ay, my lord.
Lord. Then sound the music, and I'll wake him straight,
       And see you do as erst° I gave in charge.   before
       My lord, my lord. He sleeps soundly. My lord.
Sly. Tapster, gi's° a little small° ale. Heigh ho.[9]   give us / weak
Lord. Here's wine, my lord, the purest of the grape.   11
Sly. For which lord?
Lord. For your honor, my lord.
Sly. Who I? Am I a lord? Jesus, what fine apparel have I got.
Lord. More richer far your honor hath to wear,
       And if it please you I will fetch them straight.
Will. And if your honor please to ride abroad,
       I'll fetch you lusty steeds more swift of pace

8. Early editors of this play suggested that in the religious mystery plays depict-
ing the passion of Christ, the sponge with vinegar and gall offered to Christ was
used against the Devil to make him roar.
9. An exclamation usually expressing sighing or yawning.

Than winged Pegasus[10] in all his pride
That ran so swiftly over the Persian plains.   20
Tom. And if your honor please to hunt the deer,
    Your hounds stand ready coupled at the door,
    Who in running will o'ertake the roe°   *small species of deer*
    And make the long-breathed° tiger broken-   *long-winded*
        winded.°   *out of breath*
Sly. By the mass,[11] I think I am a lord indeed. What's thy name?
Lord. Simon, and it please your honor.
Sly. Simon, that's as much to say "Si mi on" or "Simon." Put forth
    thy hand and fill the pot. Give me thy hand, Sim. Am I a lord
    indeed?
Lord. Ay, my gracious lord, and your lovely lady   30
    Long time has mournèd for your absence here,
    And now with joy behold where she doth come
    To gratulate° your honor's safe return.   *express joy at*

            Enter the boy in woman's attire.

Sly. Sim, is this she?
Lord. Ay, my lord.
Sly. Mass, 'tis a pretty wench. What's her name?
Boy. O, that my lovely lord would once vouchsafe°   *condescend*
    To look on me and leave these frantic fits,
    Or were I now but half so eloquent
    To paint in words what I'll perform in deeds,   40
    I know your honor then would pity me.
Sly. Hark you, mistress, will you eat a piece of bread?
    Come, sit down on my knee. Sim, drink to her, Sim,
    For she and I will go to bed anon.°   *immediately; soon*
Lord. May it please you, your honor's players be come
    To offer your honor a play.
Sly. A play, Sim? O brave.° Be they my players?   *excellent, bravo!*
Lord. Ay, my lord.
Sly. Is there not a fool in the play?
Lord. Yes, my lord.   50
Sly. When will they play, Sim?
Lord. Even when it please your honor; they be ready.
Boy. My lord, I'll go bid them begin their play.

10. Winged horse of the Greek gods.
11. Mild oath referring to the religious communion service; also at 2.36.

Sly. Do, but look that you come again.
Boy. I warrant° you, my lord, I will not leave you thus.   *assure*
                    Exit Boy.
Sly. Come Sim, where be the players? Sim, stand by
      me and we'll flout° the players out of their coats.   *mock*
Lord. I'll call them, my lord. Ho, where are you there?

[SCENE 3]

Sound Trumpets. Enter two young gentlemen
[Polidor and Aurelius] and a man°   *servant*
[Valeria] and a boy [Polidor's servant].

Polidor. Welcome to Athens, my beloved friend,
      To Plato's schools and Aristotle's walks;
      Welcome from Sestos, famous for the love
      Of good Leander and his tragedy
      For whom the Hellespont weeps brinish tears.[12]
      The greatest grief is I cannot, as I would,
      Give entertainment to my dearest friend.
Aurelius. Thanks, noble Polidor, my second self.
      The faithful love which I have found in thee
      Hath made me leave my father's princely court,   10
      The Duke of Sestos' thrice-renownèd seat,°   *court; throne*
      To come to Athens thus to find thee out;
      Which since I have so happily attained,
      My fortune now I do account as great
      As erst did Caesar when he conquered most.
      But tell me, noble friend, where shall we lodge,
      For I am unacquainted in this place.
Polidor. My lord, if you vouchsafe of° scholar's fare,[13]   *condescend to accept*
      My house, myself, and all is yours to use;
      You and your men shall stay and lodge with me.   20
Aurelius. With all my heart I will requite thy love.

12. Legendary Greek lover Leander nightly swam the Hellespont (the modern Dardanelles), the strait between Abydos in Asia minor and Sestos in Europe, to see his beloved Hero. The present distance is about a mile. Leander drowned in a storm; Hero then killed herself.

13. Scholars traditionally had meager food and lodgings.

Enter Signor Alfonso and his three daughters [Kate, Phylena, and Emelia].

But stay, what dames are these so bright of hue,
Whose eyes are brighter than the lamps of heaven,
Fairer than rocks of pearl and precious stone,
More lovely far than is the morning sun
When first she opes° her oriental° gates.   *opens / eastern*
Alfonso. Daughters, begone, and hie° you to the church,   *hasten*
And I will hie me down unto the quay°   *wharf*
To see what merchandise is come ashore. *Exeunt [Alfonso*
and his daughters.]
Polidor. Why, how now, my lord? What, in a dump°   *heaviness of spirit*
To see these damsels pass away so soon?   31
Aurelius. Trust me, my friend, I must confess to thee:
I took so much delight in these fair dames
As I do wish they had not gone so soon.
But if thou canst, resolve me what they be
And what old man it was that went with them,
For I do long to see them once again.
Polidor. I cannot blame your honor, good my lord,
For they are both lovely, wise, fair, and young.
And one of them—the youngest of the three—   40
I long have loved, sweet friend, and she loved me,
But never yet we could not find a means
How we might compass° our desired joys.   *achieve*
Aurelius. Why, is not her father willing to the match?
Polidor. Yes, trust me, but he hath solemnly sworn
His eldest daughter first shall be espoused
Before he grants his youngest leave° to love.   *permission*
And therefore he that means to get their loves
Must first provide for her if he will speed,°   *succeed*
And he that hath her shall be fettered° so   *shackled*
As good be wedded to the devil himself.   51
For such a scold° as she did never   *a woman addicted to abusive speech; shrew*
live;
And 'til that she be sped° none else can speed,   *satisfied; removed*
Which makes me think that all my labor's lost.
And whosoe'er can get her firm good will
A large dowry he shall be sure to have,
For her father is a man of mighty wealth
And an ancient citizen of the town.
And that was he that went along with them.

Aurelius. But he shall keep her still° by my advice.   *ever*
   And yet I needs must love his second daughter,   61
   The image of honor and nobility,
   In whose sweet person is comprised the sum
   Of nature's skill and heavenly majesty.
Polidor. I like your choice—and glad you chose not mine.
   Then if you like to follow on your love,
   We must devise a means and find someone
   That will attempt to wed this devilish scold—
   And I do know the man. Come hither, boy.
   Go your ways, sirrah, to Ferando's house.   70
   Desire him take the pains to come to me,
   For I must speak with him immediately.
Boy. I will, sir, and fetch him presently.°   *immediately*
           [Exit boy.]
Polidor. A man, I think, will fit her humor° right,   *disposition, temperament*
   As blunt in speech as she is sharp of tongue,
   And he, I think, will match her every way.
   And yet he is a man of wealth sufficient,
   And for his person worth as good as she.
   And if he compass° her to be his wife,   *achieve*
   Then may we freely visit both our loves.   80
Aurelius. O might I see the center of my soul
   Whose sacred beauty hath enchanted me:
   More fair than was the Grecian Helena
   For whose sweet sake so many princes died
   That came with thousand ships to Tenedos.[14]
   But when we come unto her father's house,
   Tell him I am a merchant's son of Sestos
   That comes for traffic° unto Athens here.   *trade*
   [To Valeria.] And here, sirrah, I will change with you for once.
   And now be thou the Duke of Sestos' son.   90
   Revel and spend as if thou wert myself,
   For I will court my love in this disguise.
Valeria. My lord, how if the Duke your father should

---

14. Helen, the epitome of female beauty, was the wife of Greek King Menelaus; she was abducted by Paris, son of King Priam of Troy (Tenedos). The Trojan War was fought over "Helen of Troy." This passage echoes Marlowe's famous description in *Doctor Faustus,* "Was this the face that launched a thousand ships?" (5.1.99).

By some means come to Athens for to see
How you do profit in these public schools°   *universities*
And find me clothèd thus in your attire?
How would he take it then, think you my lord?
Aurelius. Tush,[15] fear not, Valeria, let me alone.
But stay, here comes some other company.

Enter Ferando and his man Sander with a blue coat.[16]

Polidor. Here comes the man that I did tell you of.   100
Ferando. Good morrow, gentlemen, to all at once.
How now, Polidor. What man, still in love?
Ever wooing and canst thou never speed?°   *succeed*
God send me better luck when I shall woo.
Sander. I warrant° you, master, and° you take my counsel.   *assure / if*
Ferando. Why, sirrah, are you so cunning?
Sander. Who I? 'Twere better for you by five mark[17]
And° you could tell how to do it as well as I.   *if*
Polidor. I would thy master once were in the vein°   *mood*
To try himself how he could woo a wench.   110
Ferando. Faith, I am even now a-going.
Sander. I'faith, sir, my master's going to this gear° now.   *business*
Polidor. Whither, in faith, Ferando? Tell me true.
Ferando. To bonny° Kate, the patientest wench alive.   *lovely*
The devil himself dares scarce venture to woo her:
Signor Alfonso's eldest daughter.
And he hath promised me six thousand crowns[18]
If I can win her once to be my wife.
And she and I must woo with scolding° sure,   *loud, ranting talk*
And I will hold her to't 'til she be weary,   120
Or else I'll make her yield to grant me love.
Polidor. How like you this, Aurelius? I think he knew
Our minds before we sent to him.
But tell me, when do you mean to speak with her?

15. An exclamation of impatience or scoffing.
16. The traditional clothing for an Elizabethan servant.
17. A mark was not a coin but a monetary unit equal in value to two-thirds of a pound of pure silver—the pound sterling that is the basis of the English monetary system.
18. A crown was equal to one-quarter pound sterling.

Ferando. Faith, presently. Do you but stand aside
    And I will make her father bring her hither,°   *here*
    And she and I and he will talk alone.
Polidor. With all our hearts. Come, Aurelius,
    Let us be gone and leave him here alone. *Exeunt [all but*
        Ferando.]
Ferando. Ho, Signor Alfonso. Who's within there?   130

[Enter Alfonso.]

Alfonso. Signor Ferando, you're welcome heartily.
    You are a stranger, sir, unto my house.
    Hark you, sir, look: what I did promise you
    I'll perform—if you get my daughter's love.
Ferando. Then when I have talked a word or two with her,
    Do you step in and give her hand to me
    And tell her when the marriage day shall be—
    For I do know she would be married fain.°   *willingly*
    And when our nuptial rites be once performed,
    Let me alone to tame her well enough.   140
    Now call her forth that I may speak with her.

Enter Kate.

Alfonso. Ha, Kate, come hither, wench,° and   *endearing form of address*
    list° to me: *listen*
    Use this gentleman friendly as thou canst. *[Exit Alfonso.]*
Ferando. Twenty good morrows to my lovely Kate.
Kate. You jest I am sure. Is she yours already?
Ferando. I tell thee Kate, I know thou lov'st me well.
Kate. The devil you do. Who told you so?
Ferando. My mind, sweet Kate, doth say I am the man
    Must wed and bed and marry bonny Kate.
Kate. Was ever seen so gross an ass as this?   150
Ferando. Ay, to stand so long and never get a kiss. *[He holds her.]*
Kate. Hands off, I say, and get you from this place,
    Or I will set my ten commandments° in your face. *ten fingernails*
Ferando. I prithee,° do Kate; they say thou art a shrew, *I pray thee, please*
    And I like thee the better for I would have thee so.
Kate. Let go my hand for fear it reach your ear.
Ferando. No, Kate, this hand is mine and I thy love.
Kate. In faith, sir, no; the woodcock wants his tail.

Ferando. But yet his bill will serve if the other fail.[19]

[Enter Alfonso.]

Alfonso. How now, Ferando, what says my daughter?   160
Ferando. She's willing, sir, and loves me as her life.
Kate. 'Tis for your skin then, but not to be your wife.[20]
Alfonso. Come hither, Kate, and let me give thy hand
    To him that I have chosen for thy love,
    And thou tomorrow shalt be wed to him.
Kate. Why, father, what do you mean to do with me?
    To give me thus unto this brainsick° man   demented
    That in his mood cares not to murder me? *She turns aside*
      and speaks.
    But yet I will consent and marry him,
    For I methinks have lived too long a maid,   170
    And match him, too, or else his manhood's good.[21]
Alfonso. Give me thy hand. Ferando loves thee well
    And will with wealth and ease maintain thy state.
    Here, Ferando, take her for thy wife,
    And Sunday next shall be your wedding day.
Ferando. Why so, did I not tell thee I should be the man?
    Father, I leave my lovely Kate with you.
    Provide yourselves against° our marriage day,   *in anticipation of*
    For I must hie° me to my country house   *hurry*
    In haste to see provision may be made   180
    To entertain my Kate when she doth come.
Alfonso. Do so. Come, Kate, why dost thou look so sad?
    Be merry, wench, thy wedding day's at hand.
    Son, fare you well and see you keep your promise. *Exeunt Alfonso*
      and Kate.
Ferando. So, all thus far goes well. Ho, Sander.

---

19. Because it was easily snared, the woodcock was considered a foolish bird. Kate calls Ferando a woodcock (fool) that lacks a tail, a vital component in the bird's mating ritual. Ferando replies that if he can't display his tail, he will attract her with his bill (lips). The lines suggest that he kisses her—or tries to.

20. "If I desire him, it is to flay him rather than marry him."

21. Kate tells the audience directly that she plans to marry Ferando (match him) in order to encounter him as an adversary (match him), and finally equal him (match him) unless his valor is strong.

Enter Sander laughing.

Sander. Sander, i'faith,° you're a beast. I cry God heartily   *in faith, truly*
    mercy: my heart's ready to run out of my belly with
    laughing. I stood behind the door all this while and heard
    what you said to her.
Ferando. Why, didst thou think that I did not speak well to her?   190
Sander. You spoke like an ass to her! I'll tell you what: and° I had   *if*
    been there to have wooed her, and had this cloak on that you
    have, chud° have had her before she had gone a foot   *I would*
    further, and you talk of woodcocks with her and I cannot
    tell you what.
Ferando. Well, sirrah, and yet thou seest I have got her for all this.
Sander. Ay, merry, 'twas more by hap° than any good cunning.   *chance*
    I hope she'll make you one of the head men[22] of the parish
    shortly.
Ferando. Well, sirrah, leave your jesting and go to Polidor's house,   200
    The young gentleman that was here with me,
    And tell him the circumstance of all thou knowst.
    Tell him on Sunday next we must be married,
    And if he ask thee whither I am gone,
    Tell him into the country to my house,
    And upon Sunday I'll be here again. *Exit Ferando.*
Sander. I warrant° you, master, fear not me for doing of my   *assure*
    business. Now hang him that has not a livery coat°   *servant's coat*
    to slash it out and swash it out[23] among the proudest on°   *of*
    them. Why, look you now, I'll scarce put up° plain "Sander"   *endure*
    now at any of their hands, for and° anybody have anything   *if*
    to do with my master, straight they come crouching upon me: 212
    "I beseech you, good Master Sander, speak a good word for
    me." And then am I so stout° and takes it upon me°   *bold / act arrogantly*
    and stands upon my pantofles[24] to them out of all cry.°   *to excess*
    Why, I have a life like a giant now, but that my master hath such

22. A play on words: the forehead of a cuckold (a man whose wife was unfaithful) was said to grow horns.

23. "Slash it out" may refer to making threatening movements, or to cutting gashes in his coat so that other colors may show through or be added. "Swash it out" means to swagger.

24. "Pantofles" are exotic slippers, and to stand upon one's pantofles is "to affect an air of superiority" (*OED*).

a pestilent mind to a woman now alate,° and I have a pretty   *lately*
wench to my sister, and I had thought to have preferred my
master to her, and that would have been a good deal in my   219
way, but that he's sped° already.   *undone; satisfied*

Enter Polidor's boy.

Boy. Friend, well met.
Sander. 'Souns, "friend well met"? I hold° my life he sees not   *wager*
    my master's livery coat. Plain "friend," hop-of-my-
    thumb?° Know you who we are?   *tiny person*
Boy. Trust me, sir, it is the use° where I was born to salute   *custom*
    men after this manner. Yet notwithstanding, if you be angry
    with me for calling of you "friend," I am the more sorry for
    it, hoping the style of a "fool" will make you amends for all.
Sander. The slave is sorry for his fault; now we cannot be angry. Well,
    what's the matter that you would do with us?   230
Boy. Marry, sir, I hear you pertain° to Signor Ferando.   *are connected*
Sander. Ay, and thou beest not blind thou mayst see: *Ecce*
    signum,° here.   *"behold the sign" (Sander's blue coat)*
Boy. Shall I entreat you to do me° a message to your   *deliver for me*
    master?
Sander. Ay, it may be, and° you tell us from whence you come.   *if*
Boy. Marry, sir, I serve young Polidor, your master's friend.
Sander. Do you serve him? And what's your name?
Boy. My name, sirrah, I tell thee, sirrah, is called "Catapie."
Sander. "Cake and pie." O my teeth waters to have a piece of thee. 240
Boy. Why, slave, wouldst thou eat me?
Sander. Eat thee? Who would not eat "cake and pie"?
Boy. Why, villain, my name is "Catapie"! But wilt thou tell me where
    thy master is?
Sander. Nay, thou must first tell me where thy master is, for I have
    good news for him, I can tell thee.
Boy. Why, see where he comes.

Enter Polidor, Aurelius, and Valeria.

Polidor. Come, sweet Aurelius, my faithful friend.
    Now will we go to see those lovely dames:
    Richer in beauty than the orient pearl,   250
    Whiter than is the Alpine crystal mold,°   *snow*

And far more lovely than the Terrene plant[25]
That blushing in the air turns to a stone.
What, Sander, what news with you?

Sander. Marry, sir, my master sends you word that you must come
to his wedding tomorrow.

Polidor. What, shall he be married then?

Sander. Faith, ay. You think he stands as long about it as you do?

Polidor. Whither is thy master gone now?

Sander. Marry, he's gone to our house in the country to make all   260
  things in a readiness against° my new mistress comes   *before*
  thither, but he'll come again tomorrow.

Polidor. This is suddenly dispatched belike.°   *so it appears*
  Well, sirrah boy, take Sander in with you
  And have him to the buttery° presently.   *place for storing provisions*

Boy. I will, sir. Come, Sander. *Exit Sander and the boy.*

Aurelius. Valeria, as erst° we did devise,   *at first*
  Take thou thy lute and go to Alfonso's house
  And say that Polidor sent thee thither.

Polidor. Ay, Valeria, for he spoke to me   270
  To help him to some cunning° musician   *skillful*
  To teach his eldest daughter on the lute,
  And thou, I know will fit his turn° so well   *requirement*
  As thou shalt get great favor at his hands.
  Begone, Valeria, and say I sent thee to him.

Valeria. I will, sir,
  And stay° your coming at Alfonso's house.   *await*
                        Exit Valeria.

Polidor. Now, sweet Aurelius, by this device
  Shall we have leisure for to court our loves,
  For whilst that she is learning on the lute,   280
  Her sisters may take time to steal abroad;°   *sneak out of the house*
  For otherwise she'll keep them both within,
  And make them work whilst she herself doth play.
  But come, let's go unto Alfonso's house
  And see how Valeria and Kate agrees.
  I doubt his music scarce will please his scholar—
  But stay, here comes Alfonso.

---

25. The exact nature of this "earthly" ("Terrene") plant is unknown, although
it may be coral—that "in the air turns to a stone," as the next line puts it—from
the Mediterranean Sea ("Terrene," see 4.167). Of course, coral is not a plant.

Enter Alfonso.

Alfonso. What, Master Polidor, you are well met.
　　I thank you for the man you sent to me.
　　A good musician I think he is;　　　　　　　　　　290
　　I have set my daughter and him together.
　　But is this gentleman a friend of yours?
Polidor. He is. I pray you, sir, bid him welcome.
　　He's a wealthy merchant's son of Sestos.
Alfonso. You're welcome, sir, and if my house afford°　　*can furnish*
　　You anything that may content your mind,
　　I pray you, sir, make bold with me.°　　*take the liberty of telling me*
Aurelius. I thank you, sir, and if what I have got
　　By merchandise° or travel on the seas—　　　　*commerce*
　　Satins or lawns° or azure-colored silk　　　　*types of fabric*
　　Or precious, fiery-pointed stones of India—　　301
　　You shall command both them, myself, and all.
Alfonso. Thanks, gentle sir. Polidor, take him in
　　And bid him welcome too unto my house,
　　For thou I think must be my second son.
　　Ferando—Polidor dost thou not know
　　Must marry Kate, and tomorrow is the day.
Polidor. Such news I heard, and I came now to know.
Alfonso. Polidor, 'tis true. Go, let me alone,
　　For I must see against° the bridegroom come　　*before*
　　That all things be according to his mind.　　311
　　And so I'll leave you for an hour or two. *Exit.*
Polidor. Come then, Aurelius, come in with me,
　　And we'll go sit a while and chat with them,
　　And after bring them forth to take the air. *Exeunt.*

[SCENE 4]

Then Sly speaks.

Sly. Sim, when will the fool° come again?　　　　*(i.e., Sander)*
Lord. He'll come again, my lord, anon.°　　　　*soon*
Sly. Gi's° some more drink here. 'Souns, where's the tapster?　　*Give us*
　　Here, Sim, eat some of these things.
Lord. So I do, my lord.

Sly. Here, Sim, I drink to thee.
Lord. My lord, here comes the players again.
Sly. O brave,° here's two fine gentlewomen.   *excellent, bravo!*

Enter Valeria [as music teacher] with a lute and Kate with him.

Valeria. The senseless° trees by music have been   *lacking the sense of hearing*
    moved,
    And at the sound of pleasant-tunèd strings   10
    Have savage beasts hung down their list'ning heads
    As though they had been cast into a trance.
    Then it may be that she whom nought can please
    With music's sound in time may be surprised.
    Come, lovely mistress, will you take your lute
    And play the lesson that I taught you last?
Kate. It is no matter whether I do or no,
    For trust me, I take no great delight in it.
Valeria. I would, sweet mistress, that it lay in me
    To help you to that thing that's your delight.[26]   20
Kate. In you with a pestilence,° are you so kind?   *get away with a vengeance*
    Then make a nightcap of your fiddle's case
    To warm your head and hide your filthy face.
Valeria. If that, sweet mistress, were your heart's content,
    You should command a greater thing than that,
    Although it were ten times to my disgrace.
Kate. You're so kind, 'twere pity you should be hanged,
    And yet methinks the fool doth look asquint.[27]
Valeria. Why, mistress, do you mock me?
Kate. No, but I mean to move thee.   30
Valeria. Well, will you play a little?
Kate. Ay, give me the lute. *She plays.*
Valeria. That stop° was false, play it again.   *note*
Kate. Then mend it thou, thou filthy ass.
Valeria. What, do you bid me kiss your arse?
Kate. How now, Jack Sauce,° you're a jolly mate.   *impudent or saucy fellow*

26. Valeria's suggestion is sexual, and Kate quickly and wittily rejects it. For a
discussion of the use of Marlowe's *Doctor Faustus* as a source for this exchange,
see Houk (954–57).
27. Kate is using the proverb, "Love, being jealous, makes a good eye look
asquint" (Tilley L498).

You're best be still lest I cross your
    pate°   *You'd better be quiet or I'll slap your face.*
And make your music fly about your ears.
I'll make it and your foolish coxcomb[28] meet! *She offers to strike*
    him with the lute.

Valeria. Hold mistress, 'souns, will you break my lute?   40
Kate. Ay, on thy head and if thou speak to me.
    There—take it up and fiddle somewhere else. *She throws it down.*
    And see you come no more into this place
    Lest that I clap your fiddle on your face. *Exit Kate.*
Valeria. 'Souns, teach her to play upon the lute?
    The devil shall teach her first. I am glad she's gone,
    For I was ne'er so 'fraid in all my life
    But that my lute should fly about mine ears.
    My master shall teach her his self for me,
    For I'll keep me far enough without° her reach;   *outside of*
    For he and Polidor sent me before   51
    To be with her and teach her on the lute
    Whilst they did court the other gentlewomen.
    And here methinks they come together.

      Enter Aurelius [as a merchant], Polidor, Emelia, and Phylena.

Polidor. How now, Valeria, where's your mistress?
Valeria. At the Vengeance,[29] I think, and nowhere else.
Aurelius. Why, Valeria, will she not learn apace?°   *quickly*
Valeria. Yes, by'rlady,° she has learned too much   *by our Lady (Virgin Mary)*
    already,
    And that I had felt, had I not spoke her fair,
    But she shall ne'er be learned for° me again.   *taught by*
Aurelius. Well Valeria, go to my chamber,   61
    And bear him company that came today
    From Sestos where our agèd father dwells. *Exit Valeria.*
Polidor. Come, fair Emelia, my lovely love,
    Brighter than the burnished palace of the sun,
    The eyesight of the glorious firmament,
    In whose bright looks sparkles the radiant fire

---

28. "The cap worn by a professional fool"; "a ludicrous appellation for the head" (*OED*).

29. Perhaps an ironically named tavern, as suggested by Miller in his Cambridge edition (80), reflecting Kate's mood.

Wily Prometheus slyly stole from Jove:[30]
Infusing breath, life, motion, soul
To every object stricken by thine eyes.   70
O fair Emelia, I pine for thee
And either must enjoy thy love or die.
Emelia. Fie, man, I know you will not die for love.
    Ah, Polidor, thou needst not to complain:
    Eternal heaven sooner be dissolved
    And all that pierceth Phoebus' silver eye
    Before such hap befall to Polidor.
Polidor. Thanks, fair Emelia, for these sweet words,
    But what saith Phylena to her friend?°   *lover*
Phylena. Why, I am buying merchandise of him.   80
Aurelius. Mistress, you shall not need to buy of me,
    For when I crossed the bubbling Canibey[31]
    And sailed along the crystal Hellespont,[32]
    I filled my coffers of the wealthy mines
    Where I did cause millions of laboring Moors
    To undermine° the caverns of the earth   *dig into*
    To seek for strange and new-found precious stones,
    And dive into the sea to gather pearl
    As fair as Juno offered Priam's son;[33]
    And you shall take your liberal choice of all.   90
Phylena. I thank you, sir, and would° Phylena might   *if only*
    In any courtesy requite you so
    As she with willing heart could well bestow.

Enter Alfonso.

Alfonso. How now, daughters, is Ferando come?
Emelia. Not yet, father. I wonder he stays so long.
Alfonso. And where's your sister that she is not here?

30. The titan Prometheus stole fire from Jove and brought it to earth.

31. Apparently a fictitious river.

32. The modern Dardanelles, the strait between Asia minor and Europe. See n. 12.

33. Paris, the son of King Priam of Troy, was offered all the wealth of Asia by the goddess Hera (Juno) to name her fairer than Athena (Minerva) and Aphrodite (Venus) in an event that came to be called the Judgment of Paris.

Phylena. She is making of her ready, father,
    To go to church and if that° he were come.   *if only*
Polidor. I warrant° you, he'll not be long away.   *assure*
Alfonso. Go, daughters, get you in and bid your   100
    Sister provide herself against° that we do come,   *before*
    And see you go to church along with us. *Exeunt Phylena and*
      Emelia.
    I marvel that Ferando comes not away.°   *has not arrived*
Polidor. His tailor, it may be, hath been too slack
    In his apparel which he means to wear,
    For no question but° some fantastic suits   *without question*
    He is determinèd to wear today,
    And richly powderèd° with precious stones,   *spangled, strewn*
    Spotted with liquid gold,[34] thick set° with pearl,   *thickly ornamented*
    And such he means shall be his wedding suits.   110
Alfonso. I cared not I, what cost he did bestow
    In gold or silk so he himself were here,
    For I had rather lose a thousand crowns
    Than that he should deceive us here today.
    But soft, I think I see him come.

     Enter Ferando basely attired and a red cap on his head.

Ferando. Good morrow, father; Polidor, well met.
    You wonder, I know, that I have stayed so long.
Alfonso. Ay marry, son, we were almost persuaded
    That we should scarce have had our bridegroom here.
    But say, why art thou thus basely attired?   120
Ferando. "Thus richly," father, you should have said,
    For when my wife and I am married once,
    She's such a shrew, if we should once fall out,
    She'll pull my costly suits over mine ears.
    And therefore am I thus attired awhile,
    For many things I tell you's in my head,
    And none must know thereof but Kate and I,
    For we shall live like lambs and lions sure,
    Nor lambs to lions never was so tame,
    If once they lie within the lion's paws,   130

---

34. In George Peele's *The Arraignment of Paris* (1584), Juno says to Paris, "Xanthus shall run liquid gold for thee to wash thy hands" (2.1.135). The Trojan river Xanthus is mentioned at 4.161.

As Kate to me if we were married once.
And therefore come, let us to church presently.
Polidor. Fie, Ferando, not thus attired, for shame.
    Come to my chamber and there suit thyself
    Of twenty suits that I did never wear.
Ferando. Tush, Polidor, I have as many suits,
    Fantastic made to fit my humor so
    As any in Athens and as richly wrought
    As was the massy° robe that late adorned   massive
    The stately legate of the Persian king.   140
    And this from them have I made choice to wear.
Alfonso. I prithee, Ferando, let me entreat,
    Before thou goest unto the church with us,
    To put some other suit upon thy back.
Ferando. Not for the world if I might gain it° so,   *(i.e., the world)*
    And therefore take me thus or not at all.

                    Enter Kate.

    But soft, see where my Kate doth come.
    I must salute her: how fares my lovely Kate?
    What, art thou ready? Shall we go to church?   149
Kate. Not I with one so mad, so basely 'ttired,°   *attired*
    To marry such a filthy,° slavish groom°   *low / male attendant*
    That, as it seems, sometimes is from his wits,
    Or else he would not thus have come to us.
Ferando. Tush, Kate, these words adds greater love in me
    And makes me think thee fairer than before.
    Sweet Kate, the lovelier than Diana's purple robe,[35]
    Whiter than are the snowy Apennines,[36]
    Or icy hair that grows on Boreas' chin.[37]
    Father, I swear by Ibis'° golden beak,   *Egyptian sacred bird*
    More fair and radiant is my bonny Kate   160
    Than silver Xanthus when he doth embrace

35. Diana (Artemis), the goddess of chastity, the hunt, and the moon, is said to have transformed the maiden Amethyst into a stone that was then stained purple by Bacchus (Dionysus), god of wine. This may explain the "purple robe."

36. Mountain chain running down the center of Italy.

37. Boreas, the north wind, is pictured as having an icy beard.

The ruddy Simois at Ida's feet.[38]
And care not thou, sweet Kate, how I be clad,
Thou shalt have garments wrought of Median[39] silk,
Enchased° with precious jewels fetched from far   *set*
By Italian merchants that with Russian
    stems°   *timbers at the ends of a ship*
Plows up huge furrows in the Terrene Main,°   *Mediterranean Sea*
And better far my lovely Kate shall wear.
Then come, sweet love, and let us to the church,
For this, I swear, shall be my wedding suit.[40] *Exeunt [Ferando*
    and Kate].

Alfonso. Come, gentlemen, go along with us,   171
For thus, do what we can, he will be wed. *Exeunt.*

[SCENE 5]

Enter Polidor's boy and Sander.

Boy. Come hither, sirrah boy.
Sander. "Boy"? O, disgrace to my person. 'Souns, "boy" of your face.
    You have many boys with such pique-devants,°   *short, pointed beards*
    I am sure? 'Souns, would you not have a bloody nose for this?
Boy. Come, come, I did but jest. Where is that same piece of pie
    that I gave thee to keep?
Sander. The pie? Ay, you have more mind of your belly than to go
    see what your master does.
Boy. Tush, 'tis no matter, man. I prithee, give it me. I am very hungry,
    I promise thee.   10
Sander. Why, you may take it and the devil burst you with it. One
    cannot save a bit after supper, but you are always ready to munch
    it up.

38. A river of ancient Troy. The Xanthus and the Simois rise in the Ida mountains, the site of the Judgment of Paris that began the Trojan War. See n. 33.

39. Media is an ancient country south of northwestern Iran. The Medes were
known for their luxury.

40. As Boas notes (91–98), Ferando's speeches are strongly influenced by
Christopher Marlowe's *Tamburlaine, Parts 1* and *2*. Several phrases are directly
borrowed.

Boy. Why, come, man, we shall have good cheer anon°   *immediately; soon*
    at the bridehouse, for your master's gone to church to be married
    already, and there's such cheer as passeth.°   *surpasses everything*

Sander. O brave,° I would I had eat no meat° this week,   *excellent / food*
    for I have never a corner left in my belly to put a venison
    pasty° in. I think I shall burst myself with   *pie, baked without a dish*
    eating, for I'll so cram me down the tarts and the   20
    marchpanes° out of all cry.°   *sweets made of marzipan / to excess*

Boy. Ay, but how wilt thou do now thy master's married? Thy
    mistress is such a devil as she'll make thee forget thy eating
    quickly, she'll beat thee so.

Sander. Let my master alone with her for that, for he'll make her tame
    well enough ere long, I warrant thee. For he's such a churl waxen
    now of late° that an he be never so little   *become such a villain recently*
    angry, he thumps° me out of all cry. But in   *beats (Quarto "thum")*
    my mind, sirrah, the youngest is a very pretty wench, and if I
    thought thy master would not have her, I'd have a   30
    fling° at her myself. I'll see soon whether'twill   *throw at dice; attempt*
    be a match or no. And it will not, I'll set the matter hard for
    myself,° I warrant thee.   *pursue (Emilia) vigorously*

Boy. 'Souns, you slave, will you be a rival with my master in his love?
    Speak but such another word and I'll cut off one of thy legs.

Sander. O, cruel[41] judgment. Nay then, sirrah, my tongue shall talk
    no more to you. Marry, my timber° shall tell the trusty   *stick*
    message of his° master even on the very forehead on thee,   *its*
    thou abusious° villain; therefore, prepare thyself.   *given to abuse*

Boy. Come hither, thou imperfectious° slave. In regard   *full of imperfection*
    of° thy beggary, hold thee, there's two   *out of consideration for*
    shillings[42] for thee to pay for the healing of thy left leg which   42
    I mean furiously to invade° or to maim at the least.   *attack*

Sander. O supernodical° fool! Well, I'll take your two   *extremely silly*
    shillings, but I'll bar° striking at legs.   *prohibit*

Boy. Not I, for I'll strike anywhere.

Sander. Here, here, take your two shillings again.
    I'll see thee hanged ere° I'll fight with thee.   *before*
    I got a broken shin the other day;

---

41. In his Cambridge edition, Miller suggests a pun on "crewel," the thin wor-
sted yarn from which Sander's hose are probably made.

42. A shilling was worth one-twentieth of a pound sterling.

'Tis not whole yet, and therefore I'll not fight.   50
Come, come, why should we fall out?°   *quarrel*
Boy. Well, sirrah, your fair words hath something allayed my
    choler.° I am content for this once to put it   *anger*
    up° and be friends with thee. But soft, see   *sheathe my weapon*
where they come all from church; belike they be married already.

        Enter Ferando and Kate and Alfonso and Polidor
        and Emelia and Aurelius and Phylena.

Ferando. Father, farewell, my Kate and I must home.
    Sirrah, go make ready my horse presently.
Alfonso. Your horse! What, son, I hope you do but jest.
    I am sure you will not go so suddenly.
Kate. Let him go or tarry,° I am resolved to stay,   *linger*
    And not to travel on my wedding day.   61
Ferando. Tut,[43] Kate, I tell thee we must needs go home.
    Villain, hast thou saddled my horse?
Sander. Which horse? Your curtal?°   *horse with tail cut short*
Ferando. 'Souns, you slave, stand you prating here?
    Saddle the bay° gelding for your mistress.   *reddish-brown*
Kate. Not for me, for I'll not go.
Sander. The ostler° will not let me have him. You owe ten   *stableman*
    pence for his meat° and six pence for stuffing° my   *feed / padding*
    mistress' saddle.   70
Ferando. Here, villain, go pay him straight.
Sander. Shall I give them another peck of lavender?[44]
Ferando. Out, slave, and bring them presently° to the door.   *at once*
Alfonso. Why, son, I hope at least you'll dine with us.
Sander. I pray you, master, let's stay 'til dinner be done.
Ferando. 'Souns, villain, art thou here yet? *Exit Sander.*
    Come, Kate, our dinner is provided at home.
Kate. But not for me, for here I mean to dine.
    I'll have my will in this as well as you.

43. Mild expression of impatience or dissatisfaction.

44. Under "Spirits" in "An Alphabetical Table of Medicines," the author of *The Experienced Farrier* (1678)—who identifies himself only as "E. R., Gent."—writes that lavender is "a most excellent Cordial" for horses. However, he recommends a dose much smaller than "a peck." "Lavender" is probably Sander's error for "provender" (dry food for horses). The asinine Bottom asks for a "peck of provender" at 4.1.31 of Shakespeare's *A Midsummer Night's Dream*.

Though you in madding mood° would   *acting mad, maddening mood*
   leave your friends,
Despite of you I'll tarry with them still.   81
Ferando. Ay, Kate, so thou shalt, but at some other time.
Whenas thy sisters here shall be espoused,°   *married*
Then thou and I will keep our wedding day
In better sort than now we can provide.
For here I promise thee before them all
We will ere° long return to them again.   *before*
Come, Kate, stand not on terms;° we   *don't insist upon conditions*
   will away.
This is my day; tomorrow thou shalt rule,
And I will do whatever thou commands.   90
Gentlemen, farewell, we'll take our leaves.
It will be late before that we come home. *Exit Ferando and Kate.*
Polidor. Farewell, Ferando, since you will be gone.
Alfonso. So mad a couple did I never see.
Emelia. They're even as well matched as I would wish.
Phylena. And yet I hardly think that he can tame her,
For when he has done, she will do what she list.°   *wishes*
Aurelius. Her manhood° then is good, I do believe.   *manliness (ironic), courage*
Polidor. Aurelius, or else I miss my mark,
Her tongue will walk° if she doth hold her   *move briskly; rage*
   hands.°   *even if she doesn't strike*
I am in doubt ere half a month be past   101
He'll curse the priest that married him so soon.
And yet it may be she will be reclaimed,
For she is very patient grown of late.
Alfonso. God hold it that it may continue still.
I would be loath° that they should disagree,   *reluctant*
But he, I hope, will hold her in° a while.   *restrain her*
Polidor. Within this two days I will ride to him
And see how lovingly they do agree.
Alfonso. Now, Aurelius, what say you to this?   110
What, have you sent to Sestos, as you said,
To certify° your father of your love?   *assure*
For I would gladly he would like of it,
And if he be the man you tell to me,
I guess he is a merchant of great wealth.
And I have seen him oft at Athens here,
And for his sake assure thee thou are welcome.
Polidor. And so to me whilst Polidor doth live.

Aurelius. I find it so, right worthy gentlemen,
    And of what worth your friendship I esteem,   120
    I leave censure° of your several° thoughts.   *to the judgment / individual*
    But, for requital° of your favors past   *because recompense*
    Rests yet behind,° which when   *remains yet to come*
        occasion° serves   *opportunity*
    I vow shall be remembered to the full,
    And for my father's coming to this place,
    I do expect within this week at most—
Alfonso. Enough Aurelius! But we forget
    Our marriage dinner now the bride is gone.
    Come, let us see what there they left behind. *Exit omnes.*

[SCENE 6]

Enter Sander with two or three serving-men [Tom and Will].

Sander. Come, sirs, provide all things as fast as you can, for my master's
    hard° at hand and my new mistress and all, and he sent me   *near*
    before to see all things ready.
Tom. Welcome home, Sander. Sirrah, how looks our new mistress?
    They say she's a plaguey° shrew.   *troublesome*
Sander. Ay, and that thou shalt find, I can tell thee, an° thou dost   *if*
    not please her well. Why, my master has such ado with her as it
    passeth,° and he's even like a madman.   *exceeds everything*
Will. Why, Sander, what does he say?
Sander. Why, I'll tell you what: when they should go to church to   10
    be married, he puts on an old jerkin° and a pair of   *short jacket*
    canvas° breeches down to the small of his leg   *coarse, unbleached cloth*
    and a red cap on his head and he looks as thou wilt burst thyself
    with laughing when thou seest him. He's e'en as good as a
    fool° for me. And then, when they should go to dinner, he   *jester*
    made me saddle the horse and away he came and ne'er tarried
    for dinner. And therefore you had best get supper ready
    against° they come, for they be hard at hand I am sure,   *before*
    by this time.
Tom. 'Souns, see where they be already.   20

Enter Ferando and Kate.

Ferando. Now welcome, Kate. Where's these villains here? What, not
    supper yet upon the board?° Nor table spread nor nothing   *table*
    done at all? Where's that villain that I sent before?

Sander. Now *adsum,*° sir.   *"I am present"*

Ferando. Come hither, you villain. I'll cut your nose, you rogue. Help
    me off with my boots. Wilt please you to lay the cloth? 'Souns,
    the villain hurts my foot! Pull easily, I say. Yet again.
        He beats them all. They cover the board and fetch in the meat.
    'Souns! Burnt and scorched. Who dressed° this meat?   *prepared*

Will. Forsooth, John cook.
        He throws down the table and meat and all and beats them.

Ferando. Go, you villains. Bring you me such meat? Out of my   30
    sight, I say, and bear it hence. Come, Kate, we'll have other
    meat provided. Is there a fire in my chamber, sir?

Sander. Ay, forsooth.
         Exeunt Ferando and Kate. Manent° *serving men*   *remain*
                and eat up all the meat.

Tom. 'Souns, I think, of my conscience,° my master's mad   *in my mind*
    since he was married.

Will. I laughed° what a box° he gave Sander for pulling   *laughed at / blow*
    off his boots.

                    Enter Ferando again.

Sander. I hurt his foot for the nonce,° man.   *on purpose*

Ferando. Did you so, you damned villain. *He beats them all out again.*
    This humor° must I hold me to a while,   *idiosyncratic mood*
    To bridle and hold back my headstrong wife   41
    With curbs[45] of hunger, ease, and want of sleep.
    Nor sleep nor meat shall she enjoy tonight.
    I'll mew° her up as men do mew their hawks,   *cage*
    And make her gently come unto the lure,
    Were she as stubborn or as full of strength
    As were the Thracian horse Alcides tamed,
    That King Aegeus fed with flesh of men,[46]

---

45. "A chain or strap passing under the lower jaw of a horse, and fastened to the
upper ends of the branches of the bit; used chiefly for checking an unruly horse"
(*OED*). Cf. "bridle" in the previous line.

46. Alcides is Hercules, hero of antiquity, who performed twelve great labors.
Among them was the taming of the mares of King Diomedes of Thrace. The text
follows Marlowe's error in assigning the horses to King Aegeus of Athens.

Yet would I pull her down and make her come   49
As hungry hawks do fly unto their lure.[47] *Exit.*

[SCENE 7]

Enter Aurelius and Valeria.

Aurelius. Valeria attend;° I have a lovely love   *serve me; listen*
　　As bright as is the heaven crystalline,
　　As fair as is the milk-white way of Jove,[48]
　　As chaste as Phoebe° in her summer sports,   *Diana*
　　As soft and tender as the azure down
　　That circles Citherea's silver doves.[49]
　　Her do I mean to make my lovely bride,
　　And in her bed to breathe the sweet content
　　That I, thou knowst, long time have aimèd at.
　　Now, Valeria, it rests in thee to help   10
　　To compass° this, that I might gain my love,   *devise, accomplish*
　　Which easily thou mayst perform at will,
　　If that the merchant which thou toldst me of
　　Will, as he said, go to Alfonso's house
　　And say he is my father, and therewithal
　　Pass° over certain deeds of land to me   *sign*
　　That I thereby may gain my heart's desire,
　　And he is promisèd reward of me.
Valeria. Fear not, my lord, I'll fetch him straight° to you,   *directly*
　　For he'll do anything that you command.   20
　　But tell me, my lord, is Ferando married then?
Aurelius. He is, and Polidor shortly shall be wed,
　　And he means to tame his wife erelong.°   *before long*

---

47. Lines 44–50 feature hawking imagery: a "mew" is a cage for hawks. Falconers constructed a "lure," a bunch of feathers that attracted the hawk while it was being trained. A hawk was also tethered with leather lines so the trainer could "pull her down."

48. The phrase means "Jove's milky way" and is borrowed from Marlowe's *Tamburlaine, Part 2:* My soul "shall mount the milk-white way and meet [Jove] there" (4.3.132).

49. Venus' (Citherea's) chariot is drawn by doves who are covered ("circled") with soft down.

Valeria. He says so.
Aurelius. Faith, he's gone unto the taming school.
Valeria. The taming school? Why, is there such a place?
Aurelius. Ay, and Ferando is the master of the school.
Valeria. That's rare, but what *decorum*° does he use?   *"proper procedure" (ironic)*
Aurelius. Faith, I know not, but by some odd device or other.
    But come, Valeria, I long to see the man   30
    By whom we must comprise° our plotted drift   *put together*
    That I may tell him what we have to do.
Valeria. Then come, my lord, and I will bring you to him straight.
Aurelius. Agreed. Then let's go.   *Exeunt.*

[SCENE 8]

Enter Sander and his mistress [Kate].

Sander. Come, mistress.
Kate. Sander, I prithee, help me to some meat.
    I am so faint that I can scarcely stand.
Sander. Ay, marry, mistress, but you know my master has given me a
    charge that you must eat nothing but that which he himself
    giveth you.
Kate. Why, man, thy master needs never know it.
Sander. You say true indeed. Why, look you, mistress, what say you to
    a piece of beef and mustard now?
Kate. Why, I say 'tis excellent meat. Canst thou help me to some?   10
Sander. Ay, I could help you to some but that I doubt° the   *suspect*
    mustard is too choleric° for you. But what say you   *spicy hot, inflaming*
    to a sheep's head and garlic?
Kate. Why, anything, I care not what it be.
Sander. Ay, but the garlic, I doubt, will make your breath stink, and
    then my master will course° me for letting you eat it.   *thrash*
    But what say you to a fat capon?°   *castrated rooster*
Kate. That's meat for a king, sweet Sander; help me to some of it.
Sander. Nay, by'rlady, then 'tis too dear° for us. We   *precious; expensive*
    must not meddle with the king's meat.   20
Kate. Out, villain, dost thou mock me? Take that for thy sauciness.

She beats him.

Sander. 'Souns, are you so light-fingered° with   *prompt in giving a blow*
    a murrain?° I'll keep you fasting for it this two days.   *pestilence*

Kate. I tell thee, villain, I'll tear the flesh off thy face and eat it and°   *if*
    thou prates° to me thus.   *speak foolishly*
Sander. Here comes my master. Now he'll course° you.   *thrash*

        Enter Ferando with a piece of meat upon his
        dagger's point and Polidor with him.

Ferando. See here, Kate, I have provided meat for thee; here, take it.
    What, is't not worthy thanks? Go, sirrah. Take it away again. You
    shall be thankful for the next you have.
Kate. Why, I thank you for it.   30
Ferando. Nay, now 'tis not worth a pin. Go, sirrah, and take it hence
    I say.
Sander. Yes, sir, I'll carry it hence. Master let her have none, for she
    can fight as hungry as she is.
Polidor. I pray you, sir, let it stand,° for I'll eat some with her   *remain*
    myself.
Ferando. Well, sirrah, set it down again.
Kate. Nay, nay, I pray you, let him take it hence
    And keep it for your own diet, for I'll none.
    I'll ne'er be beholding to you for your meat.   40
    I tell thee flatly° here unto thy teeth,°   *plainly / in your face*
    Thou shalt not keep me nor feed me as thou list,°   *choose*
    For I will home again unto my father's house.
Ferando. Ay, when you're meek and gentle, but not before.
    I know your stomach° is not yet come down,   *appetite; anger; pride*
    Therefore no marvel thou canst not eat.
    And I will go unto your father's house.
    Come, Polidor, let us go in again,   48
    And, Kate, come in with us. I know ere long°   *soon*
    That thou and I shall lovingly agree. *Exeunt omnes.*

[SCENE 9]

    Enter Aurelius [as merchant], Valeria [as Prince of Sestos],
    and Phylotus the merchant [as father to Aurelius].

Aurelius. Now, Signor Phylotus, we will go
    Unto Alfonso's house, and be sure you say
    As I did tell you, concerning the man

That dwells in Sestos whose son I said I was,
For you do very much resemble him.
And fear not, you may be bold to speak your mind.
Phylotus. I warrant° you, sir, take you no care.   assure
   I'll use myself so cunning° in the cause   wisely, cleverly
   As you shall soon enjoy your heart's delight.
Aurelius. Thanks, sweet Phylotus. Then stay you here,   10
   And I will go and fetch him hither straight.°   at once
   Ho, Signor Alfonso, a word with you.

Enter Alfonso.

Alfonso. Who's there? What Aurelius, what's the matter
   That you stand so like a stranger at the door?
Aurelius. My father, sir, is newly come to town,
   And I have brought him here to speak with you
   Concerning those matters that I told you of,
   And he can certify you of the truth.
Alfonso. Is this your father? You are welcome, sir.
Phylotus. Thanks, Alfonso, for that's your name, I guess.   20
   I understand my son hath set his mind
   And bent his liking to your daughter's love,
   And for because he is my only son,
   And I would° gladly that he should do well,   desire
   I tell you, sir, I not mislike his choice.
   If you agree to give him your consent,
   He shall have living to maintain his state:
   Three hundred pounds a year I will assure
   To him and to his heirs, and if they do join
   And knit themselves in holy wedlock band,   30
   A thousand massy ingots° of pure gold   massive bars
   And twice as many bars of silver plate
   I freely give him, and in writing straight
   I will confirm what I have said in words.
Alfonso. Trust me, I must commend your liberal° mind   generous
   And loving care you bear unto your son.
   And here I give him freely my consent.
   As for my daughter, I think he knows her mind,
   And I will enlarge her dowry for your sake
   And solemnize with joy your nuptial rites.   40
   But is this gentleman° of Sestos, too?   (i.e., the disguised Valeria)

Aurelius. He is the Duke of Sestos' thrice-renownèd° son,   *much honored*
    Who for the love his honor bears to me
    Hath thus accompanied me to this place.
Alfonso. You were to blame you told me not before.
    Pardon me, my lord, for if I had known
    Your honor had been here in place with me,
    I would have done my duty to your honor.
Valeria. Thanks, good Alfonso, but I did come to see   49
    Whenas° these marriage rites should be performed,   *the time when*
    And if in these nuptials you vouchsafe°   *graciously condescend*
    To honor thus the prince of Sestos' friend
    In celebration of his spousal° rites,   *marriage*
    He shall remain a lasting friend to you.
    What says Aurelius' father?
Phylotus. I humbly thank your honor, good my lord,
    And ere we part, before your honor here,
    Shall articles° of such content° be drawn   *contracts / contents*
    As twixt° our houses and posterities°   *between / descendants*
    Eternally this league° of peace shall last   *covenant*
    Inviolate° and pure on either part.   *unbroken*
Alfonso. With all my heart. And if your honor please   62
    To walk along with us unto my house,
    We will confirm these leagues of lasting love.
Valeria. Come then, Aurelius, I will go with you. *Exeunt omnes.*

[SCENE 10]

Enter Ferando and Kate and Sander [and haberdasher].

Sander. Master, the haberdasher has brought my mistress home
    her cap here.
Ferando. Come hither, sirrah. What have you there?
Haberdasher. A velvet cap, sir, an° it please you.   *if*
Ferando. Who spoke for° it? Didst thou Kate?   *ordered*
Kate. What if I did? Come hither, sirrah; give me the cap. I'll see if
    it will fit me. *She sets it on her head.*
Ferando. O monstrous! Why, it becomes° thee not.   *suits, looks good on*
    Let me see it, Kate. Here, sirrah, take it hence.
    This cap is out of fashion quite.   10

Kate. The fashion is good enough. Belike° you mean to make   *perhaps*
    a fool of me.
Ferando. Why, true, he means to make a fool of thee,
    To have thee put on such a curtaled° cap.   *curtailed, cut short*
    Sirrah, begone with it. *[Exit haberdasher.]*

Enter the tailor with a gown.

Sander. Here is the tailor, too, with my mistress' gown.
Ferando. Let me see it, tailor. What, with cuts and
    jags?°   *slashes (to let fabric below show)*
    'Souns, you villain, thou hast spoiled the gown.
Tailor. Why, sir, I made it as your man gave me direction.
    You may read the note here.
Ferando. Come hither, sirrah. Tailor, read the note.   20
Tailor. Item, a fair round-compassed° cape.   *cut in a circular shape*
Sander. Ay, that's true.
Tailor. And a large trunk sleeve.°   *tapering from shoulder to wrist*
Sander. That's a lie, master. I said two trunk sleeves.
Ferando. Well, sir, go forward.
Tailor. Item, a loose-bodied° gown.   *loosely fitting*
Sander. Master, if ever I said "loose body's° gown," sew   *immoral woman's*
    me in a seam and beat me to death with a bottom° of   *spool, ball*
    brown thread.   29
Tailor. I made it as the note bade° me.   *instructed*
Sander. I say the note lies in his throat and thou too and° thou   *if*
    sayst it!
Tailor. Nay, nay, ne'er be so hot,° sirrah, for I fear   *angry, threatening*
    you not.
Sander. Dost thou hear, tailor, thou hast
    braved° many men. Brave not me.   *outfitted in fine clothing; challenged*
    Thou'st faced° many   *confronted, with a pun on trimmed, as tailors do garments*
    men—
Tailor. Well, sir.
Sander. Face not me. I'll neither be faced nor braved at thy hands,   40
    I can tell thee.
Kate. Come, come, I like the fashion of it well enough.
    Here's more ado than needs.° I'll have it, I,°   *is necessary / I will*
    And if you do not like it, hide your eyes.
    I think I shall have nothing by your will.
Ferando. [To the tailor] Go, I say, and take it up for your master's use.

Sander. 'Souns, villain, not for thy life, touch it not. 'Souns, "take up
    my mistress' gown to his master's use"?
Ferando. Well, sir, what's your conceit° of it?   *understanding*
Sander. I have a deeper conceit[50] in it than you think for.   50
    "Take up my mistress' gown to his master's use!"
Ferando. Tailor, come hither. For this time take it hence again, and
    I'll content thee for thy pains.
Tailor. I thank you, sir. *Exit Tailor.*
Ferando. Come, Kate, we now will go see thy father's house
    Even in these honest mean habiliments.°   *respectable humble garments*
    Our purses shall be rich, our garments plain,
    To shroud° our bodies from the winter rage,   *clothe, protect*
    And that's enough; what should we care for more?
    Thy sisters, Kate, tomorrow must be wed,   60
    And I have promised them thou shouldst be there.
    The morning is well up, let's haste away.
    It will be nine o'clock ere we come there.
Kate. Nine o'clock? Why, 'tis already past two
    In the afternoon by all the clocks in the town.
Ferando. I say 'tis but nine o'clock in the morning.
Kate. I say 'tis two o'clock in the afternoon.
Ferando. It shall be nine, then, ere we go to your father's.
    Come back again, we will not go today.   69
    Nothing but crossing° of me still.   *opposing*
    I'll have you say as I do ere you go. *Exeunt omnes.*

[SCENE 11]

Enter Polidor, Emelia, Aurelius, and Phylena.

Polidor. Fair Emelia, summer's sun-bright queen,
    Brighter of hue than is the burning clime°   *region*
    Where Phoebus° in his bright   *Apollo, the sun god*
        equator° sits   *sun's celestial sphere*
    Creating gold and precious minerals,
    What would Emelia do if I were forced

---

50. Sander's interpretation of his master's simple command is that he should raise
his mistress' gown. "Deeper" and "use" take on sexual meanings.

To leave fair Athens and to range° the world?   *roam*
Emelia. Should thou assay° to scale the seat of Jove,   *attempt*
    Mounting the subtle airy regions
    Or be snatched up, as erst° was Ganymede,[51]   *once*
    Love should give wings unto my swift desires   10
    And prune° my thoughts that I would follow thee   *preen; direct*
    Or fall and perish as did Icarus.[52]
Aurelius. Sweetly resolved, fair Emelia.
    But would Phylena say as much to me
    If I should ask a question now of thee?
    What if the duke of Sestos' only son,
    Which came with me unto your father's house,
    Should seek to get Phylena's love from me
    And make thee duchess of that stately town?
    Wouldst thou not then forsake me for his love?   20
Phylena. Not for great Neptune,° no, nor Jove himself,   *god of the sea*
    Will Phylena leave Aurelius' love.
    Could he install me empress of the world,
    Or make me queen and guideress° of the heavens,   *female ruler*
    Yet would I not exchange thy love for his.
    Thy company is poor Phylena's heaven,
    And without thee, heaven were hell to me.
Emelia. And should my love, as erst° did Hercules,[53]   *once*
    Attempt to pass° the burning vaults° of hell,   *go through / caves*
    I would with piteous looks and pleasing words,   30
    As once did Orpheus with his harmony
    And ravishing° sound of his melodious harp,   *entrancing*
    Entreat grim Pluto and of him obtain
    That thou mightest go and safe return again.[54]

51. The beautiful Trojan youth abducted from Mount Ida (see 4.162) by Jove in the guise of an eagle and taken to Olympus, the realm of the gods, to be his cupbearer.

52. Young Icarus and his father Daedalus tried to escape Crete by flying with wings of feathers and wax. Icarus flew too close to the sun, the wax melted, and he fell and drowned in the sea.

53. Another of Hercules' labors was to kidnap the three-headed dog-monster who guarded the gates of Hades.

54. The mythical poet and singer Orpheus went to the underworld to get his wife Eurydice back after she died, and charmed Pluto, god of the underworld, with his music.

Phylena. And should my love, as erst Leander did,
    Attempt to swim the boiling Hellespont
    For Hero's love, no towers of brass should hold
    But° I would follow thee through those raging floods,   *but rather*
    With locks dis-shivered° and my breast all bare.   *in disarray*
    With bended knees upon Abydos' shore,[55]   40
    I would with smoky° sighs and brinish° tears   *misty / salty*
    Importune° Neptune and the wat'ry gods   *beg*
    To send a guard of silver-scaled dolphins
    With sounding Tritons° to be our convoy°   *trumpeting sea-gods / escort*
    And to transport us safe unto the shore,
    Whilst I would hang about thy lovely neck
    Redoubling kiss on kiss upon thy cheeks
    And with our pastime° still° the swelling waves.   *recreation / calm*
Emelia. Should Polidor, as great Achilles did,
    Only employ himself to follow arms,   50
    Like to the warlike Amazonian Queen
    Penthesilea, Hector's paramour,
    Who foiled the bloody Pyrrhus, murderous Greek,[56]
    I'll thrust myself amongst the thickest throngs,
    And with my utmost force assist my love.
Phylena. Let Aeole° storm, be mild and quiet thou.   *Aeolus, lord of the winds*
    Let Neptune swell, be Aurelius calm and pleased.
    I care not, I, betide what may betide,°   *come what may come*
    Let fates and fortune do the worst they can,
    I reck° them not, they not discord with°   *regard / are not unpleasant to*
    me,
    Whilst that my love and I do well agree.   61
Aurelius. Sweet Phylena, beauty's mineral,[57]
    From whence the sun exhales his glorious shine[58]

---

55. See n. 12.

56. Emelia's mythology is confused. After Hector's death, Penthesilea, Queen of the tribe of female warriors, brought her Amazons to fight on the Trojan side. She was killed by Achilles, although some versions of the myth suggest that she was slain by Pyrrhus, the son of Achilles.

57. A mineral is a substance obtained by mining. The *OED* also gives this definition: "that variety of the philosophers' stone which was responsible for the purification of metals." It is used figuratively here.

58. "Exhales" here has the unusual meaning of "draws forth." Aurelius suggests that the sun draws its beams from Phylena, an idea that may have come

And clad° the heav'n in thy reflected rays,   *clothed*
And now my liefest° love, the time draws nigh   *dearest*
That Hymen⁵⁹ mounted° in his saffron°   *clothed / orange-yellow color*
    robe
Must with his torches wait upon thy train,
As Helen's brothers on the hornèd° moon.⁶⁰   *crescent-shaped*
Now, Juno,° to thy number shall I add   *Jupiter's wife, protectress of marriage*
The fairest bride that ever merchant had.   70
Polidor. Come, fair Emelia, the priest is gone,
And at the church your father and the rest
Do stay to see our marriage rites performed,
And knit in sight of heaven this Gordian knot,°   *indissoluble bond*
That teeth of fretting° time may ne'er untwist.   *gnawing*
Then come, fair love, and gratulate° with me   *express joy at*
This day's content and sweet solemnity. *Exeunt omnes.*

[SCENE 12]

[Then Sly speaks.]

Sly. Sim, must they be married now?
Lord. Ay, my lord.

Enter Ferando and Kate and Sander.

Sly. Look, Sim, the fool is come again now.
Ferando. Sirrah, go fetch our horses forth and bring
    Them to the back gate presently.°   *at once*
Sander. I will, sir, I warrant° you.   *promise*

---

from Tamburlaine's lament at the death of his beloved wife Zenocrate that the sun "Now wants the fuel that inflamed his beams" (2.4.4) in Marlowe's *Tamburlaine, Part 2.*

59. The god of marriage, traditionally described as wearing a "saffron robe" and carrying one or more torches.

60. Helen of Troy's brothers are Castor and Pollux, known collectively as the Dioscuri, "youths of Zeus," or (in Latin) Gemini, "twins." They were transported to the heavens where they became the brightest stars in the constellation Gemini. They are seen to accompany the moon in the night sky.

Exit Sander.

Ferando. Come, Kate, the moon shines clear tonight methinks.

Kate. The moon? Why, husband, you are deceived.
   It is the sun.

Ferando. Yet again: come back again. It shall be   10
   The moon ere° we come at your father's.   *before*

Kate. Why, I'll say as you say—it is the moon.

Ferando. Jesus save the glorious moon.

Kate. Jesus save the glorious moon.

Ferando. I am glad, Kate, your stomach is come down.[61]
   I know it well thou knowest it is the sun,
   But I did try° to see if thou wouldst speak   *test*
   And cross° me now as thou hast done before.   *oppose*
   And trust me, Kate, hadst thou not named the moon,
   We had gone back again as sure as death.   20
   But soft, who's this that's coming here?

Enter the Duke of Sestos alone.

Duke. Thus all alone from Sestos am I come
   And left my princely court and noble train
   To come to Athens, and in this disguise,
   To see what course my son Aurelius takes.
   But stay,° here's some° it may be travels   *wait / some people*
      thither.°   *there (to Athens)*
   Good sir, can you direct me the way to Athens?

Ferando speaks to the old man.

Ferando. Fair lovely maid, young and affable,°   *easy of conversation*
   More clear of hue and far more beautiful
   Than precious sardonyx[62] or purple rocks   30
   Of amethysts or glistering hyacinth,°   *glittering blue stone (sapphire)*
   More amiable far than is the plain
   Where glistering Cepheus in silver bowers°   *dwellings; canopies of trees*

61. "You have overcome your proud stubbornness."

62. A variety of onyx or quartz having layers of white in a field of yellow-orange or red.

    Gazeth upon the giant Andromede.[63]
    Sweet Kate, entertain this lovely woman.
Duke. I think the man is mad: he calls me a woman.
Kate. Fair lovely lady, bright and crystalline,°   *bright as crystal*
    Beauteous and stately as the eye-trained
      bird,°   *peacock (with eyes on its tail or "train")*
    As glorious as the morning washed with dew,
    Within whose eyes she° takes her dawning beams,   *(morning)*
    And golden summer sleeps upon thy cheeks.   41
    Wrap up thy radiations° in some cloud,   *radiance*
    Lest that thy beauty make this stately town
    Inhabitable° like the burning zone°   *not habitable / the earth's torrid zone*
    With sweet reflections of thy lovely face.
Duke. What, is she mad, too? Or is my shape transformed,
    That both of them persuade me I am a woman?
    But they are mad sure, and therefore I'll be gone,
    And leave their companies for fear of harm,   49
    And unto Athens haste to seek my son. *Exit Duke.*
Ferando. Why so, Kate, this was friendly done of° thee,   *by*
    And kindly° too. Why, thus must we   *friendly, according to nature's law*
      two live,
    One mind, one heart, and one content° for both.   *satisfaction, pleasure*
    This good old man does think that we are mad,
    And glad he is, I am sure, that he is gone.
    But come, sweet Kate, for we will after him
    And now persuade him to his shape again. *Exeunt omnes.*

[SCENE 13]

*Enter Alfonso and Phylotus [as father to Aurelius] and Valeria [as Prince
of Sestos], Polidor, Emelia, Aurelius [as merchant], and Phylena.*

Alfonso. Come, lovely sons, your marriage rites performed,
    Let's hie° us home to see what cheer° we have.   *hurry / entertainment*
    I wonder that Ferando and his wife
    Comes not to see this great solemnity.

---

63. Cepheus and his daughter Andromeda are mythological characters and constellations in the "plains" of heaven.

Polidor. No marvel if Ferando be away.
    His wife I think hath troubled so his wits
    That he remains at home to keep them° warm,   *(i.e., his wits)*
    For forward° wedlock, as the proverb says,   *well-advanced*
    Hath brought him to his nightcap long ago.[64]
Phylotus. But, Polidor, let my son and you take heed   10
    That Ferando say not, ere long, as much to you.
    And now, Alfonso, more to show my love:
    If unto Sestos you do send your ships,
    Myself will fraught° them with Arabian silks,   *load*
    Rich Afric° spices, Arras   *African*
       counterpanes,°   *quilted coverlets from Arras in France*
    Musk, cassia, sweet-smelling ambergris,[65]
    Pearl, coral, crystal, jet,° and ivory.   *hard, black stone*
    To gratulate° the favors of my son,   *express my pleasure at*
    And friendly love that you have shown to him.
Valeria. And for to honor him and this fair bride,   20

Enter the Duke of Sestos.

    I'll yearly send you from my father's court
    Chests of refined sugar severally,°   *one after another*
    Ten tun° of Tunis wine, sucket-sweet   *barrels*
       drugs,°   *spices sweet as candied fruit*
    To celebrate and solemnize this day;
    And custom-free° your merchants shall   *without tolls or duties*
       converse°   *trade*
    And interchange the profits° of your land,   *increase by exchange*
    Sending you gold for brass, silver for lead,
    Cases of silk for packs of wool and cloth,
    To bind this friendship and confirm this league.
Duke. I am glad, sir, that you would be so frank.°   *generous*
    Are you become the Duke of Sestos' son   31
    And revels with my treasure in the town
    Base villain° that thus dishonorest me?   *low-born person*

---

64. The proverb is, "Age and wedlock bring a man to his nightcap" (Tilley A63). The term "nightcap" is also associated with cuckoldry. See Fletcher's *The Tamer Tamed*, n. 54.

65. Musk and ambergris, secretions of the male musk deer and the sperm whale, respectively, are used in the making of perfume. Cassia is a kind of cinnamon.

Valeria. [Aside] 'Souns, it is the Duke. What shall I do?
　　Dishonor thee? Why, knowst thou what thou sayst?
Duke. Here's no villain; he will not know me now.
　　[To Aurelius] But what say you? Have you forgot me, too?
Phylotus. Why, sir, are you acquainted with my son?
Duke. With thy son? No, trust me, if he be thine,
　　I pray you, sir, who am I?   40
Aurelius. Pardon me, father, humbly on my knees
　　I do entreat your grace to hear me speak.
Duke. Peace,° villain. Lay hands on them   *quiet*
　　And send them to prison straight. *Phylotus and Valeria run away.*

　　　　　　　　　　Then Sly speaks.

Sly. I say, we'll have no sending to prison.
Lord. My lord, this is but the play. They're but in jest.
Sly. I tell thee, Sim, we'll have no sending to prison, that's flat.°　*for sure*
　　Why, Sim, am not I Don Chriso Vary?[66] Therefore I say they
　　shall not go to prison.
Lord. No more they shall not, my lord. They be run away.   50
Sly. Are they run away, Sim? That's well.
　　Then gi's° some more drink and let them play again.   *give us*
Lord. Here, my lord. *Sly drinks and then falls asleep.*
Duke. Ah, treacherous boy that durst° presume   *dares to*
　　To wed thyself without thy father's leave,°   *permission*
　　I swear by fair Cynthia's° burning rays,   *the moon's*
　　By Meroe's head and by seven-mouthed Nile,[67]

66. Sly gives himself a fanciful name, perhaps a mishearing of "Christopher." The Spanish title "Don" is often used by Shakespeare for humor as "Don Adriano de Armado" from *Love's Labor's Lost.*

67. The quartos all read "*Merops*" and editors have (without enthusiasm) suggested a King of Ethiopia by that name. In his Cambridge edition, Miller, following Sugden (367), conjectured that "*Meroe*" might be the proper reading (115), and there is more evidence to support that name. Meroe is "the ancient name for the district in Nubia lying East of Khartoum, between the Nile, the Atbara, and the Rahad" (Sugden 342). It was considered the upper end or "head" of the Nile River, where it branches into "a number of channels, usually reckoned as 7" (Sugden 367). Thus "Meroe's head" refers to the "seven-mouthed Nile." The two are connected in the anonymous play *The Tragedy of Caesar and Pompey or Caesar's Revenge* (1607): Caesar speaks of Pompey as " . . . aided with the unresisted power / The *Meroe* or the seven-mouthed Nile can yield" (11.328–29). Moreover, the term is preceded by "burning rays" (albeit of

Had I but known ere° thou hadst wedded her,   *before*
Were in thy breast the world's immortal soul,[68]
This angry sword should rip thy hateful chest   60
And hew thee smaller than the Libyan sands.
Turn hence° thy face, O cruel, impious° boy.   *away / wicked*
Alfonso, I did not think you would presume
To match your daughter with my princely house
And ne'er make me acquainted with the cause.°   *the matter*
Alfonso. My lord, by heavens I swear unto your grace,
I knew none other but Valeria your man
Had been the Duke of Sestos' noble son,
Nor did my daughter, I dare swear for her.
Duke. That damned villain that hath deluded me,   70
Whom I did send guide° unto my son,   *as a guide*
O that my furious force could cleave° the earth   *open*
That I might muster° bands of hellish fiends   *enlist*
To rack° his heart and tear his impious soul.   *tear apart*
The ceaseless turning of celestial orbs
Kindles not greater flames in flitting° air   *unstable*
Than passionate anguish of my raging breast.
Aurelius. Then let my death, sweet father, end your grief,
For I it is that thus have wrought your woes.
Then be revenged on me, for here I swear   80
That they are innocent of what I did.
O, had I charge to cut off Hydra's° head,   *many-headed monster*
To make the topless° Alps a champion field,°   *immensely high / level plain*
To kill untamèd monsters with my sword,
To travel daily in the hottest sun,
And watch° in winter when the nights be cold,   *stay awake*
I would with gladness undertake them all
And think the pain but pleasure that I felt
So that my noble father at my return
Would but forget and pardon my offence.   90
Phylena. Let me entreat your grace upon my knees
To pardon him and let my death discharge°   *release, exonerate*
The heavy wrath your grace hath vowed 'gainst him.

---

the moon), and a character in *Locrine* (1595), by an anonymous "W.S.," speaks
of "wat'ry *Meroe,* / Where fiery *Phoebus* in his chariot . . . Casts such a heat, yea
such a scorching heat" (2.5.48–49, 51).

68. "If the whole world's soul were in your breast."

Polidor. And, good my lord, let us entreat your grace
    To purge your stomach° of this melancholy.   *seat of passions and emotions*
    Taint° not your princely mind with grief, my lord,   *stain*
    But pardon and forgive these lovers' faults,
    That kneeling crave your gracious favor here.
Emelia. Great prince of Sestos, let a woman's words
    Entreat a pardon in your lordly breast,   100
    Both for your princely son and us, my lord.
Duke. Aurelius, stand up. I pardon thee.
    I see that virtue will have enemies,
    And fortune will be thwarting honor still.°   *continually*
    And you, fair virgin too, I am content
    To accept you for my daughter since 'tis done,
    And see you princely used° in Sestos' court.   *royally treated*
Phylena. Thanks, good my lord, and I° no longer live   *and may I*
    Than I obey and honor you in all.
Alfonso. Let me give thanks unto your royal grace   110
    For this great honor done to me and mine.
    And if your grace will walk unto my house,
    I will, in humblest manner I can, show
    The eternal service I do owe your grace.
Duke. Thanks, good Alfonso, but I came alone
    And not as did beseem the Sestian duke,
    Nor would I have it known within the town
    That I was here and thus without my train,°   *body of attendants*
    But as I came alone so will I go
    And leave my son to solemnize his feast.   120
    And ere't be long I'll come again to you
    And do him honor as beseems the son
    Of mighty Jerobel[69] the Sestian duke.
    'Til when, I'll leave you. Farewell, Aurelius.
Aurelius. Not yet my lord; I'll bring you to your ship. *Exeunt omnes.*

---

69. This name is of unknown origin although it may come from the biblical
name "Jerobaal," another name for Gideon at Judges 6:32.

[SCENE 14]

Sly sleeps.

Lord. Who's within there? Come hither, sirs. My lord's
 Asleep again. Go take him easily up,
 And put him in his own apparel again,
 And lay him in the place where we did find him,
 Just underneath the alehouse side, below;
 But see you wake him not in any case.
Boy. It shall be done, my lord. Come, help to bear him hence. *Exeunt.*

   Enter Ferando, Aurelius, and Polidor
   and his boy, and Valeria and Sander.

Ferando. Come, gentlemen, now that supper's done,
 How shall we spend the time 'til we go to bed?
Aurelius. Faith, if you will, in trial of our wives,   10
 Who will come soonest at their husband's call.
Polidor. Nay then, Ferando he must needs sit out,°   *take no part*
 For he may call, I think, 'til he be weary
 Before his wife will come before she list.°   *wants to*
Ferando. 'Tis well for you that have such gentle wives,
 Yet in this trial will I not sit out.
 It may be Kate will come as soon as yours.
Aurelius. My wife comes soonest for a hundred pound.
Polidor. I take it. I'll lay° as much to yours°   *wager / as you do*
 That my wife comes as soon as I do send.   20
Aurelius. How now, Ferando, you dare not lay belike.° *probably dare not bet*
Ferando. Why, true. I dare not lay indeed;
 But how, so little money on so sure a thing?
 A hundred pound: why, I have laid as much
 Upon my dog, in running at a deer.
 She shall not come so far for such a trifle.
 But will you lay five hundred marks[70] with me?
 And whose wife soonest comes when he doth call,
 And shows herself most loving unto him,
 Let him enjoy the wager I have laid.   30
 Now, what say you? Dare you adventure thus?

---

70. Three and one-third times the £100 wager.

Polidor. Ay, were it a thousand pound I durst presume
    On my wife's love, and I will lay with thee.

Enter Alfonso.

Alfonso. How now, sons, what, in conference so
        hard.°   such intense conversation
    May I without offence know whereabouts?
Aurelius. Faith, father, a weighty cause° about our wives.   matter
    Five hundred marks already we have laid,
    And he whose wife doth show most love to him,
    He must enjoy the wager to himself.
Alfonso. Why then, Ferando he is sure to lose.   40
    I promise thee, son, thy wife will hardly come,
    And therefore I would not wish thee lay so much.
Ferando. Tush, father, were it ten times more,
    I durst adventure on my lovely Kate.
    But if I lose I'll pay, and so shall you.
Aurelius. Upon mine honor, if I lose I'll pay.
Polidor. And so will I, upon my faith, I vow.
Ferando. Then sit we down, and let us send for them.
Alfonso. I promise thee, Ferando, I am afraid thou wilt lose.
Aurelius. I'll send for my wife first. Valeria,   50
    Go bid your mistress come to me.
Valeria. I will, my lord.   *Exit Valeria.*
Aurelius. Now for my hundred pound.
    Would any lay ten hundred more with me,
    I know I should obtain it by her love.
Ferando. I pray God you have not laid too much already.
Aurelius. Trust me, Ferando, I am sure you have,
    For you I dare presume have lost it all.

Enter Valeria again.

    Now, sirrah, what says your mistress?
Valeria. She is something° busy but she'll come anon.   somewhat
Ferando. Why, so, did not I tell you this before?   61
    She is "busy" and cannot come.
Aurelius. I pray God your wife send you so good an answer.
    She may be busy, yet she says she'll come.
Ferando. Well, well. Polidor, send you for your wife.
Polidor. Agreed. Boy, desire your mistress to come hither.

Boy. I will, sir. *Exit boy.*
Ferando. Ay so, so he "desires" her to come.
Alfonso. Polidor, I dare presume for thee.
    I think thy wife will not deny to come.   70
    And I do marvel much, Aurelius,
    That your wife came not when you sent for her.

Enter the boy again.

Polidor. Now, where's your mistress?
Boy. She bade me tell you that she will not come.
    An° you have any business, you must come to her.   *if*
Ferando. O monstrous, intolerable presumption,
    Worse than a blazing star,° or snow at midsummer,   *comet*
    Earthquakes or anything unseasonable.
    She will not come, but he must come to her.
Polidor. Well, sir, I pray you, let's hear what   80
    Answer your wife will make.
Ferando. Sirrah, command your mistress to come
    To me presently.°   *immediately*
Exit Sander.
Aurelius. I think my wife for all she did not come,
    Will prove most kind, for now I have no fear,
    For I am sure Ferando's wife, she will not come.
Ferando. The more's the pity: then I must lose.

Enter Kate and Sander.

    But I have won, for see where Kate doth come.
Kate. Sweet husband, did you send for me?
Ferando. I did, my love. I sent for thee to come.   90
    Come hither, Kate. What's that upon thy head.
Kate. Nothing, husband, but my cap, I think.
Ferando. Pull it off and tread it under thy feet.
    'Tis foolish. I will not have thee wear it. *She takes off her cap and*
      treads on it.
Polidor. O wonderful metamorphosis.
Aurelius. This is a wonder almost past belief.
Ferando. This is a token of her true love to me.
    And yet I'll try° her further, you shall see.   *test*
    Come hither, Kate. Where are thy sisters?
Kate. They be sitting in the bridal chamber.   100

Ferando. Fetch them hither, and if they will not come,
  Bring them perforce° and make them come with thee.   *forcibly*
Kate. I will. *[Exit Kate.]*
Alfonso. I promise thee, Ferando, I would have sworn
  Thy wife would ne'er have done so much for thee.
Ferando. But you shall see she will do more than this:
  For see where she brings her sisters forth by force.

        Enter Kate thrusting Phylena and Emelia before her
          and makes them come unto their husbands' call.

Kate. See husband, I have brought them both.
Ferando. 'Tis well done, Kate.
Emelia. Ay, sure, and like a loving piece,° you're   *person (often derogatory)*
    worthy
  To have great praise for this attempt.   111
Phylena. Ay, for making a fool of herself and us.
Aurelius. Beshrew° thee, Phylena, thou hast   *curse*
  Lost me a hundred pound tonight.
  For I did lay° that thou wouldst first have come.   *wager*
Polidor. But thou, Emelia, has lost me a great deal more.
Emelia. You might have kept it better then.
    Who bade you lay?
Ferando. Now, lovely Kate, before their husbands here,
  I prithee, tell unto these headstrong women   120
  What duty wives do owe unto their husbands.
Kate. Then you that live thus by your pampered wills,
  Now list° to me and mark what I shall say: *listen*
  Th'eternal power that with his only breath°[71]   *only with his breath*
  Shall cause this end and this beginning frame—
  Not in time, nor before time, but with time confused—
  For all the course of years, of ages, months,
  Of seasons temperate, of days and hours,
  Are tuned and stopped by measure of his hand.
  The first world was a form without a form,   130
  A heap confused, a mixture all deformed,
  A gulf of gulfs, a body bodyless

71. Lines 124–38 are borrowed from *La Création du Monde ou Première Sepmaine*
(known in English as *The Divine Weeks*) of the French poet Du Bartas. See
Miller's Cambridge edition of this play, Appendix 3 (147–52).

Where all the elements were orderless
Before the great commander of the world,
The King of Kings, the glorious God of heaven,
Who in six days did frame his heavenly work
And made all things to stand in perfect course.
Then to his image he did make a man,
Old Adam, and from his side, asleep,
A rib was taken, of which the Lord did make   140
The "woe of man" so termed by Adam then
"Woman" for that.[72] By her came sin to us,
And for her sin was Adam doomed to die.
As Sara[73] to her husband, so should we,
Obey them, love them, keep and nourish them.
If they by any means do want our helps,
Laying our hands under their feet to tread,
If that by that we might procure their ease,
And for a precedent I'll first begin,
And lay my hand under my husband's feet. *She lays her hand under*
      her husband's feet.

Ferando. Enough, sweet, the wager thou hast won,   151
      And they I am sure cannot deny the same.
Alfonso. Ay, Ferando, the wager thou hast won.
      And for to show thee how I am pleased in this,
      A hundred pounds I freely give thee more,
      Another dowry for another daughter,
      For she is not the same she was before.
Ferando. Thanks, sweet father. Gentlemen, goodnight,
      For Kate and I will leave you for tonight.   159
      'Tis Kate and I am wed, and you are sped.°   *undone*
      And so farewell, for we will to our beds. *Exeunt Ferando and Kate*
      and Sander.
Alfonso. Now, Aurelius, what say you to this?
Aurelius. Believe me, father, I rejoice to see
      Ferando and his wife so lovingly agree.
            Exeunt Aurelius and Phylena and Alfonso and Valeria.
Emelia. How now, Polidor, in a dump;° what sayst thou, man? *low spirits*
Polidor. I say thou art a shrew.

---

72. This punning false etymology of "woman" was current at the time.
73. The wife of Abraham in Genesis.

Emelia. That's better than a sheep.[74]

Polidor. Well, since 'tis done, let it go. Come, let's in.   *Exeunt Polidor*
    and Emelia.

[SCENE 15]

Then enter two bearing of Sly in his own apparel again, and leaves him
where they found him and then goes out. Then enter the tapster.

Tapster. Now that the darksome night is overpast,
    And dawning day appears in crystal sky,
    Now must I haste abroad. But soft, who's this?
    What, Sly? O wondrous, hath he lain here all night?
    I'll wake him. I think he's starved by this,
    But that his belly was so stuffed with ale.
    What how, Sly, awake, for shame.

Sly. Sim, gi's° some more wine. What's all the players gone? Am   *give us*
    not I a lord?   9

Tapster. A lord with a murrain.° Come, art thou drunken still?   *disease*

Sly. Who's this? Tapster? O lord, sirrah, I have had the bravest°   *best*
    dream tonight that ever thou heard'st in all thy life.

Tapster. Ay, marry, but you had best get you home, for your wife will
    course° you for dreaming here tonight.   *thrash*

Sly. Will she? I know now how to tame a shrew. I dreamt upon it all
    this night 'til now, and thou hast waked me out of the best dream
    that ever I had in my life. But I'll to my wife presently and tame
    her, too, an if she anger me.

Tapster. Nay tarry, Sly, for I'll go home with thee
    And hear the rest that thou hast dreamt tonight.   20
                    Exeunt omnes.

F I N I S.

74. The *OED* gives one sense of "sheep" as "a person who is as stupid, timid,
or poor-spirited as a sheep." There are two proverbs that explain this line: "It is
better to be a shrew than a sheep" and "One shrew is worth two sheep" (Tilley
S412 and S413).

THE TAMING
OF THE SHREW

WILLIAM SHAKESPEARE

[The Names of All the Characters

A lord, later acting as servant to Sly
Christopher Sly, a beggar treated as a lord
A hostess
Bartholomew, servant to the lord, acting as wife to Sly
Huntsmen, servants, players

In the play performed for Sly

BAPTISTA MINOLA, a gentleman of Padua
KATHERINA, a shrewish daughter of Baptista
BIANCA, daughter of Baptista
VINCENTIO, a merchant of Pisa
PETRUCHIO, a gentleman of Verona, a suitor to Katherina
LUCENTIO, son to Vincentio, suitor to Bianca in disguise as Cambio
GREMIO, a pantaloon,° suitor to Bianca   *foolish old man*
HORTENSIO, suitor to Bianca, sometimes in disguise as Litio
TRANIO, servant to Lucentio, suitor to Bianca, sometimes in
            disguise as Lucentio
BIONDELLO, servant to Lucentio
GRUMIO, servant to Petruchio
CURTIS, servant to Petruchio
A PEDANT, an itinerant scoundrel, induced to pretend to be
            Vincentio
A WIDOW, married by Hortensio
Tailor, haberdasher, and servants attending on Baptista and Petruchio]

THE TAMING OF THE SHREW

ACT 1, SCENE 1

Enter beggar (Christopher Sly) and hostess.

Sly. I'll feeze° you, in faith.   drive away, beat
Hostess. A pair of stocks, you rogue.
Sly. Y'are a baggage;° the Slys are no rogues. Look in the   strumpet
    chronicles: we came in with Richard Conqueror.[1] Therefore,
    paucas pallabris,° let the world slide.° Sessa.[2]   *"few words" / pass away*
Hostess. You will not pay for the glasses you have burst?
Sly. No, not a denier.° Go, by Saint Jeronimy,[3] go   *French coin of small value*
    to thy cold bed and warm thee.
Hostess. I know my remedy. I must go fetch the third-
    borough.°   *petty constable*

Exit.

Sly. Third, or fourth, or fifth borough, I'll answer him by law. I'll   11
    not budge an inch, boy; let him come, and kindly.   *fittingly (ironic)*

Falls asleep.

Wind horns. Enter a lord from hunting with his train.

Lord. Huntsman, I charge thee, tender° well my hounds—   attend to
    Brach° Merriman, the poor cur, is embossed,°   *bitch-hound / exhausted*
    And couple° Clowder with the deep-   *leash together in pairs*
      mouthed° brach.   *sonorous barking*
    Saw'st thou not, boy, how Silver made it good
    At the hedge corner, in the coldest fault?°   *a break in the scent trail*
    I would not lose the dog for twenty pound.
Huntsman. Why, Belman is as good as he, my lord;

---

1. Probably a mistake for William the Conqueror, whose conquest of England in 1066 meant the beginning of a new era in law.

2. The meaning of the exclamation "sessa" is not clear, although Shakespeare also uses it in *King Lear*. The term "sess" is used to call dogs, and "cessa" is Spanish for "be quiet."

3. Instead of invoking St. Jerome, Sly corrupts Hieronimo, the name of the hero of Thomas Kyd's popular *The Spanish Tragedy*.

He cried upon it at the merest loss,[4] 20
And twice today picked out the dullest scent.
Trust me, I take him for the better dog.
Lord. Thou art a fool. If Echo were as fleet,
I would esteem him worth a dozen such.
But sup° them well, and look unto them all; *feed*
Tomorrow I intend to hunt again.
Huntsman. I will, my lord.
Lord. What's here? One dead, or drunk? See, doth he breathe?
2 Huntsman. He breathes, my lord. Were he not warmed with ale,
This were a bed but cold to sleep so soundly. 30
Lord. O monstrous beast, how like a swine he lies.
Grim death, how foul and loathsome is thine
image.° *likeness (sleep resembling death)*
Sirs, I will practice on° this drunken man. *trick*
What think you if he were conveyed to bed,
Wrapped in sweet clothes, rings put upon his fingers,
A most delicious banquet by his bed,
And brave° attendants near him when he wakes— *finely dressed*
Would not the beggar then forget himself?
1 Huntsman. Believe me, lord, I think he cannot choose.
2 Huntsman. It would seem strange unto him when he waked. 40
Lord. Even as a flatt'ring dream or worthless fancy.° *fantasy*
Then take him up, and manage well the jest:
Carry him gently to my fairest chamber,
And hang it round with all my wanton° pictures; *lewd*
Balm his foul head in warm distillèd° waters, *purified*
And burn sweet wood to make the lodging sweet.
Procure me music ready when he wakes,
To make a dulcet° and a heavenly sound; *sweet*
And if he chance to speak, be ready straight,° *immediately*
And with a low submissive reverence 50
Say, "What is it your honor will command?"
Let one attend° him with a silver basin *wait on*
Full of rose-water and bestrewed with flowers;
Another bear the ewer,° the third a diaper,° *pitcher / towel or napkin*
And say, "Will't please your lordship cool your hands?"
Someone be ready with a costly suit,
And ask him what apparel he will wear.

4. Kept up his cry (barking) even when the scent was completely lost.

Another tell him of his hounds and horse,
And that his lady mourns at his disease;°   *malady*
Persuade him that he hath been lunatic,   60
And, when he says he is, say that he dreams,
For he is nothing but a mighty lord.
This do, and do it kindly,° gentle sirs.   *convincingly, naturally*
It will be pastime passing° excellent   *exceedingly*
If it be husbanded° with modesty.°   *managed / moderation*
1 Huntsman. My lord, I warrant° you, we will play our part   *assure*
As he shall think by our true diligence
He is no less than what we say he is.
Lord. Take him up gently, and to bed with him;   69
And each one to his office when he wakes. *[Sly is carried out.]*
                    Sound trumpets.
Sirrah,[5] go see what trumpet 'tis that sounds.
                    [Exit Servant.]
Belike° some noble gentleman that means,   *probably*
Traveling some journey, to repose him here.

                    Enter a serving-man.

How now! Who is it?
Servant. An't° please your honor, players   *and if it*
That offer service to your lordship.
Lord. Bid them come near.

                    Enter players.

Now, fellows, you are welcome.
Players. We thank your honor.
Lord. Do you intend to stay with me tonight?   80
2 Player. So please° your lordship to accept our duty.   *if it please*
Lord. With all my heart. This fellow I remember
Since once he played a farmer's eldest son;
'Twas where you wooed the gentlewoman so well.
I have forgot your name, but, sure, that part
Was aptly fitted and naturally performed.
2 Player. I think 'twas Soto[6] that your honor means.

5. Form of address to male inferiors.
6. There are a couple of characters named Soto in sixteenth-century plays, but neither fits the description given.

Lord. 'Tis very true; thou didst it excellent.
  Well, you are come to me in happy time,
  The rather for I have some sport in hand   90
  Wherein your cunning° can assist me much.   *skill*
  There is a lord will hear you play tonight;
  But I am doubtful of your modesties,°   *self-restraint*
  Lest,° over-eying° of his odd behavior— *for fear that / watching over*
  For yet his honor never heard a play—
  You break into some merry passion°   *fit of merriment*
  And so offend him. For I tell you, sirs,
  If you should smile, he grows impatient.
Player. Fear not, my lord; we can contain ourselves, 99
  Were he the veriest antic° in the world. *most strange person*
Lord. Go, sirrah, take them to the buttery,° *place for storing provisions*
  And give them friendly welcome every one;
  Let them want° nothing that my house affords.   *lack*
      Exit one with the players.
  Sirrah, go you to Bartholomew, my page,
  And see him dressed in all suits° like a lady. *respects; garments*
  That done, conduct him to the drunkard's chamber,
  And call him "madam"; do him obeisance.° *make a bow to him (Sly)*
  Tell him° from me (as° he will win my love)— *(Bartholomew) / if*
  He bear himself with honorable action
  Such as he hath observed in noble ladies   110
  Unto their lords, by them accomplishèd.° *performed*
  Such duty to the drunkard let him do,
  With soft low tongue and lowly courtesy,
  And say, "What is't your honor will command,
  Wherein your lady and your humble wife
  May show her duty and make known her love?"
  And then with kind embracements, tempting kisses,
  And with declining head into his bosom,
  Bid him shed tears, as being overjoyed
  To see her noble lord restored to health,   120
  Who for this seven years hath esteemèd him° *considered himself*
  No better than a poor and loathsome beggar.
  And if the boy have not a woman's gift
  To rain a shower of commanded tears,
  An onion will do well for such a shift,° *purpose, subterfuge*
  Which, in a napkin° being close conveyed, *handkerchief*
  Shall in despite° enforce a watery eye. *notwithstanding anything*
  See this dispatched with all the haste thou canst.

Anon° I'll give thee more instructions.   *immediately; soon*
                    Exit a Servingman.
I know the boy will well usurp the grace,   130
Voice, gait, and action, of a gentlewoman.
I long to hear him call the drunkard "husband,"
And how my men will stay° themselves from laughter   *restrain*
When they do homage to this simple peasant.
I'll in to counsel them; haply° my presence   *perhaps*
May well abate° the over-merry spleen,°   *calm down / gaiety*
Which otherwise would grow into extremes.
                    [Exeunt.]

[ACT 1, SCENE 2]

Enter aloft the drunkard with attendants,
some with apparel, basin and ewer,°   *pitcher*
and other appurtenances;° and lord.   *accessories*

Sly. For God's sake, a pot of small° ale.   *weak*
1 Servant. Will't please your lordship drink a cup of
   sack°?   *Spanish wine*
2 Servant. Will't please your honor taste of these conserves?° *candied fruit*
3 Servant. What raiment° will your honor wear today?   *clothing*
Sly. I am Christophero Sly; call not me "honor" nor "lordship." I
   ne'er drank sack in my life; and if you give me any conserves,
   give me conserves of beef. Ne'er ask me what raiment I'll wear,
   for I have no more doublets° than backs, no more   *body garments*
   stockings than legs, nor no more shoes than feet—nay, sometime
   more feet than shoes, or such shoes as my toes look through   10
   the overleather.
Lord. Heaven cease this idle humor° in your honor.   *disposition, whim*
   O, that a mighty man of such descent,
   Of such possessions, and so high esteem,
   Should be infusèd° with so foul a spirit.   *imbued, instilled*
Sly. What, would you make me mad? Am not I Christopher Sly, old
   Sly's son of Burton-Heath,[7] by birth a pedlar, by education a

---

7. Generally identified as Burton-on-the-Heath, a village sixteen miles from
Stratford, where Shakespeare's aunt, Joan Lambert, lived.

cardmaker,[8] by transmutation a bear-herd,° and   *keeper of a tame bear*
now by present profession a tinker?° Ask   *mender of pots and kettles*
Marian Hacket, the fat ale-wife of Wincot,[9] if she know me   20
not. If she say I am not fourteen pence on the score° for   *in debt*
sheer° ale, score° me up for the lying'st knave in   *undiluted / mark*
Christendom. What, I am not bestraught.° Here's—   *distracted*

3 Servant. O, this it is that makes your lady mourn.

2 Servant. O, this is it that makes your servants droop.

Lord. Hence comes it that your kindred shuns your house,
    As beaten hence by your strange lunacy.
    O, noble lord, bethink thee of° thy birth.   *recollect*
    Call home thy ancient thoughts from
        banishment,°   *recall the memories you've suppressed*
    And banish hence these abject° lowly dreams.   *dejected*
    Look how thy servants do attend on thee,   31
    Each in his office ready at thy beck.
    Wilt thou have music? Hark, Apollo° plays,   *god of music*
                    Music.
    And twenty cagèd nightingales do sing.
    Or wilt thou sleep? We'll have thee to a couch
    Softer and sweeter than the lustful bed
    On purpose trimmed up° for Semiramis.°   *attired / Queen of Assyria*
    Say thou wilt walk: we will
        bestrew° the ground.   *cover (with flowers or rushes)*
    Or wilt thou ride? Thy horses shall be trapped,°   *adorned with trappings*
    Their harness studded all with gold and pearl.   40
    Dost thou love hawking? Thou hast hawks will soar
    Above the morning lark. Or wilt thou hunt?
    Thy hounds shall make the welkin° answer them   *sky*
    And fetch shrill echoes from the hollow earth.

1 Servant. Say thou wilt course:° thy greyhounds are as swift   *hunt*
    As breathèd° stags; ay, fleeter than the roe.°   *strong-winded / deer*

2 Servant. Dost thou love pictures? We will fetch thee
        straight°   *immediately*
    Adonis[10] painted by a running brook,
    And Cytherea all in sedges° hid,   *grassy plants*

---

8. "Cards" are implements with iron teeth used for combing out wool.

9. Perhaps a real person and related to the Cicely Hacket of 1.2.87. Wincot is four miles south of Stratford.

10. Beautiful boy beloved of Venus (Cytheria).

    Which seem to move and wanton° with her breath   *frolic*

    Even as the waving sedges play with wind.   51

Lord. We'll show thee Io[11] as she was a maid

    And how she was beguilèd and surprised,

    As lively painted as the deed was done.

3 Servant. Or Daphne[12] roaming through a thorny wood,

    Scratching her legs, that one shall swear she bleeds,

    And at that sight shall sad Apollo weep,

    So workmanly the blood and tears are drawn.

Lord. Thou art a lord, and nothing but a lord.

    Thou hast a lady far more beautiful   60

    Than any woman in this waning age.

1 Servant. And, 'til the tears that she hath shed for thee

    Like envious floods o'er-run her lovely face,

    She was the fairest creature in the world;

    And yet she is inferior to none.

Sly. Am I a lord, and have I such a lady?

    Or do I dream? Or have I dreamed 'til now?

    I do not sleep: I see, I hear, I speak;

    I smell sweet savors, and I feel soft things.

    Upon my life, I am a lord indeed,   70

    And not a tinker, nor Christopher Sly.

    Well, bring our lady hither to our sight.

    And once again, a pot o'th' smallest° ale.   *weakest*

2 Servant. Will't please your mightiness to wash your hands?

    O, how we joy to see your wit restored.

    O, that once more you knew but what you are:

    These fifteen years you have been in a dream,

    Or, when you waked, so waked as if you slept.

Sly. These fifteen years? By my fay,° a goodly nap.   *faith*

    But did I never speak of all that time?   80

1 Servant. O, yes, my lord, but very idle words.

    For though you lay here in this goodly chamber,

    Yet would you say ye were beaten out of door

    And rail upon° the hostess of the house,   *cry out against*

    And say you would present her at the leet°   *bring her to trial in court*

---

11. A maiden beloved of Jupiter, who turned her into a cow to conceal her from his queen Juno.

12. A nymph beloved of Apollo, the god of poetry, music, and the sun. She fled him and was rescued by being changed into a laurel tree.

   Because she brought stone jugs and no sealed quarts.[13]
   Sometimes you would call out for Cicely Hacket.[14]
Sly. Ay, the woman's maid of the house.
3 Servant. Why, sir, you know no house nor no such maid,
   Nor no such men as you have reckoned up: 90
   As Stephen Sly, and old John Naps of Greece,
   And Peter Turph, and Henry Pimpernell,
   And twenty more such names and men as these,
   Which never were, nor no man ever saw.
Sly. Now, Lord be thankèd for my good amends.
All. Amen.

        Enter [the page Bartholomew as] lady, with attendants.

Sly. I thank thee; thou shalt not lose by it.
Page. How fares my noble lord?
Sly. Marry, I fare well; for here is cheer enough.
   Where is my wife?   100
Page. Here, noble lord; what is thy will with her?
Sly. Are you my wife and will not call me husband?
   My men should call me "lord"; I am your goodman.°   *husband*
Page. My husband and my lord, my lord and husband;
   I am your wife in all obedience.
Sly. I know it well. What must I call her?
Lord. Madam.
Sly. Alice madam, or Joan madam?
Lord. Madam, and nothing else; so lords call ladies.
Sly. Madam wife, they say that I have dreamed   110
   And slept above some fifteen year or more.
Page. Ay, and the time seems thirty unto me,
   Being all this time abandoned from your bed.
Sly. 'Tis much. Servants, leave me and her alone. *[Exeunt lord and*
        servants.]
   Madam, undress you, and come now to bed.
Page. Thrice noble lord, let me entreat of you
   To pardon me yet for a night or two;
   Or, if not so, until the sun be set.
   For your physicians have expressly charged,

13. Containers officially stamped to guarantee they held a quart.
14. See n. 9.

In peril to incur your former malady,   120
That I should yet absent me from your bed.
I hope this reason stands for my excuse.
Sly. Ay, it stands so that I may hardly tarry so long. But I would
be loath to fall into my dreams again. I will therefore tarry in
despite of the flesh and the blood.

Enter a messenger.

Messenger. Your honor's players, hearing your amendment,
Are come to play a pleasant comedy,
For so your doctors hold it very meet,°   *proper*
Seeing too much sadness hath congealed your blood,
And melancholy is the nurse of frenzy.   130
Therefore they thought it good you hear a play
And frame your mind to mirth and merriment,
Which bars° a thousand harms and lengthens life.   *prevents*
Sly. Marry, I will let them play; it is not a comonty,° a   *mistake for "comedy"*
Christmas gambol or a tumbling-trick!
Page. No, my good lord, it is more pleasing stuff.
Sly. What, household stuff.
Page. It is a kind of history.
Sly. Well, we'll see't. Come, madam wife, sit by my side and let
the world slip. We shall ne'er be younger.   140

Flourish.° Enter Lucentio and his man Tranio.   *fanfare*

Lucentio. Tranio, since for the great desire I had
To see fair Padua, nursery of arts,
I am arrived for° fruitful Lombardy,[15]   *in*
The pleasant garden of great Italy,
And by my father's love and leave am armed
With his good will and thy good company.
My trusty servant, well approved in all,
Here let us breathe° and haply institute°   *pause / perhaps begin*
A course of learning and ingenious° studies.   *suitable for my rank, liberal*
Pisa, renownèd for grave citizens,   150

15. The details of the text seem to suggest that Padua, famous for its university,
was a seaport in Lombardy. It is neither. Padua is twenty-five miles west of
Venice.

Gave me my being and my father first,
A merchant of great traffic° through the world,   *business*
Vincentio, come of the Bentivolii.[16]
Vincentio's son, brought up in Florence,
It shall become to serve all hopes
    conceived,°   *it is fitting to fulfill expectation*
To deck° his fortune with his virtuous deeds.   *adorn*
And therefore, Tranio, for the time I study,
Virtue and that part of philosophy
Will I apply° that treats of happiness   *apply myself to*
By virtue specially to be achieved.   160
Tell me thy mind; for I have Pisa left
And am to Padua come, as he that leaves
A shallow plash° to plunge him in the deep,   *pool*
And with satiety° seeks to quench his thirst.   *excess*
Tranio. Mi perdonato,° gentle master mine,   *"excuse me"*
    I am in all affected° as yourself: *inclined*
Glad that you thus continue your resolve
To suck the sweets of sweet philosophy.
Only, good master, while we do admire
This virtue and this moral discipline,   170
Let's be no Stoics nor no stocks,° I pray,   *repressed or stupid people*
Or so devote to Aristotle's checks°   *devoted to Aristotle's restraints*
As Ovid[17] be an outcast quite abjured.°   *rejected*
Balk° logic with acquaintance that you have,°   *shun / people you know*
And practice rhetoric in your common talk;
Music and poesy use to quicken° you;   *enliven*
The mathematics and the metaphysics,
Fall to them as you find your stomach serves° you.   *inclination moves*
No profit grows where is no pleasure ta'en.   179
In brief, sir, study what you most affect.°   *desire*
Lucentio. Gramercies,° Tranio, well dost thou advise.   *thanks*
    If, Biondello, thou wert come ashore,
    We could at once put us in readiness,

16. Historically, the Bentivogli were from Bologna, not Pisa.

17. Ovid is the author of *Ars Amatoria* ("Art of Love"), and Tranio is anxious that the rigor of their study would not rule out loving encounters. Ovid also wrote *Heroides,* which Lucentio seems to be using as a pretext for his lovemaking in 3.1.27–36.

And take a lodging fit to entertain
Such friends as time in Padua shall beget.

Enter Baptista with his two daughters, Katherina and Bianca; Gremio, a
pantaloon; Hortensio, suitor to Bianca. Lucentio and Tranio stand by.

But stay awhile, what company is this?
Tranio. Master, some show to welcome us to town.
Baptista. Gentlemen, importune° me no farther,   *urge*
    For how I firmly am resolved you know:
    That is, not to bestow my youngest daughter   190
    Before I have a husband for the elder.
    If either of you both love Katherina,
    Because I know you well and love you well,
    Leave shall you have to court her at your pleasure.
Gremio. To cart[18] her rather. She's too rough for me.
    There, there, Hortensio, will you any wife?
Katherina. I pray you, sir, is it your will
    To make a stale° of me amongst these   *spinster; prostitute*
      mates?°   *fellows; husbands*
Hortensio. Mates, maid, how mean you that? No mates for you,
    Unless you were of gentler, milder mold.   200
Katherina. I'faith, sir, you shall never need to fear:
    Iwis° it is not halfway to her° heart,   *indeed / (i.e., her own)*
    But if it were, doubt not her care should be
    To comb your noddle° with a three-legged stool,   *beat you over the head*
    And paint your face, and use you like a fool.
Hortensio. From all such devils, good Lord deliver us.
Gremio. And me, too, good Lord.
Tranio. Hush, master, here's some good pastime toward.°   *coming*
    That wench is stark mad or wonderful froward.°   *perverse, ungovernable*
Lucentio. But in the other's silence do I see   210
    Maid's mild behavior and sobriety.
    Peace, Tranio!
Tranio. Well said, master; mum, and gaze your fill.
Baptista. Gentlemen, that I may soon make good
    What I have said—Bianca, get you in;
    And let it not displease thee, good Bianca,
    For I will love thee ne'er the less, my girl.

18. "Carting," carrying through the streets on display in a cart, was a punishment. "Cart" is also a homonym for "court."

Katherina. A pretty peat!° It is best   *pet*
    Put finger in the eye, an° she knew why.   *if*
Bianca. Sister, content you in my discontent.   220
    Sir, to your pleasure humbly I subscribe;
    My books and instruments shall be my company,
    On them to look, and practice by myself.
Lucentio. Hark, Tranio, thou mayst hear Minerva°   *Roman goddess of wisdom*
    speak.
Hortensio. Signor Baptista, will you be so strange?°   *difficult*
    Sorry am I that our good will effects°   *causes*
    Bianca's grief.
Gremio. Why will you mew° her up,   *cage (as a hawk)*
    Signor Baptista, for this fiend of hell,
    And make her° bear the penance of her° tongue?   *(Bianca) / (Katherina)*
Baptista. Gentlemen, content ye; I am resolved.   231
    Go in, Bianca. *[Exit Bianca.]*
    And for I know she taketh most delight
    In music, instruments, and poetry,
    Schoolmasters will I keep within my house
    Fit to instruct her youth. If you, Hortensio,
    Or, Signor Gremio, you, know any such,
    Prefer them hither, for to cunning° men   *skillful, expert*
    I will be very kind, and liberal
    To mine own children in good bringing-up.   240
    And so, farewell. Katherina, you may stay;
    For I have more to commune with Bianca.   *Exit*
Katherina. Why, and I trust I may go too, may I not?
    What, shall I be appointed hours, as though,
    Belike° I knew not what to take and what to leave? Ha!   *maybe*
                      Exit.
Gremio. You may go to the devil's dam. Your gifts are so good
    here's none will hold you. Their° love is not so great,   *(women's)*
    Hortensio, but we may blow our nails together, and fast it fairly
    out. Our cake's dough on both sides.[19] Farewell. Yet, for the
    love I bear my sweet Bianca, if I can by any means light on   250
    a fit man to teach her that wherein she delights, I will wish
    him to her father.

---

19. These lines combine expressions for waiting patiently ("blow our nail," Dent 10.1) and disappointment for a failed undertaking ("our cake's dough on both sides," Tilley C12).

Hortensio. So will I, Signor Gremio. But a word, I pray. Though
the nature of our quarrel yet never brooked parle,°   *allowed negotiations*
know now, upon advice, it toucheth us both—that we may yet
again have access to our fair mistress and be happy rivals in
Bianca's love—to labor and effect one thing specially.

Gremio. What's that, I pray?

Hortensio. Marry, sir, to get a husband for her sister.

Gremio. A husband: a devil.   260

Hortensio. I say a husband.

Gremio. I say a devil. Think'st thou, Hortensio, though her father
be very rich, any man is so very° a fool to be married   *complete*
to hell?

Hortensio. Tush,[20] Gremio. Though it pass° your patience and   *surpass*
mine to endure her loud alarums,° why, man,   *disturbances, outcries*
there be good fellows in the world, and° a man could light   *if*
on them, would take her with all faults, and money enough.

Gremio. I cannot tell; but I had as lief° take her dowry with this   *as soon*
condition: to be whipped at the high cross[21] every morning.   270

Hortensio. Faith, as you say, there's small choice in rotten
apples. But, come: since this bar in law°   *obstacle (Baptista's decision)*
makes us friends, it shall be so far forth friendly maintained
'til by helping Baptista's eldest daughter to a husband we set
his youngest free for a husband, and then have to't°   *go at it*
afresh. Sweet Bianca, happy man be his dole.°   *may the best man win*
He that runs fastest gets the ring. How say you, Signor Gremio?

Gremio. I am agreed, and would I had given him° the best   *(some man)*
horse in Padua to begin his wooing that would thoroughly woo
her, wed her, and bed her, and rid the house of her. Come on.   280

> *Exeunt ambo° [Gremio and Hortensio]*   *two together*
> *Manent° Tranio and Lucentio.*   *remain*

Tranio. I pray, sir, tell me, is it possible
That love should of a sudden take such hold?

Lucentio. O, Tranio, 'til I found it to be true,
I never thought it possible or likely.
But see, while idly I stood looking on,

---

20. An exclamation of impatience or scoffing.

21. The *OED* provides the definition, "a cross set on a pedestal in a market-place
or in the centre of a town or village."

I found the effect of love in idleness;[22]
And now in plainness do confess to thee,
That art to me as secret and as dear
As Anna to the Queen of Carthage[23] was—
Tranio, I burn, I pine, I perish, Tranio,   290
If I achieve not this young modest girl.
Counsel me, Tranio, for I know thou canst;
Assist me, Tranio, for I know thou wilt.

Tranio. Master, it is no time to chide you now;
Affection is not rated° from the heart.   *scolded*
If love have touched you, nought remains but so:
"*Redime te captum quam queas minimo.*"[24]

Lucentio. Gramercies, lad. Go forward; this contents;°   *this helps*
The rest will comfort, for thy counsel's sound.   299

Tranio. Master, you looked so longly° on the maid,   *for such a long time*
Perhaps you marked not what's the pith° of all.   *essence*

Lucentio. O, yes, I saw sweet beauty in her face,
Such as the daughter of Agenor[25] had,
That made great Jove to humble him to her hand,
When with his knees he kissed the Cretan strand.

Tranio. Saw you no more? Marked you not how her sister
Began to scold and raise up such a storm
That mortal ears might hardly endure the din?°   *noise*

Lucentio. Tranio, I saw her coral lips to move,
And with her breath she did perfume the air.   310
Sacred and sweet was all I saw in her.

Tranio. Nay, then 'tis time to stir him° from his trance.   *(Lucentio)*
I pray, awake, sir. If you love the maid,
Bend thoughts and wits to achieve her. Thus it stands:
Her elder sister is so curst and shrewd°   *cantankerous and sharp-tongued*
That, 'til the father rid his hands of her,

22. It was thought that idleness begot love. The pansy is called "love-in-idleness" and is the flower used for the love potion in *A Midsummer Night's Dream.*

23. In Vergil's *Aeneid,* Anna is the sister and confidante of Dido, Queen of Carthage, the abandoned paramour of Aeneas.

24. "Ransom yourself (from love) as cheaply as you can." The quotation is from Lily's *Latin Grammar,* which Shakespeare probably used as a schoolboy.

25. Agenor was the father of Europa, the paramour of Jove (Jupiter) who transformed himself into a bull to carry Europa across the sea to Crete for his pleasure.

    Master, your love must live a maid at home;
    And therefore has he closely mewed her up,
    Because she will not be annoyed with suitors.
Lucentio. Ah, Tranio, what a cruel father's he.   320
    But art thou not advised he took some care
    To get her cunning schoolmasters to instruct her?
Tranio. Ay, marry, am I, sir, and now 'tis plotted.
Lucentio. I have it, Tranio.
Tranio. Master, for my hand,°   *I assure you*
    Both our inventions meet and jump° in one.   *coincide*
Lucentio. Tell me thine first.
Tranio. You will be schoolmaster,
    And undertake the teaching of the maid.
    That's your device.°   *scheme*
Lucentio. It is. May it be done?   331
Tranio. Not possible. For who shall bear your part
    And be in Padua here Vincentio's son;
    Keep house and ply° his book, welcome his friends, *work at*
    Visit his countrymen, and banquet them?
Lucentio. Basta,° content thee, for I have it full.   *"Enough"*
    We have not yet been seen in any house,
    Nor can we be distinguished by our faces
    For man or master. Then it follows thus:
    Thou shalt be master, Tranio, in my stead,   340
    Keep house and port° and servants, as I should. *social station*
    I will some other be: some Florentine,
    Some Neapolitan, or meaner man of Pisa.
    'Tis hatched and shall be so. Tranio, at once
    Uncase thee;° take my con-lord[26] hat and *take off your outer garments*
        cloak.
    When Biondello comes, he waits on thee;
    But I will charm° him first to keep his tongue. *influence*
Tranio. So had you need. *[They exchange clothing.]*
    In brief, sir, sith° it your pleasure is,   *since*
    And I am tied to be obedient,   350

---

26. *Conlord* is the folio reading. The *n* is usually taken for a turned *u* (as occurs another time in F1) and the word interpreted as *coulord* ("coulor'd") and printed "colored." According to the *OED,* the prefix "con" can mean "with," and "confrere" and "con-brethren" are given as compounds with "con." Perhaps, by analogy, "con-lord" means "lordly" or "as lords wear."

For so your father charged me at our parting:
"Be serviceable to my son" quoth he—
Although I think 'twas in another sense—
I am content to be Lucentio,
Because so well I love Lucentio.

Lucentio. Tranio, be so because Lucentio loves;
And let me be a slave t'achieve that maid
Whose sudden sight hath thralled° my wounded eye.   *enslaved*

Enter Biondello.

Here comes the rogue. Sirrah, where have you been?

Biondello. Where have I been? Nay, how now, where are you?   360
Master, has my fellow Tranio stol'n your clothes, or you stol'n
his, or both? Pray, what's the news?

Lucentio. Sirrah, come hither. 'Tis no time to jest,
And therefore frame your manners to the time.
Your fellow Tranio here, to save my life,
Puts my apparel and my count'nance° on,   *manner*
And I for my escape have put on his.
For in a quarrel since I came ashore
I killed a man, and fear I was descried.°   *observed*
Wait you on him, I charge you, as becomes,   370
While I make way from hence to save my life.
You understand me?

Biondello. Ay, sir, ne'er a whit.

Lucentio. And not a jot of Tranio in your mouth—
Tranio is changed into Lucentio.

Biondello. The better for him; would I were so too.

Tranio. So could I, 'faith, boy, to have the next wish after, that
Lucentio indeed had Baptista's youngest daughter. But, sirrah,
not for my sake but your master's, I advise you use your manners
discreetly in all kind of companies. When I am alone, why,   380
then I am Tranio. But in all places else your master Lucentio.

Lucentio. Tranio, let's go.
One thing more rests, that thyself execute:
To make one among these wooers. If thou ask me why,
Sufficeth, my reasons are both good and weighty. *Exeunt.*

The presenters above [Sly, page, and servant] speak.

Servant. My lord, you nod; you do not mind° the play.   *pay attention to*

Sly. Yes, by Saint Anne, do I. A good matter, surely; comes there
    any more of it?
Page. My lord, 'tis but begun.
Sly. 'Tis a very excellent piece of work, madam lady. Would   390
    'twere done.

                    They sit and mark.

     Enter Petruchio and his man Grumio.

Petruchio. Verona, for a while I take my leave,
    To see my friends in Padua; but of all
    My best belovèd and approvèd friend,
    Hortensio. And I trow° this is his house.   *believe*
    Here, sirrah Grumio, knock, I say.
Grumio. Knock, sir? Whom should I knock? Is there any man has
    rebused° your worship?   *(i.e., abused)*
Petruchio. Villain, I say, knock me[27] here soundly.
Grumio. Knock you here, sir? Why, sir, what am I, sir, that I   400
    should knock you here, sir?
Petruchio. Villain, I say, knock me at this gate,
    And rap me well, or I'll knock your knave's pate°   *head*
Grumio. My master is grown quarrelsome. I should knock you first,
    And then I know after who comes by the
    worst.°   *I hit you and then you beat me*
Petruchio. Will it not be?
    Faith, sirrah, an° you'll not knock, I'll ring it;   *if*
    I'll try how you can sol-fa,° and sing it.   *notes in scale*
             He wrings him by the ears.
Grumio. Help, masters,[28] help! My master is mad.   410
Petruchio. Now knock when I bid you, sirrah villain.°   *slave, wretch*

            Enter Hortensio.

Hortensio. How now, what's the matter? My old friend, Grumio,
    and my good friend, Petruchio? How do you all at Verona?

27. Petruchio's "me" in this line is the old-fashioned ethical dative, described
by the *OED* as "used to imply that a person, other than the subject or object,
has an indirect interest in the fact stated." Thus the phrase may be rendered,
"Knock for me." In the following line, Grumio interprets the order as a request
to "Knock" (punch) Petruchio.
28. Here, and again at 4.5.5 and 4.5.43, it appears that an abbreviation in the
manuscript led the compositors to set "mistris" for "master(s)."

Petruchio. Signor Hortensio, come you to part the fray?

    Con tutto il cuore ben trovato,° may I say.   *"With all my heart well met."*

Hortensio. Alla nostra casa ben venuto,

    Molto honorato signor mio

        Petruchio.°   *"Welcome to our house my much-honored Petruchio."*

    Rise, Grumio, rise; we will compound° this quarrel.   settle

Grumio. Nay, 'tis no matter, sir, what he 'leges° in Latin. If this   alleges

    be not a lawful cause for me to leave his service: look you, sir: 420

    he bid me knock him and rap him soundly, sir. Well, was it fit

    for a servant to use his master so; being, perhaps, for aught I

    see, two and thirty, a pip out?[29] Whom would to God I

    had well knocked at first. Then had not Grumio come

    by the worst.

Petruchio. A senseless villain. Good Hortensio,

    I bade the rascal knock upon your gate,

    And could not get him for my heart to do it.

Grumio. Knock at the gate? O, heavens. Spake you not these words

    plain: "Sirrah, knock me here, rap me here, knock me well,   430

    and knock me soundly"? And come you now with "knocking

    at the gate"?

Petruchio. Sirrah, be gone, or talk not, I advise you.

Hortensio. Petruchio, patience; I am Grumio's pledge.°   bond, security

    Why, this's a heavy chance° 'twixt him and you,   sad misunderstanding

    Your ancient, trusty, pleasant servant Grumio.

    And tell me now, sweet friend, what happy gale

    Blows you to Padua here from old Verona?

Petruchio. Such wind as scatters young men through the world

    To seek their fortunes farther than at home,   440

    Where small experience grows but in a few.

    Signor Hortensio, thus it stands with me:

    Antonio, my father, is deceased,

    And I have thrust myself into this maze,°   labyrinth

    Haply° to wive and thrive as best I may.   with luck

    Crowns[30] in my purse I have, and goods at home,

    And so am come abroad to see the world.

---

29. Apparently a reference to the card game "Thirty-One," where the object was to get a hand where the cards (marked with "pips" or "spots") add up to thirty-one. Grumio is suggesting that Petruchio has one "pip" over and thus has lost. This game is alluded to again at 3.4.59.

30. A crown was equal to five shillings or one-quarter pound sterling.

Hortensio. Petruchio, shall I then come roundly° to thee   *speak plainly*
   And wish thee to a shrewd, ill-favored°   *shrewish, endued with bad qualities*
      wife?
   Thou'dst thank me but a little for my counsel,   450
   And yet I'll promise thee she shall be rich,
   And very rich. But th'art too much my friend,
   And I'll not wish thee to her.
Petruchio. Signor Hortensio, 'twixt such friends as we
   Few words suffice; and therefore, if thou know
   One rich enough to be Petruchio's wife,
   As wealth is burden° of my wooing dance,   *musical accompaniment*
   Be she as foul as was Florentius'[31] love,
   As old as Sibyl,[32] and as curst and shrewd°   *shrewish, scolding*
   As Socrates' Xanthippe[33] or a worse,   460
   She moves me not, or not removes at least
   Affection's edge in me, were she as rough
   As are the swelling Adriatic seas.
   I come to wive it wealthily in Padua;
   If wealthily, then happily in Padua.
Grumio. Nay, look you, sir, he tells you flatly what his mind is.
   Why, give him gold enough and marry him to a puppet or an
   aglet-baby,° or an old trot° with   *doll decorated with ornamental tags / hag*
   ne'er a tooth in her head, though she have as many diseases as
   two and fifty horses. Why, nothing comes amiss, so money   470
   comes withal.
Hortensio. Petruchio, since we are stepped thus far in,
   I will continue that I broached in jest.
   I can, Petruchio, help thee to a wife
   With wealth enough, and young and beauteous;
   Brought up as best becomes a gentlewoman.
   Her only fault, and that is faults enough,

---

31. In John Gower's *Confessio Amantis,* Florentius is a knight who keeps his promise to marry an ugly hag, because she answered the question upon which his life depends: "What is it that all women desire?" She answers that all women want to "be sovereign of man's love." On their wedding night she turns into a beautiful woman. Chaucer tells the tale in *The Wife of Bath's Tale.* The story may be at the heart of this play.

32. Apollo granted the Cumaean Sybil a life of as many years as the grains in a handful of sand.

33. Xanthippe, the wife of Socrates, was notorious for her ill temper, nagging, and scolding.

Is that she is intolerable curst,
And shrewd and froward,° so beyond all measure,   *perverse*
That, were my state° far worser than it is,   *fortune, estate*
I would not wed her for a mine of gold.   481
Petruchio. Hortensio, peace; thou know'st not gold's effect.
Tell me her father's name, and 'tis enough;
For I will board° her though she chide as loud   *woo*
As thunder when the clouds in autumn crack.
Hortensio. Her father is Baptista Minola,
An affable and courteous gentleman;
Her name is Katherina Minola,
Renowned in Padua for her scolding tongue.
Petruchio. I know her father, though I know not her;   490
And he knew my deceasèd father well.
I will not sleep, Hortensio, 'til I see her;
And therefore let me be thus bold with you
To give you over° at this first encounter,   *leave you*
Unless you will accompany me thither.
Grumio. I pray you, sir, let him go while the humor°   *disposition, whim*
lasts. O' my word, and° she knew him as well as I do, she   *if*
would think scolding would do little good upon him. She may
perhaps call him half a score knaves or so. Why, that's
nothing; and he begin once, he'll rail in his rope-tricks.[34]   500
I'll tell you what, sir: and she stand him but a little, he will
throw a figure° in her face, and so disfigure her   *figure of speech*
with it that she shall have no more eyes to see withal than
a cat. You know him not, sir.
Hortensio. Tarry, Petruchio, I must go with thee,
For in Baptista's keep my treasure is.
He hath the jewel of my life in hold—
His youngest daughter, beautiful Bianca,
And her withholds from me. Other more
Suitors to her and rivals in my love: 510
Supposing it a thing impossible,
For those defects I have before rehearsed,
That ever Katherina will be wooed:

34. The meaning of Grumio's coinage has been debated. It seems to combine
suggestions of "rhetoric" and "tropes" (Thomas Nashe uses the compound
"rope-rhetoric" in a pamphlet); in *Romeo and Juliet,* Mercutio's indecent jesting
is described by Juliet's Nurse as "roperipe" or "ropery" (2.4.144).

Therefore this order hath Baptista ta'en,
That none shall have access unto Bianca
'Til Katherine the curst have got a husband.

Grumio. Katherine the curst,
A title for a maid of all titles the worst.

Hortensio. Now shall my friend Petruchio do me grace,
And offer me disguised in sober robes   520
To old Baptista as a schoolmaster,
Well seen° in music, to instruct Bianca;   *highly qualified*
That so I may by this device at least
Have leave and leisure to make love to her,
And unsuspected court her by herself.

Enter Gremio with Lucentio disguised [as Cambio].

Grumio. Here's no knavery. See, to beguile the old folks, how the
young folks lay their heads together. Master, master, look about
you. Who goes there, ha?

Hortensio. Peace, Grumio. It is the rival of my love. Petruchio,
stand by awhile.   530

Grumio. A proper stripling,° and an amorous.   *(ironic—Gremio is old)*

Gremio. O, very well; I have perused the note.°   *list of books*
Hark you, sir; I'll have them very fairly° bound: *handsomely*
All books of love, see that at any hand;
And see you read no other lectures to her.
You understand me: over and beside
Signor Baptista's liberality,
I'll mend it with a largess.° Take your paper, too,   *gift*
And let me have them very well perfumed;
For she is sweeter than perfume itself   540
To whom they go to. What will you read to her?

Lucentio. Whate'er I read to her, I'll plead for you
As for my patron, stand you so assured,
As firmly as yourself were still in place;
Yea, and perhaps with more successful words
Than you, unless you were a scholar, sir.

Gremio. O, this learning, what a thing it is.

Grumio. O, this woodcock,° what an ass it is.   *bird easily snared, hence a fool*

Petruchio. Peace, sirrah.

Hortensio. Grumio, mum. God save you, Signor Gremio.   550

Gremio. And you are well met, Signor Hortensio.
Trow you whither I am going? To Baptista Minola.

I promised to enquire carefully
About a schoolmaster for the fair Bianca,
And by good fortune I have lighted well
On this young man—for learning and behavior
Fit for her turn, well read in poetry
And other books, good ones, I warrant° ye.   assure
Hortensio. 'Tis well; and I have met a gentleman
Hath promised me to help one° to another,   another suitor (i.e., himself)
A fine musician to instruct our mistress;   561
So shall I no whit° be behind in duty   in no way
To fair Bianca, so beloved of me.
Gremio. Beloved of me, and that my deeds shall prove.
Grumio. And that his bags° shall prove.   moneybags
Hortensio. Gremio, 'tis now no time to vent° our love.   express
Listen to me, and if you speak me fair
I'll tell you news indifferent° good for either.   equally
Here is a gentleman whom by chance I met,
Upon agreement from us to his liking,   570
Will undertake to woo curst Katherine;
Yea, and to marry her, if her dowry please.
Gremio. So said, so done, is well.°   Sooner said than done.
Hortensio, have you told him all her faults?
Petruchio. I know she is an irksome, brawling scold.
If that be all, masters, I hear no harm.
Gremio. No, say'st me so,° friend? What   Is that what you tell me?
countryman?
Petruchio. Born in Verona, old Antonio's³⁵ son.
My father dead, my fortune lives for me,
And I do hope good days and long to see.   580
Gremio. O, sir, such a life with such a wife were strange,
But if you have a stomach,° to't a God's name;   inclination
You shall have me assisting you in all.
But will you woo this wild cat?
Petruchio. Will I live?
Grumio. Will he woo her? Ay, or I'll hang her.
Petruchio. Why came I hither but to that intent?
Think you a little din can daunt mine ears?
Have I not in my time heard lions roar?
Have I not heard the sea, puffed up with winds,   590

---

35. F1 prints "Butonios" but the correct name is given at line 444 above.

Rage like an angry boar chafèd° with sweat?   *irritated*
Have I not heard great ordnance° in the field,   *cannons*
And heaven's artillery thunder in the skies?
Have I not in a pitchèd battle heard
Loud 'larms, neighing steeds, and trumpets' clang?
And do you tell me of a woman's tongue,
That gives not half so great a blow to hear
As will a chestnut in a farmer's fire.
Tush, tush, fear boys with bugs.°   *frighten children with bugbears (hobgoblins)*
Grumio. For he fears none.   600
Gremio. Hortensio, hark,
    This gentleman is happily arrived,
    My mind presumes, for his own good and yours.
Hortensio. I promised we would be contributors
    And bear his charge of wooing, whatsoe'er.
Gremio. And so we will, provided that he win her.
Grumio. I would I were as sure of a good dinner.

          Enter Tranio, brave° *[as Lucentio], and Biondello.*   *finely dressed*

Tranio. Gentlemen, God save you. If I may be bold,
    Tell me, I beseech you, which is the readiest way
    To the house of Signor Baptista Minola?   610
Biondello. He that has the two fair daughters; is't he you mean?
Tranio. Even he, Biondello.
Gremio. Hark you, sir, you mean not her to—
Tranio. Perhaps him and her, sir. What have you to do?
Petruchio. Not her that chides,° sir, at any hand, I pray.   *finds fault*
Tranio. I love no chiders, sir. Biondello, let's away.
Lucentio. Well begun, Tranio.
Hortensio. Sir, a word ere° you go.   *before*
    Are you a suitor to the maid you talk of, yea or no?
Tranio. And if I be, sir, is it any offence?   620
Gremio. No, if without more words you will get you hence.
Tranio. Why, sir, I pray, are not the streets as free
    For me as for you?
Gremio. But so is not she.
Tranio. For what reason, I beseech you.
Gremio. For this reason, if you'll know,
    That she's the choice love of Signor Gremio.
Hortensio. That she's the chosen of Signor Hortensio.

Tranio. Softly, my masters. If you be gentlemen,
    Do me this right: hear me with patience.   630
    Baptista is a noble gentleman,
    To whom my father is not all unknown,
    And, were his daughter fairer than she is,
    She may more suitors have, and me for one.
    Fair Leda's daughter[36] had a thousand wooers.
    Then well one more may fair Bianca have;
    And so she shall: Lucentio shall make one,
    Though Paris came in hope to speed° alone.   *succeed*
Gremio. What, this gentleman will out-talk us all.
Lucentio. Sir, give him head; I know he'll prove a jade.°   *worn-out horse*
Petruchio. Hortensio, to what end are all these words?   641
Hortensio. Sir, let me be so bold as ask you,
    Did you yet ever see Baptista's daughter?
Tranio. No, sir, but hear I do that he hath two:
    The one as famous for a scolding tongue
    As is the other for beauteous modesty.
Petruchio. Sir, sir, the first's for me; let her go by.
Gremio. Yea, leave that labor to great Hercules,
    And let it be more than Alcides' twelve.[37]
Petruchio. Sir, understand you this of me, in sooth: 650
    The youngest daughter, whom you hearken for,
    Her father keeps from all access of suitors,
    And will not promise her to any man
    Until the elder sister first be wed.
    The younger then is free, and not before.
Tranio. If it be so, sir, that you are the man
    Must stead° us all, and me amongst the rest;   *help*
    And if you break the ice, and do this seek,
    Achieve the elder, set the younger free
    For our access, whose hap° shall be to have her   *he whose luck*
    Will not so graceless be to be ingrate.[38]   661
Hortensio. Sir, you say well, and well you do conceive;

36. Leda's daughter is Helen of Troy, whose kidnapping at the hands of Paris began the Trojan War.

37. Hercules (Alcides) is the ancient hero who performed twelve great labors. Among them was the taming of the horses of King Diomedes of Thrace.

38. "Whoever is fortunate to obtain Bianca will not be so lacking in manners as to fail to show his gratitude."

And since you do profess to be a suitor,
    You must, as we do, gratify° this gentleman,   *reward*
    To whom we all rest generally beholding.°   *in debt to, obligated*
Tranio. Sir, I shall not be slack; in sign whereof,
    Please ye we may contrive this afternoon,
    And quaff carouses° to our mistress' health;   *drink toasts*
    And do as adversaries do in law:
    Strive mightily, but eat and drink as friends.   670
Grumio, Biondello. O, excellent motion. Fellows, let's be gone.
Hortensio. The motion's good indeed, and be it so.
    Petruchio, I shall be your *ben venuto.*°   *"welcome"*
                         Exeunt.

[ACT 2, SCENE 1]

Enter Katherina and Bianca.

Bianca. Good sister, wrong me not, nor wrong yourself,
    To make a bondmaid and a slave of me.
    That I disdain; but for these other goods,°   *(clothes and jewels)*
    Unbind my hands, I'll pull them off myself,
    Yea, all my raiment, to my petticoat.
    Or what you will command me will I do,
    So well I know my duty to my elders.
Katherina. Of all thy suitors here I charge thee, tell
    Whom thou lov'st best. See thou dissemble°   *conceal your true opinions*
        not.
Bianca. Believe me, sister, of all the men alive   10
    I never yet beheld that special face
    Which I could fancy more than any other.
Katherina. Minion,° thou liest. Is't not   *term of endearment or subservience*
        Hortensio?
Bianca. If you affect° him, sister, here I swear   *like*
    I'll plead for you myself but you shall have him.
Katherina. O, then, belike,° you fancy riches more: *perhaps*
    You will have Gremio to keep you fair.°   *finely dressed*
Bianca. Is it for him you do envy me so?
    Nay, then you jest. And now I well perceive
    You have but jested with me all this while.   20
    I prithee, sister Kate, untie my hands.

Katherina. If that be jest, then all the rest was so. *Strikes her.*

Enter Baptista.

Baptista. Why, how now, dame! Whence grows this insolence?
    Bianca, stand aside—poor girl, she weeps.
    Go ply° thy needle; meddle not° with her.   *work at / have nothing to do*
    For shame, thou hilding° of a devilish spirit,   *base wretch*
    Why dost thou wrong her that did ne'er wrong thee?
    When did she cross thee with a bitter word?   28
Katherina. Her silence flouts° me, and I'll be revenged.   *insults*
               Flies after Bianca.
Baptista. What, in my sight? Bianca, get thee in. *Exit [Bianca.]*
Katherina. What, will you not suffer° me? Nay, now I see *tolerate, bear with*
    She is your treasure, she must have a husband;
    I must dance barefoot on her wedding-day,[39]
    And for your love to her lead apes in hell.[40]
    Talk not to me; I will go sit and weep,
    'Til I can find occasion of revenge. *[Exit.]*
Baptista. Was ever gentleman thus grieved as I?
    But who comes here?

> *Enter Gremio, Lucentio [as Cambio] in*
> *the habit of a mean° man, Petruchio*   *of low status*
> *[with Hortensio as a musician, Litio;*
> *and] with Tranio [as Lucentio], with his*
> *boy [Biondello], bearing a lute and books.*

Gremio. Good morrow, neighbor Baptista.
Baptista. Good morrow, neighbor Gremio.   40
    God save you, gentlemen.
Petruchio. And you, good sir. Pray, have you not a daughter
    Called Katherina, fair and virtuous?
Baptista. I have a daughter, sir, called Katherina.
Gremio. You are too blunt; go to it orderly.°   *properly*
Petruchio. You wrong me, Signor Gremio; give me leave.
    I am a gentleman of Verona, sir,

39. Unmarried elder sisters were supposed to dance barefoot at their younger sisters' wedding, and thus the phrase became proverbial for being unmarried.

40. "Leading apes in hell" was a proverbial occupation of old maids, since they lack children to lead to heaven.

That, hearing of her beauty and her wit,
Her affability and bashful modesty,
Her wondrous qualities and mild behavior,   50
Am bold to show myself a forward guest
Within your house, to make mine eye the witness
Of that report which I so oft have heard.
And, for an entrance° to my entertainment,°   *entrance fee / reception*
I do present you with a man of mine,
Cunning in music and the mathematics,
To instruct her fully in those sciences,°   *branches of knowledge*
Whereof I know she is not ignorant.
Accept of him, or else you do me wrong.
His name is Litio, born in Mantua.   60

Baptista. Y'are welcome, sir, and he for your good sake.
But for my daughter Katherine, this I know,
She is not for your turn,° the more my grief.   *suitable for you*

Petruchio. I see you do not mean to part with her,
Or else you like not of my company.

Baptista. Mistake me not; I speak but as I find.
Whence° are you, sir? What may I call your name?   *from where*

Petruchio. Petruchio is my name, Antonio's son,
A man well known throughout all Italy.

Baptista. I know him well; you are welcome for his sake.   70

Gremio. Saving° your tale, Petruchio, I pray, let us that   *with all respect for*
are poor petitioners speak too. *Baccare!*° You are   *"Stand back!"*
marvelous forward.°   *bold*

Petruchio. O, pardon me, Signor Gremio, I would fain be
doing.°   *I am eager to get started*

Gremio. I doubt it not, sir, but you will curse° your   *bring bad luck to*
wooing neighbors. This is a gift very grateful,° I am   *welcome*
sure of it. To express the like kindness, myself, that have been
more kindly beholding to you° than any, freely give   *(i.e., Baptista)*
unto you this young scholar that hath been long studying at
Rheims;° as cunning in Greek, Latin,   *a city in France with a university*
and other languages, as the other in music and mathematics.   81
His name is Cambio. Pray accept his service.

Baptista. A thousand thanks, Signor Gremio. Welcome, good
Cambio. But, gentle sir, methinks you walk like a stranger.
May I be so bold to know the cause of your coming?

Tranio. Pardon me, sir, the boldness is mine own,
That, being a stranger in this city here,
Do make myself a suitor to your daughter,

Unto Bianca, fair and virtuous.
Nor is your firm resolve unknown to me   90
In the preferment of° the eldest sister.   *giving precedence to*
This liberty is all that I request:
That, upon knowledge of my parentage,
I may have welcome 'mongst the rest that woo,
And free access and favor as the rest.
And toward the education of your daughters,
I here bestow a simple instrument,
And this small packet of Greek and Latin books.
If you accept them, then their worth is great.
Baptista. Lucentio is your name? Of whence, I pray?   100
Tranio. Of Pisa, sir; son to Vincentio.
Baptista. A mighty° man of Pisa, by report;   *illustrious*
I know him well. You are very welcome, sir.
Take you the lute, and you the set of books;
You shall go see your pupils presently.
Holla, within.°   *a call to servants in the inner part of the house*

Enter a servant.

Sirrah, lead these gentlemen
To my daughters; and tell them both
These are their tutors. Bid them use them well. *[Exeunt servant,*
     Hortensio, and Lucentio.]
We will go walk a little in the orchard,   110
And then to dinner. You are passing° welcome,   *very*
And so I pray you all to think yourselves. *[Exeunt Gremio, Tranio,*
     and Biondello.]
Petruchio. Signor Baptista, my business asketh haste,
And every day I cannot come to woo.
You knew my father well, and in him me,
Left solely heir to all his lands and goods,
Which I have bettered° rather than decreased.   *increased*
Then tell me, if I get your daughter's love,
What dowry shall I have with her to wife?
Baptista. After my death, the one half of my lands   120
And, in possession, twenty thousand crowns.
Petruchio. And for that dowry, I'll assure her of
Her widowhood, be it that she survive me,
In all my lands and leases whatsoever.

Let specialities° be therefore drawn between us,   *detailed contracts*
That covenants may be kept on either hand.
Baptista. Ay, when the special thing is well obtained,
    That is, her love; for that is all in all.
Petruchio. Why, that is nothing; for I tell you, father,
    I am as peremptory° as she proud-minded;   *intolerant of contradiction*
    And where two raging fires meet together,   131
    They do consume the thing that feeds their fury.
    Though little fire grows great with little wind,
    Yet extreme gusts will blow out fire and all.
    So I to her, and so she yields to me;
    For I am rough, and woo not like a babe.
Baptista. Well mayst thou woo, and happy be thy speed,°   *good luck to you*
    But be thou armed for some unhappy words.
Petruchio. Ay, to the proof,° as mountains are for   *point of impenetrability*
    winds,
    That shake not though they blow perpetually.   140

        Enter Hortensio with his head broke.°   *bruised, bleeding*

Baptista. How now, my friend, why dost thou look so pale?
Hortensio. For fear, I promise you, if I look pale.
Baptista. What, will my daughter prove° a good   *become, turn out to be*
    musician?
Hortensio. I think she'll sooner prove a soldier.
    Iron may hold with her,° but never lutes.   *stand up to her*
Baptista. Why, then thou canst not break° her to the lute?   *train*
Hortensio. Why, no, for she hath broke the lute to me.
    I did but tell her she mistook her frets,°   *ridges on lute fingerboard*
    And bowed her hand to teach her fingering,
    When, with a most impatient devilish spirit,   150
    "Frets,° call you these?" quoth she, "I'll   *irritations*
        fume° with them."   *rage (as in "fret and fume")*
    And with that word she struck me on the head,
    And through the instrument my pate made way.
    And there I stood amazèd for a while,
    As on a pillory,° looking   *wooden punishment frame for head and feet; stocks*
        through the lute,
    While she did call me rascal,° fiddler°   *base man / trifler*
    And twangling Jack,° with twenty such vile terms,   *base or silly fellow*
    As° she had studied to misuse me so.   *as if*

Petruchio. Now, by the world, it is a lusty° wench.   *high-spirited*

    I love her ten times more than e'er I did.   160

    O, how I long to have some chat° with her.   *conversation*

Baptista. Well, go with me, and be not so discomfited.°   *thwarted, defeated*

    Proceed in practice with my younger daughter.

    She's apt to learn, and thankful for good turns.

    Signor Petruchio, will you go with us,

    Or shall I send my daughter Kate to you?

Petruchio. I pray you do.

        Exeunt [Baptista and Hortensio]. Manet° Petruchio.   *remain*

    I'll attend her here,

    And woo her with some spirit when she comes.

    Say that she rail; why, then I'll tell her plain   170

    She sings as sweetly as a nightingale.

    Say that she frown; I'll say she looks as clear°   *serenely beautiful*

    As morning roses newly washed with dew.

    Say she be mute, and will not speak a word;

    Then I'll commend her volubility,°   *fluency of speech*

    And say she uttereth piercing eloquence.

    If she do bid me pack,° I'll give her thanks,   *leave*

    As though she bid me stay by her a week.

    If she deny° to wed, I'll crave the day   *refuse*

    When I shall ask the banns,[41] and when be married.   180

    But here she comes, and now, Petruchio, speak.

                Enter Katherina.

    Good morrow, Kate, for that's your name, I hear.

Katherina. Well have you heard, but something hard of hearing:

    They call me Katherine that do talk of me.

Petruchio. You lie, in faith, for you are called plain Kate,

    And bonny° Kate, and sometimes Kate the   *lovely*

        curst;°   *shrewish*

    But Kate, the prettiest Kate in Christendom,

    Kate of Kate Hall, my super-dainty Kate,

    For dainties are all cates,° and therefore, Kate,   *edible delicacies*

    Take this of me, Kate of my consolation:°   *comfort*

---

41. Public notice in church of the intention to marry. The process took three weeks. While it is mentioned again at 3.2.16, the long process is omitted in the play.

Hearing thy mildness praised in every town,   191
Thy virtues spoke of, and thy beauty sounded,°   *proclaimed*
Yet not so deeply as to thee belongs,
Myself am moved to woo thee for my wife.

Katherina. Moved? In good time.° Let him that moved you   *indeed*
    hither
    Remove you hence. I knew you at the first
    You were a moveable.°   *easily moved, as furniture, or person given to change*

Petruchio. Why, what's a moveable?

Katherina. A joint-stool.°   *low wooden stool made by a joiner*

Petruchio. Thou hast hit it. Come, sit on me.   200

Katherina. Asses are made to bear,° and so are you.   *carry burdens*

Petruchio. Women are made to bear, and so are you.

Katherina. No such jade° as you, if me you mean.   *worn-out horse*

Petruchio. Alas, good Kate, I will not burden thee,
    For, knowing thee to be but young and light.°   *slender; wanton*

Katherina. Too light° for such a swain° as you to   *quick-witted / bumpkin*
    catch,
    And yet as heavy as my weight°   *carrying the proper weight for my position*
    should be.

Petruchio. Should be? Should—buzz!

Katherina. Well ta'en, and like a buzzard.

Petruchio. O, slow-winged turtle, shall a buzzard take thee?   210

Katherina. Ay, for a turtle, as he takes a buzzard.[42]

Petruchio. Come, come, you wasp; i'faith, you are too angry.[43]

Katherina. If I be waspish, best beware my sting.

Petruchio. My remedy is then to pluck it out.

Katherina. Ay, if the fool could find it where it lies.

Petruchio. Who knows not where a wasp does wear his sting?
    In his tail.

Katherina. In his tongue!

Petruchio. Whose tongue?

Katherina. Yours, if you talk of tales, and so farewell.   220

---

42. The exchange is brilliant. Petruchio puns on "be" and "bee," and on "buzz" (the sound bees make), also meaning rumor or scandal, and a term of dismissal. Katherine retorts by turning "buzz" into "buzzard," "a worthless, stupid, or ignorant person." "Turtle" is the "turtledove," "a symbol of faithful love" (*OED*).

43. It is proverbial that "Women are wasps if angered" (Tilley W705) and that "The sting is in the tail" (Tilley S858). Shakespeare often puns on "tales" (stories, gossip) and "tails" (buttocks and genitals).

Petruchio. What, with my tongue in your tail.

    Nay, come again,° good Kate; I am a   *come back; renew the combat*
        gentleman.

Katherina. That I'll try. *She strikes him.*

Petruchio. I swear I'll cuff you, if you strike again.

Katherina. So may you lose your
        arms.°   *loosen your hold on me; forfeit your coat-of-arms*
    If you strike me, you are no gentleman;
    And if no gentleman, why then no arms.

Petruchio. A herald, Kate? O, put me in thy books.

Katherina. What is your crest[44]—a coxcomb?°   *rooster's crest; jester's cap*

Petruchio. A combless cock,[45] so° Kate will be my hen.   *provided that*

Katherina. No cock of mine: you crow too like a
        craven.°   *a fighting-cock afraid to fight*

Petruchio. Nay, come, Kate, come, you must not look so sour.   232

Katherina. It is my fashion when I see a crab.°   *crab-apple; sour-faced person*

Petruchio. Why, here's no crab, and therefore look not sour.

Katherina. There is, there is.

Petruchio. Then show it me.

Katherina. Had I a glass° I would.   *mirror*

Petruchio. What, you mean my face.

Katherina. Well aimed of° such a young° one.   *guessed by / inexperienced*

Petruchio. Now, by Saint George, I am too young° for you.   *vigorous*

Katherina. Yet you are withered.   241

Petruchio. 'Tis with cares.

Katherina. I care not.

Petruchio. Nay, hear you, Kate. In sooth, you 'scape° not so.   *escape*

Katherina. I chafe° you, if I tarry. Let me go.   *irritate; excite*

Petruchio. No, not a whit; I find you passing° gentle.   *extremely*
    'Twas told me you were rough, and coy, and sullen,
    And now I find report a very liar;
    For thou art pleasant, gamesome,° passing° courteous,   *playful / very*
    But slow in speech, yet sweet as springtime flowers.   250
    Thou canst not frown, thou canst not look askance,°   *scornfully*

---

44. The College of Heralds awarded coats-of-arms to gentlemen and recorded them in their "books." Each coat-of-arms had a "crest," a figure or device.

45. A rooster without his comb is traditionally considered humbled and unaggressive. Although the *OED* lists the first written record of "cock" meaning "penis" in 1618, Williams declares that "the relationship of cock and phallus is ancient" (258).

Nor bite the lip, as angry wenches will,
Nor hast thou pleasure to be cross° in talk;   *contradicting*
But thou with mildness entertain'st° thy wooers: *receive*
With gentle conference, soft and affable.
Why does the world report that Kate doth limp?
O, sland'rous world. Kate like the hazel twig
Is straight and slender, and as brown in hue
As hazelnuts, and sweeter than the kernels.
O, let me see thee walk. Thou dost not halt.   260
Katherina. Go, fool, and whom thou keep'st,
    command.°   *order your servants around, not me*
Petruchio. Did ever Dian° so   *Diana, goddess of chastity and hunting*
    become° a grove   *adorn*
As Kate this chamber with her princely gait?
O, be thou Dian, and let her be Kate;
And then let Kate be chaste, and Dian sportful.°   *amorous*
Katherina. Where did you study all this goodly speech?
Petruchio. It is extempore,° from my mother   *unstudied, unprepared*
    wit.°   *natural intelligence*
Katherina. A witty mother, witless else her son.
Petruchio. Am I not wise?
Katherina. Yes, keep you warm.[46]   270
Petruchio. Marry, so I mean, sweet Katherine, in thy bed.
And therefore, setting all this chat aside,
Thus in plain terms: your father hath consented
That you shall be my wife, your dowry 'greed° on,   *agreed*
And will you, nill you,° I will marry you.   *whether or not you want*
Now, Kate, I am a husband for your turn;°   *right for you*
For, by this light, whereby I see thy beauty,
Thy beauty that doth make me like thee well.
Thou must be married to no man but me,
For I am he am° born to tame you, Kate,   *I am he who is*
And bring you from a wild Kate to a Kate   281
Conformable° as other household cates.   *compliant*

Enter Baptista, Gremio, Tranio.

Here comes your father. Never make denial.
I must and will have Katherine to my wife.

---

46. "He is wise enough that can keep himself warm" (Tilley K10).

Baptista. Now, Signor Petruchio, how speed° you with my   *succeed*
    daughter?
Petruchio. How but well, sir? How but well?
    It were impossible I should speed amiss.
Baptista. Why, how now, daughter Katherine, in your
    dumps?°   *low spirits*
Katherina. Call you me daughter? Now I promise you
    You have showed a tender fatherly regard   290
    To wish me wed to one half lunatic,
    A madcap ruffian and a swearing Jack,°   *common fellow*
    That thinks with oaths to face the matter out.°   *brazen it out*
Petruchio. Father, 'tis thus: yourself and all the world
    That talked of her have talked amiss of her.
    If she be curst, it is for policy,°   *for her own public purpose*
    For she's not froward,° but modest as the dove;   *perverse*
    She is not hot, but temperate as the morn;
    For patience she will prove a second Grissel,
    And Roman Lucrece for her chastity.[47]   300
    And, to conclude, we have 'greed so well together
    That upon Sunday is the wedding-day.
Katherina. I'll see thee hanged on Sunday first.
Gremio. Hark, Petruchio; she says she'll see thee hanged first.
Tranio. Is this your speeding?° Nay, then good   *success*
    night° our part.   *goodbye to*
Petruchio. Be patient, gentlemen. I choose her for myself;
    If she and I be pleased, what's that to you?
    'Tis bargained 'twixt us twain, being alone,
    That she shall still be curst° in company.   *continue to appear shrewish*
    I tell you 'tis incredible to believe   310
    How much she loves me. O, the kindest Kate,
    She hung about my neck, and kiss on kiss
    She vied° so fast, protesting oath on oath,   *redoubled*
    That in a twink° she won me to her love.   *instant*
    O, you are novices. 'Tis a world° to see,   *it's a treat*
    How tame, when men and women are alone,
    A meacock° wretch can make the curstest shrew.   *spiritless*

47. Patient Griselda is the model of wifely virtue in tales by Boccaccio and
Chaucer, among others. Shakespeare himself wrote about the Roman heroine
Lucrece who committed suicide after being raped by Tarquin (*The Rape of
Lucrece,* 1594).

Give me thy hand, Kate; I will unto Venice,

To buy apparel 'gainst° the wedding-day.   *against, in preparation for*

Provide the feast, father, and bid the guests;   320

I will be sure my Katherine shall be fine.

Baptista. I know not what to say, but give me your hands.

God send you joy, Petruchio. 'Tis a match.

Gremio, Tranio. Amen, say we; we will be witnesses.

Petruchio. Father and wife and gentlemen, adieu.

I will to Venice; Sunday comes apace.°   *quickly*

We will have rings and things and fine array;

And kiss me, Kate; we will be married a-Sunday.   *Exit Petruchio*
and Katherina.

Gremio. Was ever match clapped up° so suddenly?   *arranged*

Baptista. Faith, gentlemen, now I play a merchant's part,   330

And venture madly on a desperate mart.°   *chancy piece of business*

Tranio. 'Twas a commodity° lay fretting°   *article of trade (Kate) / rotting, chafing*
by you;

'Twill bring you gain, or perish on the seas.

Baptista. The gain I seek is quiet in the match.

Gremio. No doubt but he hath got a quiet catch

But now, Baptista, to your younger daughter.

Now is the day we long have lookèd for.

I am your neighbor and was suitor first.

Tranio. And I am one that love Bianca more

Than words can witness or your thoughts can guess   340

Gremio. Youngling,° thou canst not love so dear as I.   *novice*

Tranio. Greybeard, thy love doth freeze.

Gremio. But thine doth fry.

Skipper,° stand back; 'tis age that   *young one*
nourisheth.°   *provides good things*

Tranio. But youth in ladies' eyes that flourisheth.°   *prospers*

Baptista. Content you, gentlemen; I will compound° this strife.   *settle*

'Tis deeds must win the prize, and he of both°   *one of you two*

That can assure my daughter greatest
dower°   *portion of a deceased husband's estate*

Shall have my Bianca's love.

Say, Signor Gremio, what can you assure her?   350

Gremio. First, as you know, my house within the city

Is richly furnishèd with plate° and gold,   *domestic utensils of silver and gold*

Basins and ewers° to lave° her dainty hands;   *pitchers / wash*

My hangings all of Tyrian tapestry;[48]
In ivory coffers° I have stuffed my crowns;°   *strongboxes / coins*
In cypress chests my Arras
    counterpoints,°   *quilted counterpanes from Arras, France*
Costly apparel, tents, and canopies,°   *material on frame to cover bed*
Fine linen, Turkey cushions bossed° with pearl,   *embossed*
Valance° of Venice gold in needlework;   *fringes on bed canopy*
Pewter and brass, and all things that belongs   360
To house or housekeeping. Then at my farm
I have a hundred milch kine to the
    pail,°   *cows whose milk doesn't go to calves*
Six score° fat oxen standing in my stalls,   *six times twenty*
And all things answerable° to this portion. *commensurate, corresponding to*
Myself am struck° in years, I must confess;   *well along*
And if I die tomorrow this is hers,
If whilst I live she will be only mine.

Tranio. That "only" came well in.° Sir, list to me.   *is appropriate*
I am my father's heir and only son;
If I may have your daughter to my wife,   370
I'll leave her houses three or four as good
Within rich Pisa's walls as any one
Old Signor Gremio has in Padua;
Besides, two thousand ducats° by the year   *about £900*
Of fruitful land, all which shall be her
    jointure.°   *the estate the groom gives the bride*
What, have I pinched you,° Signor Gremio?   *gained an advantage*

Gremio. Two thousand ducats by the year of land.
My land amounts not to so much in all—
That she shall have, besides an argosy°   *large merchant ship*
That now is lying in Marseilles road.°   *anchorage in Marseilles, France*
What, have I choked you with an argosy?   381

Tranio. Gremio, 'tis known my father hath no less
Than three great argosies, besides two
    galliasses,°   *heavy, low-built ships, larger than a galley*
And twelve tight°   *sound*
    galleys.° These I will assure her,   *low, flat-built ships*
And twice as much whate'er thou off'rest next.

---

48. Hangings included tapestries and draperies. Gremio boasts that his are from Tyre, famous for its scarlet or purple dyes.

Gremio. Nay, I have off'red all; I have no more;
    And she can have no more than all I have.
    If you like me, she shall have me and mine.
Tranio. Why, then the maid is mine from all the world
    By your firm promise; Gremio is outvied.°   *outdone*
Baptista. I must confess your offer is the best;   391
    And, let your father make her the assurance,
    She is your own. Else, you must pardon me;
    If you should die before him, where's her dower?
Tranio. That's but a cavil;° he is old, I young.   *frivolous objection*
Gremio. And may not young men die as well as old?
Baptista. Well, gentlemen, I am thus resolved:
    On Sunday next you know
    My daughter Katherine is to be married;
    Now, on the Sunday following shall Bianca   400
    Be bride to you, if you make this assurance;
    If not, to Signor Gremio.
    And so I take my leave, and thank you both. *Exit.*
Gremio. Adieu, good neighbor. Now, I fear thee not.
    Sirrah, young gamester,° your father were a fool   *gambler*
    To give thee all, and in his waning age
    Set foot under thy table.° Tut,[49] a toy.°   *live on your charity / nonsense*
    An old Italian fox is not so kind, my boy. *Exit.*
Tranio. A vengeance on your crafty withered hide.
    Yet I have faced it with a card of ten.[50]   410
    'Tis in my head to do my master good.
    I see no reason but supposed Lucentio
    Must get a father, called supposed Vincentio;[51]
    And that's a wonder:° fathers commonly   *miracle*
    Do get° their children; but in this case   *beget, make a woman pregnant*
        of wooing
    A child shall get a sire, if I fail not of my cunning.°   *ingenuity*
                        Exit.

---

49. Expression of impatience or dissatisfaction.

50. "To outface with a card of ten" is proverbial for bluffing (Tilley C75).

51. "It is necessary that the pretended Lucentio must get a father called pretended Vincentio."

ACT 3, [SCENE 1]

Enter Lucentio [as Cambio], Hortensio [as Litio], and Bianca.

Lucentio. Fiddler, forbear; you grow too forward, sir.
    Have you so soon forgot the entertainment°   *reception*
    Her sister Katherine welcomed you withal?°   *with*
Hortensio. But, wrangling pedant, this is
    The patroness of heavenly harmony.
    Then give me leave to have prerogative;°   *precedence*
    And when in music we have spent an hour,
    Your lecture° shall have leisure for as much.   *lesson*
Lucentio. Preposterous[52] ass, that never read so far
    To know the cause why music was ordained.°   *created*
    Was it not to refresh the mind of man   11
    After his studies or his usual pain?°   *customary work*
    Then give me leave to read philosophy,
    And while I pause serve in your harmony.
Hortensio. Sirrah, I will not bear these braves° of thine.   *challenges*
Bianca. Why, gentlemen, you do me double wrong
    To strive for that which resteth in my choice.
    I am no breeching scholar° in the schools;   *young scholar subject to flogging*
    I'll not be tied to hours nor 'pointed° times,   *appointed*
    But learn my lessons as I please myself.   20
    And to cut off all strife, here sit we down;
    Take you your instrument, play you the whiles.°   *in the meantime*
    His lecture will be done ere you have tuned.
Hortensio. You'll leave his lecture when I am in tune?
Lucentio. That will be never. Tune your instrument.
Bianca. Where left we last?
Lucentio. Here, madam:
    "*Hic ibat Simois, hic est Sigeia tellus,*
    Hic steterat Priami regia celsa senis."[53]   29
Bianca. Construe° them.   *interpret, translate*

---

52. "Absurd, ridiculous." This is a pedant's insult that literally means "placing last what should be first" (*OED*).

53. "Here ran the [river] Simois; here is the Sigeian land [Troy]; / here stood old Priam's lofty palace." These lines are from the first poem of Ovid's *Heroides,* an imaginary letter from Penelope to Ulysses. Penelope repeats for her husband what those returning from the war say to her to describe it.

Lucentio. "*Hic ibat*"—as I told you before, "*Simois*"—I am Lucentio,
"*hic est*"—son unto Vincentio of Pisa, "*Sigeia tellus*"—disguised
thus to get your love, "*Hic steterat*"—and that Lucentio that
comes a-wooing, "*Priami*"—is my man Tranio, "*regia*"—bearing
my port,° "*celsa senis*"—that we might beguile the old   *state, style*
pantaloon.°   *foolish old man*
Hortensio. Madam, my instrument's in tune.
Bianca. Let's hear. O, fie,° the treble jars.   *exclamation of disgust or reproach*
Lucentio. Spit in the hole, man, and tune again.[54]
Bianca. Now let me see if I can construe it: "*Hic ibat Simois*"—   40
    I know you not, "*hic est Sigeia tellus*"—I trust you not, "*Hic
    steterat Priami*"—take heed he hear us not, "*regia*"—presume not,
    "*celsa senis*"—despair not.
Hortensio. Madam, 'tis now in tune.
Lucentio. All but the bass.
Hortensio. The bass is right; 'tis the base knave that jars.
Lucentio. How fiery and forward our pedant is.[55]
    Now, for my life, the knave doth court my love.
    Pedascule,° I'll watch you better yet.   *little pedant (coined)*
    In time I may believe, yet I mistrust.   50
Bianca. Mistrust it not—for sure, Aeacides[56]
    Was Ajax,[57] called so from his grandfather.
Hortensio. I must believe my master; else, I promise you,

---

54. Although the proposal sounds facetious, some have suggested that spitting
in the treble peg-hole might help the peg to grip and make it easier to tune the
notoriously difficult-to-tune lute.

55. This and the next ten lines of this scene are assigned differently in most
modern texts, which have Hortensio continue saying, "How fiery . . . I'll watch
you better yet"; Bianca saying, "In time I may believe, yet I mistrust"; Lucentio
saying, "Mistrust it not . . . from his grandfather"; and Bianca saying, "I must
believe . . . thus pleasant with you both." We follow the F1 readings.

56. Bianca looks ahead to the next line in the text they are reading: "*Illic Aeacides,
illic tendebat Ulixes*" ("There Aeacides, there Ulysses pitched his tent").

57. Ajax, son of Telamon, was called Aeacides after his grandfather Aeacus, but
so was Achilles, son of Peleus. Both heroes could be called by this patronymic
because they had the same grandfather. Bianca's statement goes against all other
translators and commentators on this passage, who would construe Aeacides as
Achilles here. Ajax could also be pronounced a-jakes, with a pun on "jakes," a
word for privy. Sir John Harington's ingenious satire, *The Metamorphosis of Ajax:
A New Discourse on a Stale Subject* (1596), contains a design for a watercloset or
toilet.

> I should be arguing still upon that doubt;
> But let it rest. Now Litio[58] to you.
> Good master, take it not unkindly, pray,
> That I have been thus pleasant with you both.

Hortensio.[59] You may go walk and give me leave awhile;
> My lessons make no music in three parts.

Lucentio. Are you so formal, sir. Well, I must wait   60
> And watch withal, for, but° I be deceived,   *unless*
> Our fine musician groweth amorous.

Hortensio. Madam, before you touch the instrument,
> To learn the order of my fingering,
> I must begin with rudiments of art,
> To teach you gamut° in a briefer sort,   *the musical scale*
> More pleasant, pithy,° and effectual,°   *condensed / effective*
> Than hath been taught by any of my trade;
> And there it is in writing fairly drawn.

Bianca. Why, I am past my gamut long ago.   70

Hortensio. Yet read the gamut of Hortensio.

Bianca. *[Reads]* "Gamut I am, the ground of all accord,° *basis of all harmony*
> A *re*—to plead Hortensio's passion,
> B *mi*—Bianca, take him for thy lord,
> C *fa ut*—that loves with all affection,
> D *sol re*—one clef, two notes have I,[60]
> E *la mi*—show pity or I die."

58. Hortensio is referring to himself under the name he has assumed, as he refers to himself by his actual name in the last line of this scene (3.1.91), and as do characters throughout this play (e.g., Petruchio at 2.1.181). Hortensio says, in effect, "Now it is Litio's (my) turn to teach you." Most editions assigning the speech to Bianca make "Litio" a noun of address.

59. Two speeches in succession assigned to the same speaker is a rare event in early dramatic texts and is usually, though not always, an error. In subsequent folios of 1632, 1663–1664, and 1685, the anomaly is removed by changing the speaker of "You may go walk . . . " to Bianca. Nicholas Rowe, in his edition of 1709, avoids it by making the phrase "I must believe my master . . . thus pleasant with you both" a continuation of Bianca's speech, "Mistrust it not . . . ."

60. "Clef" is the symbol that designates pitch, but this note has two names: "sol" in one "gamut" ("six-tone scale") and "re" in the second. Hortensio may be suggesting his own double identity. There is also a bawdy suggestion, since "clef" (or "cliff") can refer to the female genitals. Foul-mouthed Thersites says of Cressida, "And any man may sing her, if he can take her clef" (*Troilus and Cressida,* 5.2.10–11). See Thompson Appendix 3 (186–188).

Call you this gamut? Tut, I like it not.
Old fashions please me best; I am not so nice
To change true rules for odd inventions.[61]   80

Enter a messenger [Nick].[62]

Nick. Mistress, your father prays you leave your books
And help to dress your sister's chamber up.
You know tomorrow is the wedding-day.
Bianca. Farewell, sweet masters, both; I must be gone.
                    [Exeunt Bianca and servant.]
Lucentio. Faith, mistress, then I have no cause to stay.
                    [Exit.]
Hortensio. But I have cause to pry into this pedant.
Methinks he looks as though he were in love.
Yet if thy thoughts,° Bianca, be so humble°   inclinations / low
To cast thy wand'ring eyes on every stale,°   bawdy decoy-bird, dupe
Seize thee that list.° If once I find thee   let anyone who wants you get you
    ranging,°   straying
Hortensio will be quit with thee by
    changing.°   get even with you by loving another
                    Exit.

[ACT 3, SCENE 2]

*Enter Baptista, Gremio, Tranio [as Lucentio], Katherina,
Bianca, and others [i.e., Lucentio as Cambio], attendants.*

Baptista. Signor Lucentio, this is the 'pointed° day   appointed
That Katherine and Petruchio should be married,
And yet we hear not of our son-in-law.
What will be said, what mockery will it be

61. "I am not so whimsical as to exchange true rules for fantastical new ideas."
F1 reads "charge" where we print "change" and "old" for "odd." F1's reading
might be interpreted, "I am not so foolish (nice) as to make well-established
custom bear the burden (charge) of stale jokes."
62. Nick, to whom F1 assigns the next speech, may be the name of an actor,
but it is unlikely that Shakespeare thought of a specific minor actor for these
three lines.

To want° the bridegroom when the priest attends   *lack*
To speak the ceremonial rites of marriage?
What says Lucentio to this shame of ours?

Katherina. No shame but mine; I must, forsooth, be forced
To give my hand, opposed against my heart,
Unto a madbrain rudesby,° full of   *unmannered fellow*
  spleen,°   *whims, caprices*
Who wooed in haste and means to wed at leisure.   11
I told you, I, he was a frantic fool,
Hiding his bitter jests in blunt behavior,
And, to be noted for° a merry man.   *to be known as*
He'll woo a thousand, 'point° the day of marriage,   *appoint*
Make friends, invite and proclaim the banns;[63]
Yet never means to wed where he hath wooed.
Now must the world point at poor Katherine,
And say, "Lo, there is mad Petruchio's wife,
If it would please him come and marry her."   20

Tranio. Patience, good Katherine, and Baptista, too.
Upon my life, Petruchio means but well,
Whatever fortune stays° him from his word.°   *accident detains / promise*
Though he be blunt, I know him passing° wise;   *exceedingly*
Though he be merry,° yet withal° he's   *facetious, pleasant / all in all*
  honest.

Katherina. Would Katherine had never seen him though.   *Exit, weeping.*

Baptista. Go, girl, I cannot blame thee now to weep,
For such an injury would vex a very saint,
Much more a shrew of impatient humor.°   *temperament*

Enter Biondello.

Biondello. Master, master, news, and such old news as you never   30
  heard of.
Baptista. Is it new and old, too? How may that be?
Biondello. Why, is it not news to hear of Petruchio's coming?
Baptista. Is he come?
Biondello. Why, no, sir.
Baptista. What then?

63. This line is often emended to "Make feast, invite friends, and," following
Petruchio's "Provide the feast, father, and bid the guests" (2.1.320). For "banns"
see n. 41.

Biondello. He is coming.

Baptista. When will he be here?

Biondello. When he stands where I am and sees you there.

Tranio. But, say, what to thine old news?   40

Biondello. Why, Petruchio is coming in a new hat and an old
    jerkin;° a pair of old breeches thrice   *short coat*
    turned;° a pair of boots that have been   *turned inside out*
    candle-cases,° one buckled, another laced;   *used to store candle ends*
    an old rusty sword ta'en out of the town armory, with a
    broken hilt, and chapeless;° with two broken   *lacking a sheath*
    points;° his horse hipped,° with an old   *tagged laces / lame in the hip*
    mothy saddle and stirrups of no kindred;° besides,   *unmatched*
    possessed with the glanders[64] and like to *mourn in the chine*,
    troubled with the lampass, infected with the fashions, full of   50
    windgalls, sped with° spavins, rayed° with the   *ruined by / defiled*
    yellows, past cure of the fives, stark spoiled with°   *wrecked by*
    the staggers, begnawn° with the bots, swayed in the   *gnawed at*
    back and shoulder-shotten, near-legged before, and with a
    half-cheeked bit, and a head-stall° of sheep's   *bridle part over horse's head*
    leather which, being restrained to keep him from stumbling,
    hath been often burst, and now repaired with knots; one
    girth° six times pieced, and a woman's   *leather band holding saddle on*
    crupper° of velure,° which   *strap from saddle that goes around tail / velvet*
    hath two letters for her name fairly set down in studs, and here 60
    and there pieced with packthread.

Baptista. Who comes with him?

Biondello. O, sir, his lackey, for all the world caparisoned° like   *dressed*
    the horse, with a linen stock° on one leg and a   *stocking*
    kersey° boot-hose on the other, gart'red with a red   *coarse woollen*
    and blue list;° an old hat, and the humor of forty   *strip of cloth*
    fancies° pricked° in't for a feather; a   *some fantastic ornament / pinned*
    monster, a very monster in apparel, and not like a Christian
    footboy or a gentleman's lackey.   69

---

64. A staggering list of horse diseases and their symptoms follows: "glanders"
(swollen jaw and mucus discharge; French "*mourn in the chine*," is the last stage);
"lampass" (swelling in the mouth); "fashions" (farcy), very like "glanders";
"windgalls" (soft leg tumors); "spavins" (swelling of the leg joint); "yellows"
(jaundice); "fives" (strangles, swelling of the salivary glands); "staggers" (giddi-
ness); "bots" (intestinal worms); "swayed" (strained back); "shoulder-shotten"
(dislocated shoulder); and "near-legged" (knock-kneed in the forelegs).

Tranio. 'Tis some odd humor pricks° him to this   *strange fancy incites*
    fashion;
    Yet oftentimes he goes but mean-apparelled.°   *poorly dressed*
Baptista. I am glad he's come, howsoe'er he comes.
Biondello. Why, sir, he comes not.
Baptista. Didst thou not say he comes?
Biondello. Who, that Petruchio came?
Baptista. Ay, that Petruchio came.
Biondello. No, sir. I say his horse comes with him on his back.
Baptista. Why, that's all one.°   *just the same, doesn't matter*
Biondello. Nay, by Saint Jamy,°   *James*
    I hold you a penny,   80
    A horse and a man
    Is more than one,
    And yet not many.

Enter Petruchio and Grumio.

Petruchio. Come, where be these gallants? Who's at home?
Baptista. You are welcome, sir.
Petruchio. And yet I come not well.
Baptista. And yet you halt not.
Tranio. Not so well appareled as I wish you were.
Petruchio. Were it better, I should rush in thus.
    But where is Kate? Where is my lovely bride?   90
    How does my father? Gentles,° methinks you frown;   *gentlefolk*
    And wherefore gaze this goodly company
    As if they saw some wondrous monument,°   *strange portent*
    Some comet, or unusual prodigy?°   *omen*
Baptista. Why, sir, you know this is your wedding-day.
    First, were we sad, fearing you would not come;
    Now, sadder that you come so unprovided.°   *improperly dressed*
    Fie, doff this habit,° shame to your estate,°   *take off this outfit / rank*
    An eyesore to our solemn festival.
Tranio. And tell us what occasion of import°   *important reason*
    Hath all so long detained you from your wife,   101
    And sent you hither so unlike yourself?
Petruchio. Tedious it were to tell, and harsh to hear;
    Sufficeth° I am come to keep my word,   *it is enough that*
    Though in some part enforcèd° to   *forced*
        digress,°   *deviate from my promise*

Which at more leisure I will so excuse
As you shall well be satisfied withal.
But where is Kate? I stay too long from her;
The morning wears;° 'tis time we were at church.   *marches on*
Tranio. See not your bride in these unreverent° robes;   *disrespectful*
Go to my chamber; put on clothes of mine.   111
Petruchio. Not I, believe me; thus I'll visit her.
Baptista. But thus, I trust, you will not marry her.
Petruchio. Good sooth,° even thus; therefore ha' done with   *yes indeed*
    words;
To me she's married, not unto my clothes.
Could I repair what she will wear° in me   *wear out, use up (bawdy)*
As I can change these poor accoutrements,°   *clothes*
'Twere well for Kate and better for myself.
But what a fool am I to chat with you,
When I should bid good morrow to my bride   120
And seal the title with a lovely° kiss.   *loving*
                    Exit [with Grumio].
Tranio. He hath some meaning in his mad attire.
We will persuade him, be it possible,
To put on better ere° he go to church.   *before*
Baptista. I'll after him and see the event° of this.   *outcome*

        Exit [with Gremio, Biondello, Bianca, and attendants].

Tranio. But, sir, to love concerneth° us to add   *it concerns*
Her father's liking;° which to bring to pass,   *good will*
As I before imparted to your worship,
I am to get a man—whate'er he be
It skills not much;° we'll fit him to our turn   *doesn't much matter*
And he shall be Vincentio of Pisa,   131
And make assurance here in Padua
Of greater sums than I have promisèd.
So shall you quietly enjoy your hope
And marry sweet Bianca with consent.
Lucentio. Were it not that my fellow schoolmaster
Doth watch Bianca's steps° so narrowly,   *actions*
'Twere good, methinks, to steal our marriage;°   *marry secretly*
Which once performed, let all the world say no,
I'll keep mine own despite of all the world.   140
Tranio. That, by degrees, we mean to look into
And watch our vantage° in this business.   *opportunity*

We'll overreach° the greybeard, Gremio,   *dupe*
The narrow, prying father, Minola,
The quaint° musician, amorous Litio—   *crafty, scheming*
All for my master's sake, Lucentio.

                        Enter Gremio.

   Signor Gremio, came you from the church?
Gremio. As willingly as e'er I came from school.
Tranio. And is the bride and bridegroom coming home?
Gremio. A bridegroom, say you? 'Tis a groom° indeed,   *male attendant*
   A grumbling groom, and that the girl shall find.   151
Tranio. Curster° than she? Why, 'tis impossible.   *more shrewish*
Gremio. Why, he's a devil, a devil, a very fiend.
Tranio. Why, she's a devil, a devil, the devil's dam.°   *mother*
Gremio. Tut, she's a lamb, a dove, a fool,° to him.   *a gentle innocent*
   I'll tell you, Sir Lucentio: when the priest
   Should ask if Katherine should be his wife,
   "Ay, by Gog's woun's,"° quoth he, and swore so   *God's wounds (oath)*
      loud
   That, all amazed, the priest let fall the book;
   And as he stooped again to take it up,   160
   This mad-brained bridegroom took him° such a cuff   *gave him*
   That down fell priest and book, and book and priest.
   "Now, take them up," quoth he, "if any list."[65]
Tranio. What said the wench, when he rose again?
Gremio. Trembled and shook, for why° he stamped and swore   *because*
   as if the vicar meant to cozen° him. But after many   *cheat*
   ceremonies done he calls for wine:[66] "A health!" quoth
   he, as if he had been aboard,° carousing to his mates   *on shipboard*
   after a storm; quaffed off the muscatel, and threw the sops all in
   the sexton's face, having no other reason but that his beard   170
   grew thin and hungerly° and seemed to ask him sops as he   *sparsely*

65. Although it is possible that Petruchio is daring anyone to lift up the priest
and his book, it is more likely that he is accusing the bending priest of improp-
erly interfering with the skirt of Katherine's dress ("take them up").

66. It was traditional at the conclusion of a wedding that the bride and groom
shared a cup of "muscatel," a strong, sweet wine, with "sops," cakes, in it.
Petruchio drains the wine himself and throws the soggy cake at the sexton
because, he says, the sexton's thin beard looked hungry.

was drinking. This done, he took the bride about the neck, and
kissed her lips with such a clamorous smack that at the parting
all the church did echo. And I, seeing this, came thence for very
shame. And after me, I know, the rout° is coming.   *crowd of guests*
Such a mad marriage never was before. Hark, hark, I hear
the minstrels play. *Music plays.*

Enter Petruchio, Katherina, Bianca, Hortensio, Baptista,
[with Grumio, and attendants.]

Petruchio. Gentlemen and friends, I thank you for your pains.
　　I know you think° to dine with me today,   *expect*
　　And have prepared great store of wedding cheer   180
　　But so it is: my haste doth call me hence,
　　And therefore here I mean to take my leave.
Baptista. Is't possible you will away tonight?
Petruchio. I must away today before night come.
　　Make it no wonder;° if you knew my business,   *don't be surprised*
　　You would entreat me rather go than stay.
　　And, honest company, I thank you all
　　That have beheld me give away myself
　　To this most patient, sweet, and virtuous wife.
　　Dine with my father, drink a health to me.   190
　　For I must hence;° and farewell to you all.   *away*
Tranio. Let us entreat you stay 'til after dinner.
Petruchio. It may not be.
Gremio. Let me entreat you.
Petruchio. It cannot be.
Katherina. Let me entreat you.
Petruchio. I am content.
Katherina. Are you content to stay?
Petruchio. I am content you shall entreat me stay;
　　But yet not stay, entreat me how you can.   200
Katherina. Now, if you love me, stay.
Petruchio. Grumio, my horse.
Grumio. Ay, sir, they be ready; the oats have eaten the
　　horses.°   *the horses have eaten their fill*
Katherina. Nay, then,
　　Do what thou canst, I will not go today;
　　No, nor tomorrow, not 'til I please myself.
　　The door is open, sir; there lies your way;

You may be jogging whiles your boots are
    green;°   *fresh (i.e., hit the road)*
For me, I'll not be gone 'til I please myself.   209
'Tis like you'll prove a jolly° surly groom   *extremely*
That take it on you° at the first so roundly.°   *carry on / thoroughly*
Petruchio. O, Kate, content thee;° prithee be not angry.   *compose yourself*
Katherina. I will be angry; what hast thou to do?°   *what business is it of yours?*
    Father, be quiet; he shall stay my leisure.°   *wait until I am ready*
Gremio. Ay, marry,[67] sir, now it begins to work.
Katherina. Gentlemen, forward to the bridal dinner.
    I see a woman may be made a fool
    If she had not a spirit to resist.
Petruchio. They shall go forward, Kate, at thy command.
    Obey the bride, you that attend on her;   220
    Go to the feast, revel and domineer,°   *feast riotously*
    Carouse full measure to her maidenhead;
    Be mad and merry, or go hang yourselves.
    But for° my bonny Kate, she must with me.   *as for*
    Nay, look not big, nor stamp, nor stare, nor fret;
    I will be master of what is mine own.
    She is my goods, my chattels, she is my house,
    My household stuff, my field, my barn,
    My horse, my ox, my ass, my anything,[68]
    And here she stands; touch her whoever dare.   230
    I'll bring mine action° on the proudest he   *legal proceedings*
    That stops my way in Padua. Grumio,
    Draw forth thy weapon; we are beset with thieves;
    Rescue thy mistress, if thou be a man.
    Fear not, sweet wench; they shall not touch thee, Kate;
    I'll buckler° thee against a million.   *shield*
          Exeunt Petruchio, Katherina, [and Grumio].
Baptista. Nay, let them go, a couple of quiet ones.
Gremio. Went they not quickly,° I should die with   *had they not gone quickly*
    laughing.
Tranio. Of all mad matches, never was the like.
Lucentio. Mistress, what's your opinion of your sister?   240

---

67. An interjection adding emphasis to the speaker's words.

68. The list of nouns echoes the several items in the list of things humans are forbidden to covet in the last commandment in the Decalogue ("Ten Commandments") of Exodus 20.

Bianca. That, being mad herself, she's madly
      mated.°   *matched; married; defeated*
Gremio. I warrant him, Petruchio is Kated.
Baptista. Neighbors and friends, though bride and bridegroom wants
    For to supply° the places at the table,   *are not here to fill*
    You know there wants no junkets° at the feast.   *lacks no delicacies*
    Lucentio, you shall supply the bridegroom's place;
    And let Bianca take her sister's room.
Tranio. Shall sweet Bianca practice how to bride it?°   *play the bride*
Baptista. She shall, Lucentio. Come, gentlemen, let's go. *Exeunt.*

[ACT 3, SCENE 3]

Enter Grumio.

Grumio. Fie, fie on all tired jades,° on all mad masters,   *worn-out horses*
    and all foul ways.° Was ever man so beaten? Was ever   *dirty roads*
    man so rayed?° Was ever man so weary? I am sent before   *dirtied*
    to make a fire, and they are coming after to warm them.
    Now were not I "a little pot and soon hot,"[69] my very lips might
    freeze to my teeth, my tongue to the roof of my mouth, my heart
    in my belly, ere I should come by a fire to thaw me. But I with
    blowing the fire shall warm myself; for, considering the weather,
    a taller° man than I will take cold. Holla, ho! Curtis.   *bolder*

Enter Curtis.

Curtis. Who is that calls so coldly?   10
Grumio. A piece of ice. If thou doubt it, thou mayst slide from my
    shoulder to my heel with no greater a run but my head and my
    neck. A fire, good Curtis.
Curtis. Is my master and his wife coming, Grumio?
Grumio. O, ay, Curtis, ay; and therefore "fire, fire; cast on no water."[70]
Curtis. Is she so hot a shrew as she's reported?

69. This proverb (Tilley P497) suggests that short men are quick to anger.
Grumio is short.
70. Grumio is playing with the early modern round: "Scotland's burning,
Scotland's burning, / Fire, fire, fire, fire, cast on water, cast on water." See
n. 73.

Grumio. She was, good Curtis, before this frost; but thou know'st
    winter tames man, woman, and beast;[71] for it hath tamed my old
    master and my new mistress and myself, fellow Curtis.   19

Curtis. Away, you three-inch° fool. I am no beast.   *(diminutive)*

Grumio. Am I but three inches? Why, thy horn is a foot, and so long
    am I at the least.[72] But wilt thou make a fire, or shall I complain
    on° thee to our mistress, whose hand (she being now at   *about*
    hand) thou shalt soon feel, to thy cold comfort, for being slow
    in thy hot office.°   *(i.e., making a fire)*

Curtis. I prithee, good Grumio, tell me how goes the world?

Grumio. A cold world, Curtis, in every office but thine; and
    therefore fire. Do thy duty, and have thy duty,° for   *what is due you*
    my master and mistress are almost frozen to death.

Curtis. There's fire ready; and therefore, good Grumio, the news.   30

Grumio. Why, "Jack boy, ho boy,"[73] and as much news as wilt thou.

Curtis. Come, you are so full of cony-catching!°   *trickery*

Grumio. Why, therefore, fire; for I have caught extreme cold.
    Where's the cook? Is supper ready, the house trimmed, rushes
    strewed,[74] cobwebs swept, the servingmen in their new
    fustian,° the white stockings, and every   *coarse cloth of cotton and flax*
    officer his wedding-garment on? Be the jacks fair within, the
    jills fair without, the carpets laid,[75] and everything in order?

Curtis. All ready; and therefore, I pray thee, news.

Grumio. First, know my horse is tired; my master and mistress   40
    fall'n out.

Curtis. How?

Grumio. Out of their saddles into the dirt; and thereby hangs a tale.

---

71. Another proverb: "Age (winter) and wedlock tame both man and beast"
(Tilley A64). Note that Grumio adds "woman" as well.

72. Grumio suggests that if the "three-inch" insult is aimed at his manhood, he
is enough of a man to have cuckolded Curtis by having sex with his wife.

73. The opening line of a popular Renaisssance "catch" or round: "Jack boy,
ho boy, news: / The cat is in the well / Let us sing now for her knell / Ding
dong, ding dong, bell."

74. The straight stalks of rushes were spread over the interior floors of homes
before carpets were used. It is proverbial that fresh rushes were spread for visitors
(Tilley R213). See next note.

75. "Jacks" are both man-servants and leather drinking vessels; "jills" are maid-
servants and metal drinking vessels. Carpets are laid on tables and chests since
there are rushes on the floor.

Curtis. Let's ha't,° good Grumio.   have it
Grumio. Lend thine ear.
Curtis. Here.
Grumio. There. *[Strikes him.]*
Curtis. This 'tis to feel a tale, not to hear a tale.
Grumio. And therefore 'tis called a sensible°   capable of being felt; understandable
    tale; and this cuff was but to knock at your ear and beseech   50
    list'ning. Now I begin. *Imprimis,*° we came down a foul   "first"
    hill, my master riding behind my mistress—
Curtis. Both of° one horse?   on
Grumio. What's that to thee?
Curtis. Why, a horse.
Grumio. Tell thou the tale.° But hadst thou not   so you finish the story
    crossed me, thou shouldst have heard how her horse
    fell and she under her horse; thou shouldst have
    heard in how miry° a place, how she was   swampy, muddy
    bemoiled,° how he left her with the horse   covered in dirt and mire
    upon her, how he beat me because her horse stumbled, how   61
    she waded through the dirt to pluck him off me, how he swore,
    how she prayed that never prayed before, how I cried, how
    the horses ran away, how her bridle was burst, how I lost my
    crupper°—with many things of worthy   part of a saddle
    memory,° which now shall die in oblivion, and   worth remembrance
    thou return unexperienced° to thy grave.   ignorant of them
Curtis. By this reck'ning he is more shrew than she.
Grumio. Ay, and that thou and the proudest of you all shall find
    when he comes home. But what° talk I of this? Call forth   why
    Nathaniel, Joseph, Nicholas, Philip, Walter, Sugarsop, and   71
    the rest; let their heads be sleekly° combed, their blue   smoothly
    coats° brushed, and their garters of an indifferent   (livery of servant)
    knit;° let them curtsy with their left legs, and not   matching style
    presume to touch a hair of my master's horse-tail 'til
    they kiss their hands.° Are they all ready?   (a mark of respect)
Curtis. They are.
Grumio. Call them forth.
Curtis. Do you hear, ho? You must meet my master, to
    countenance° my mistress.   honor
Grumio. Why, she hath a face of her own.   81
Curtis. Who knows not that?
Grumio. Thou, it seems, that calls for company to countenance her.
Curtis. I call them forth to credit° her.   do credit to

Grumio. Why, she comes to borrow nothing of them.

Enter four or five servingmen [Nathaniel, Philip, Joseph, Nicholas, Gregory].

Nathaniel. Welcome home, Grumio.
Philip. How now, Grumio.
Joseph. What, Grumio.
Nicholas. Fellow Grumio.
Nathaniel. How now, old lad.   90
Grumio. "Welcome," you; "how now," you; "what," you; "fellow,"
    you; and thus much for greeting. Now, my spruce°   *lively*
    companions, is all ready and all things neat?
Nathaniel. All things is ready. How near is our master?
Grumio. E'en at hand, alighted by this; and therefore be not—
    Cock's passion,[76] silence. I hear my master.

Enter Petruchio and Kate.

Petruchio. Where be these knaves? What, no man at door
    To hold my stirrup nor to take my horse?
    Where is Nathaniel, Gregory, Philip?
All servants. Here, here, sir; here, sir.   100
Petruchio. "Here, sir; here, sir; here, sir; here, sir."
    You logger-headed° and unpolished grooms.   *stupid*
    What, no attendance? No regard? No duty?
    Where is the foolish knave I sent before?
Grumio. Here, sir; as foolish as I was before.
Petruchio. You peasant, swain,° you whoreson malt-horse   *rascal bumpkin*
    drudge.[77]
    Did I not bid thee meet me in the
        park°   *enclosed area attached to a country house*
    And bring along these rascal knaves with thee?
Grumio. Nathaniel's coat, sir, was not fully made,   109
    And Gabriel's pumps were all unpinked° i'th' heel;   *unornamented*
    There was no link° to color Peter's hat,   *blacking from burnt torches*

76. "God's passion," a mild oath.
77. While "whoreson" literally means "son of a whore," the term is used loosely as a modifier to express contempt and reprobation. "Malt-horse drudge" is a slow, heavy horse used to grind malt by walking a treadmill. The malt-horse was proverbially stupid.

And Walter's dagger was not come from
    sheathing.°   *being fitted for a scabbard*
There were none fine but Adam, Ralph, and Gregory;
The rest were ragged, old, and beggarly;
Yet, as they are, here are they come to meet you.

Petruchio. Go, rascals, go and fetch my supper in. *Exeunt servingmen.*
    [Sings] Where is the life that late I led?
    Where are those—
    Sit down, Kate, and welcome. Soud, soud, soud, soud.[78]

      Enter servants [one named Peter] with supper.

    Why, when, I say? Nay, good sweet Kate, be merry.   120
    Off with my boots, you rogues. You villains, when?
    [Sings] It was the friar of orders grey,
    As he forth walkèd on his way—
    Out,° you rogue. You pluck my foot awry;°   *expression of anger / crookedly*
    Take that, and mend the plucking of the other. *[Strikes him.]*
    Be merry, Kate. Some water, here, what, ho.

      Enter one with water.

    Where's my spaniel Troilus? Sirrah, get you hence,
    And bid my cousin Ferdinand come hither: *[Exit servingman.]*
    One, Kate, that you must kiss and be acquainted with.
    Where are my slippers? Shall I have some water?   130
    Come, Kate, and wash, and welcome heartily.
    You whoreson villain, will you let it fall? *[Strikes him.]*
Katherina. Patience, I pray you; 'twas a fault unwilling.
Petruchio. A whoreson, beetle°-headed, flap°-   *heavy wooden mallet / pendulous*
    eared knave.
    Come, Kate, sit down; I know you have a stomach.°   *appetite*
    Will you give thanks,° sweet Kate, or else shall I?   *say grace*
    What's this? Mutton?

78. Petruchio's "soud," repeated four times, has defied explication. Oliver suggests that Petruchio is humming, while other editors have called it some sort of exclamation, perhaps of fatigue or impatience (Onions). Perhaps it is a noise to frighten Kate. Many editors emend "soud" to "food" due to "the easy confusion of 'f' and long 's' in Secretary hand" (Thompson). The capital "f," however, is quite distinct from the capital "s."

1 Servant. Ay.

Petruchio. Who brought it?

Peter. I.   140

Petruchio. 'Tis burnt; and so is all the meat.
    What dogs are these? Where is the rascal cook?
    How durst you villains bring it from the
        dresser°   *kitchen table upon which food was prepared*
    And serve it thus to me that love it not?
    There, take it to you, trenchers, cups, and all; *[Throws the meat*
        and dishes at them.]
    You heedless joltheads° and unmannered slaves.   *careless blockheads*
    What, do you grumble? I'll be with you straight. *[Exeunt*
    servants.]

Katherina. I pray you, husband, be not so disquiet;°   *upset*
    The meat was well, if you were so contented.

Petruchio. I tell thee, Kate, 'twas burnt and dried away,   150
    And I expressly am forbid to touch it,
    For it engenders choler,° planteth anger;   *anger, rashness*
    And better 'twere that both of us did fast,°   *go without food*
    Since, of ourselves,° ourselves are choleric,   *by nature*
    Than feed it with such over-roasted flesh.°   *meat*
    Be patient; tomorrow 't shall be mended.°   *put right*
    And for this night we'll fast for company.°   *companionship*
    Come, I will bring thee to thy bridal chamber. *Exeunt.*

        Enter servants [Nathanial, Peter, Grumio] severally.°   *one by one*

Nathaniel. Peter, didst ever see the like?   159

Peter. He kills her in her own humor.°   *masters her by behaving as she does*

        Enter Curtis, a servant.

Grumio. Where is he?

Curtis. In her chamber, making a sermon of
        continency° to her;   *moderation; sexual self-restraint*
    And rails,° and swears, and rates,° that she, poor soul,   *rants / scolds*
    Knows not which way to stand, to look, to speak,
    And sits as one new risen from a dream.
    Away, away, for he is coming hither. *[Exeunt.]*

        Enter Petruchio.

Petruchio. Thus have I politicly° begun my reign,   *prudently, cunningly*
    And 'tis my hope to end successfully.   168
    My falcon[79] now is sharp° and passing° empty.   *famished / extremely*
    And 'til she stoop she must not be full-gorged,°   *allowed to eat her fill*
    For then she never looks upon her lure.°   *decoy bird made of feathers*
    Another way I have to man my haggard,°   *tame my wild hawk*
    To make her come, and know her keeper's call,
    That is, to watch her,° as we watch these kites°   *keep her awake / falcons*
    That bate and beat,° and will not be obedient.   *flutter and flap wings*
    She ate no meat today, nor none shall eat;
    Last night she slept not, nor tonight she shall not;
    As with the meat, some undeservèd fault
    I'll find about the making of the bed;   179
    And here I'll fling the pillow, there the bolster,°   *stuffed cushion*
    This way the coverlet, another way the sheets;
    Ay, and amid this hurly° I intend   *commotion*
    That all is done in reverend° care of her.   *respectful*
    And, in conclusion, she shall watch° all night;   *stay awake*
    And if she chance to nod I'll rail and brawl
    And with the clamor keep her still° awake,   *always*
    This is a way to kill a wife with kindness,°   *apparent affection*
    And thus I'll curb her mad and headstrong humor.
    He that knows better how to tame a shrew,   189
    Now let him speak; 'tis charity to show.°   *explain what he knows*
                               Exit.

[ACT 3, SCENE 4]

Enter Tranio [as Lucentio with Lucentio as Cambio] and Hortensio [as Litio].

Tranio. Is 't possible, friend Litio, that Mistress Bianca
    Doth fancy any other but Lucentio?
    I tell you, sir, she bears me fair in hand.°   *is deluding me with false pretense*

79. Petruchio reveals to the audience his plan for taming Katherina just as a falconer tames a wild hawk or "haggard." The hawk is trained to "stoop," or fly to the "lure," by being kept hungry and awake until the hawk responds to the master's call.

Lucentio.[80] Sir, to satisfy you in° what I have said,   *convince you of*
　　　Stand by and mark the manner of his teaching.

　　　　　　　　　Enter Bianca.

Hortensio. Now, mistress, profit you in what you read?
Bianca. What master read you first; resolve me that?
Hortensio. I read, that I profess,° "The Art to   *what I practice*
　　　Love."°   *(see n. 17)*
Bianca. And may you prove, sir, master of your art.
Lucentio. While you, sweet dear, prove mistress of my heart.   10
Hortensio. Quick proceeders,° marry. Now tell me, I pray,   *apt students*
　　　You that durst swear that your Mistress Bianca
　　　Loved me in the world so well as Lucentio.
Tranio. O, despiteful love, unconstant womankind,
　　　I tell thee, Litio, this is wonderful.°   *incredible*
Hortensio. Mistake no more; I am not Litio,
　　　Nor a musician as I seem to be;
　　　But one that scorn to live in this disguise
　　　For such a one as leaves a gentleman
　　　And makes a god of such a cullion.°   *base fellow*
　　　Know, sir, that I am called Hortensio.   21
Tranio. Signor Hortensio, I have often heard
　　　Of your entire affection° to Bianca;   *pure love*
　　　And since mine eyes are witness of her lightness,°   *loose behavior*
　　　I will with you, if you be so contented,
　　　Forswear Bianca and her love for ever.
Hortensio. See, how they kiss and court. Signor Lucentio,

80. F1 has no entrance for Lucentio, although he is clearly in the scene. Since the opening stage direction in F1 is "Enter Tranio and Hortensio," whoever prepared the text for F2 (1632) switched the speakers of the second and third speeches and also gave the next speech that is assigned to Hortensio in F1 to Lucentio. Tranio's opening speech is addressed to Litio (Hortensio), but there is no reason that Cambio (Lucentio) might not respond, especially if he was the one who told "Lucentio" (Tranio) that Bianca's affection for the man to whom she is betrothed (him) is compromised by her affection to another ("to satisfy you in what I have said"). If he is just now telling "Lucentio" the rumor, they would enter together. Litio (Hortensio) refers to the rumor that Bianca is betraying her betrothed with him in 3.4.12–13. Rowe (1709) rationalized the F2 assignments by adding Lucentio to Bianca's entrance into the scene and changing "me" to "none" in 3.4.13. We follow F1 here.

Here is my hand, and here I firmly vow
Never to woo her more, but do forswear her,
As one unworthy all the former favors   30
That I have fondly° flattered her withal.   *foolishly*

Tranio. And here I take the like unfeignèd oath,
Never to marry with her though she would entreat;
Fie on her. See how beastly° she doth court him.   *like an animal*

Hortensio. Would all the world but he had quite forsworn
For me,[81] that I may surely keep mine oath.
I will be married to a wealthy widow,
Ere three days pass, which hath as long loved me
As I have loved this proud disdainful haggard.°   *wild hawk*
And so farewell, Signor Lucentio.   40
Kindness in women, not their beauteous looks,
Shall win my love; and so I take my leave,
In resolution° as I swore before.   *firmly determined*

                    Exit.

Tranio. Mistress Bianca, bless you with such grace
As 'longeth° to a lover's blessèd case.   *belongs*
Nay, I have ta'en you napping,° gentle love,   *surprised you (embracing?)*
And have forsworn you with Hortensio.

Bianca. Tranio, you jest; but have you both forsworn me?

Tranio. Mistress, we have.

Lucentio. Then we are rid of Litio.   50

Tranio. I'faith, he'll have a lusty° widow now,   *high-spirited*
That shall be wooed and wedded in a day.

Bianca. God give him joy.

Tranio. Ay, and he'll tame her.

Bianca. He says so, Tranio?

Tranio. Faith, he is gone unto the taming-school.

Bianca. The taming-school. What, is there such a place?

Tranio. Ay, mistress; and Petruchio is the master,
That teacheth tricks eleven and twenty long,[82]
To tame a shrew and charm her chattering tongue.   60

81. It is not clear what Hortensio is saying here in F1. Perhaps he means that if everybody but Cambio broke the promises they made (to him? or to Bianca?), he would find it easier not to love her himself. Many modern editors put a full stop after "forsworn" and a comma after "oath" in 3.4.36. This punctuation does not do much to clarify 3.4.35, however.

82. Tricks of exactly the right kind for the game "Thirty-One." See n. 29.

Enter Biondello.

Biondello. O, master, master, I have watched so long
    That I am dog-weary;° but at last I spied   *worn out*
    An ancient angel[83] coming down the hill
    Will serve the turn.°   *our purposes*
Tranio. What is he, Biondello?
Biondello. Master, a *marcantant*° or a   *corruption of Italian for "merchant"*
    pedant,°   *scholar*
    I know not what, but formal in apparel,
    In gait and countenance surely like a father.
Lucentio. And what of him, Tranio?   69
Tranio. If he be credulous and trust my tale,°   *believe my story*
    I'll make him glad to seem° Vincentio,   *appear to be*
    And give assurance to Baptista Minola
    As if he were the right Vincentio.
    Take me[84] your love, and then let me alone. *[Exeunt Lucentio and*
    Bianca.]

Enter a pedant.

Pedant. God save you, sir.
Tranio. And you, sir; you are welcome.
    Travel you far on, or are you at the farthest?
Pedant. Sir, at the farthest for a week or two;
    But then up farther, and as far as Rome;
    And so to Tripoli,° if God lend me life.   *(in north Africa)*
Tranio. What countryman, I pray?   81
Pedant. Of Mantua.
Tranio. Of Mantua, sir, marry, God forbid,
    And come to Padua, careless° of your life.   *without regard for*
Pedant. My life, sir? How, I pray? For that goes hard.
Tranio. 'Tis death for any one in Mantua

---

83. An "ancient angel" is defined in Randle Cotgrave's early dictionary as "a fellow of th'old, sound, honest, and worthy stamp." An "angel" is both a heavenly messenger and a coin worth half a pound sterling, so called because it was stamped with the angel Michael battling a dragon.

84. Another example of the ethical dative (see n. 27). Thus the phrase may be rendered, "Take, I say, your love in." Compare "Go, hop me over . . . " (4.1.102), where the initial "me" is often emended to "in."

To come to Padua. Know you not the cause?
Your ships are stayed° at Venice; and the Duke,   *held up*
For° private quarrel 'twixt your duke and him,   *on account of*
Hath published and proclaimed it openly.   90
'Tis marvel°—but° that you are but newly come,   *strange / except*
You might have heard it else proclaimed about.°   *throughout the city*
Pedant. Alas, sir, it is worse for me than so,
For I have bills for money by exchange°   *promissory notes*
From Florence, and must here deliver them.
Tranio. Well, sir, to do you courtesy,
This will I do, and this I will advise you.
First, tell me, have you ever been at Pisa?
Pedant. Ay, sir, in Pisa have I often been,
Pisa renownèd for grave citizens.   100
Tranio. Among them know you one Vincentio?
Pedant. I know him not, but I have heard of him,
A merchant of incomparable wealth.
Tranio. He is my father, sir; and, sooth to say,
In count'nance somewhat doth resemble you.
Biondello. As much as an apple doth an oyster,° and all one.   *(proverbial)*
Tranio. To save your life in this extremity,
This favor will I do you for his sake;
And think it not the worst of all your fortunes
That you are like to Sir Vincentio.   110
His name and credit° shall you undertake,   *reputation*
And in my house you shall be friendly lodged;
Look that you take upon you° as you should.   *play your part*
You understand me, sir. So shall you stay
'Til you have done your business in the city.
If this be court'sy, sir, accept of it.
Pedant. O, sir, I do, and will repute° you ever   *consider*
The patron of my life and liberty.
Tranio. Then go with me to make the matter good.°   *put the plan into effect*
This, by the way, I let you understand: 120
My father is here looked for° every day   *expected*
To pass assurance° of a dow'r in marriage   *settle*
'Twixt me and one Baptista's daughter here.
In all these circumstances I'll instruct you.
Go with me to clothe you as becomes you. *Exeunt.*

ACT 4, SCENE 1

Enter Katherina and Grumio.

Grumio. No, no, forsooth; I dare not for my life.
Katherina. The more my wrong,° the more his   *the greater the injustice I suffer*
    spite appears.
    What, did he marry me to famish me?
    Beggars that come unto my father's door
    Upon entreaty have a present° alms;   *immediate*
    If not, elsewhere they meet with charity;
    But I, who never knew how to entreat,
    Nor never needed that I should entreat,
    Am starved for meat,° giddy for lack of sleep.   *food*
    With oaths kept waking, and with brawling fed.   10
    And that which spites° me more than all these wants: *vexes*
    He does it under name of perfect love;
    As who should say,° if I should sleep or eat,   *as if to say*
    'Twere deadly sickness or else present death.
    I prithee go and get me some repast;°   *food*
    I care not what, so it be wholesome food.
Grumio. What say you to a neat's foot?°   *ox or calf foot*
Katherina. 'Tis passing° good; I prithee let me have it.   *exceedingly*
Grumio. I fear it is too choleric° a meat.   *inducing anger or rashness*
    How say you to a fat tripe finely
        broiled?°   *stomach of a sheep or cow cooked over coals*
Katherina. I like it well; good Grumio, fetch it me.   21
Grumio. I cannot tell; I fear 'tis choleric.
    What say you to a piece of beef and mustard?
Katherina. A dish that I do love to feed upon.
Grumio. Ay, but the mustard is too hot a little.
Katherina. Why then the beef, and let the mustard rest.
Grumio. Nay, then I will not; you shall have the mustard,
    Or else you get no beef of Grumio.
Katherina. Then both, or one, or anything thou wilt.
Grumio. Why then the mustard without the beef.   30
Katherina. Go, get thee gone, thou false deluding slave, *Beats him.*
    That feed'st me with the very name° of meat.   *nothing but the word*
    Sorrow on thee and all the pack of you
    That triumph thus upon my misery.
    Go, get thee gone, I say.

Enter Petruchio and Hortensio with meat.

Petruchio. How fares my Kate? What, sweeting,°   *sweetheart*
    all amort?°   *lifeless, dejected*
Hortensio. Mistress, what cheer?°   *How are you?; What mood (cheer) are you in?*
Katherina. Faith, as cold° as can be.   *dejected, void of passion*
Petruchio. Pluck up thy spirits, look cheerfully upon me.
    Here, love, thou seest how diligent I am,   40
    To dress° thy meat myself and bring it thee.   *prepare*
    I am sure, sweet Kate, this kindness merits thanks.
    What, not a word? Nay then, thou lov'st it not,
    And all my pains is sorted to no proof.°   *all my labor has been in vain*
    Here, take away this dish.
Katherina. I pray you, let it stand.
Petruchio. The poorest° service is repaid with thanks;   *slightest*
    And so shall mine, before you touch the meat.
Katherina. I thank you, sir.
Hortensio. Signor Petruchio, fie, you are to blame.°   *too much at fault*
    Come, Mistress Kate, I'll bear you company.   51
Petruchio. Eat it up all, Hortensio, if thou lovest me;
    Much good do it unto thy gentle heart—
    Kate, eat apace.° And now, my honey love,   *quickly*
    Will we return unto thy father's house
    And revel it as bravely° as the best,   *splendidly dressed*
    With silken coats and caps, and golden rings,
    With ruffs and cuffs and farthingales° and things,   *hooped petticoats*
    With scarfs and fans and double change of brav'ry.° *variation of finery*
    With amber bracelets, beads, and all this knav'ry.°   *tricks of dress*
    What, hast thou dined? The tailor stays thy leisure,   61
    To deck thy body with his ruffling° treasure. *swaggering, rising in ruffles*

Enter tailor.

Come, tailor, let us see these ornaments;
Lay forth the gown.

Enter haberdasher.

    What news with you, sir?
Haberdasher. Here is the cap your worship did bespeak.°   *order*
Petruchio. Why, this was molded on a porringer,°   *soup or porridge bowl*
    A velvet dish. Fie, fie, 'tis lewd and filthy.°   *cheap and nasty*
    Why, 'tis a cockle° or a walnut-shell,   *cockleshell*

A knack,° a toy, a trick,° a baby's cap.   *trifle / bauble*

Away with it. Come, let me have a bigger.   71

Katherina. I'll have no bigger; this doth fit the time,

And gentlewomen wear such caps as these.

Petruchio. When you are gentle, you shall have one too,

And not 'til then.

Hortensio. That will not be in haste.

Katherina. Why, sir, I trust I may have leave to speak;

And speak I will. I am no child, no babe.

Your betters have endured° me say my mind,   *allowed*

And if you cannot, best you stop your ears.   80

My tongue will tell the anger of my heart,

Or else my heart, concealing it, will break;

And rather than it shall, I will be free

Even to the uttermost, as I please, in words.

Petruchio. Why, thou say'st true; it is paltry cap,

A custard-coffin,° a bauble, a   *crust of pastry in which a custard was baked*

silken pie;

I love thee well in that thou lik'st it not.

Katherina. Love me or love me not, I like the cap;

And it I will have, or I will have none. *[Exit haberdasher.]*

Petruchio. Thy gown. Why, ay. Come, tailor, let us see't.   90

O, mercy, God, what masquing

stuff° is here?   *costume for a masque, strange and elaborate*

What's this? A sleeve? 'Tis like a demi-cannon.°   *large gun*

What, up and down, carved like an appletart?

Here's snip and nip and cut and slish and

slash,°   *slit that lets other colors show through*

Like to a censer[85] in a barber's shop.

Why, what a devil's name, tailor, call'st thou this?

Hortensio. I see she's like to have neither cap nor gown.

Tailor. You bid me make it orderly and well,

According to the fashion and the time.

Petruchio. Marry, and did;° but if you be rememb'red,°   *indeed I did / recollect*

I did not bid you mar it to the time.   101

Go, hop me° over every kennel° home,   *hop, I say / gutter, street gutter*

---

85. F1 "censor" would appear to be "censer," an incense burner with holes in the top. The *OED* cites this line under that spelling but says, "The commentators are not agreed as to what exactly is referred to." Such fumigators have not been found connected with barbers, but the reference appears to be to the designs cut in the top of the censer where the odor escapes.

For you shall hop without my custom,° sir.   *business*
I'll none of it; hence, make your best of it.
Katherina. I never saw a better-fashioned gown,
    More quaint,° more pleasing, nor more   *artfully made, elegant*
        commendable.
    Belike° you mean to make a puppet of me.   *perhaps*
Petruchio. Why, true; he means to make a puppet of thee.
Tailor. She says your worship means to make a puppet of her.
Petruchio. O, monstrous arrogance. Thou liest, thou thread, thou
        thimble,   110
    Thou yard, three-quarters, half-yard, quarter,
        nail,°   *one-sixteenth of a yard*
    Thou flea, thou nit,° thou winter-cricket thou.   *gnat*
    Braved° in mine own house with a skein of thread.   *defied*
    Away, thou rag,° thou quantity,° thou   *bit of cloth; shabby person / scrap*
        remnant,
    Or I shall so bemete° thee with thy yard   *measure*
    As thou shalt think on prating° whilst thou   *think better of talking saucily*
        liv'st.
    I tell thee, I, that thou hast marred her gown.
Tailor. Your worship is deceived; the gown is made
    Just as my master had direction.
    Grumio gave order how it should be done.   120
Grumio. I gave him no order; I gave him the stuff.°   *material*
Tailor. But how did you desire it should be made?
Grumio. Marry, sir, with needle and thread.
Tailor. But did you not request to have it cut?
Grumio. Thou hast faced° many things.   *trimmed with braid; bullied*
Tailor. I have.
Grumio. Face not me. Thou hast braved° many men;   *dressed in finery; defied*
    brave not me. I will neither be faced nor braved. I say unto thee,
    I bid thy master cut out the gown, but I did not bid him cut it to
    pieces. *Ergo,*° thou liest.   *"therefore"*
Tailor. Why, here is the note of the fashion to testify.   131
Petruchio. Read it.
Grumio. The note lies in's throat, if he say I said so.
Tailor. "*Imprimis,*° a loose-bodied° gown—"   *"first" / loose fitting*
Grumio. Master, if ever I said "loose-bodied° gown,"   *immoral woman's*
    sew me in the skirts of it and beat me to death with a
    bottom° of brown thread; I said a gown.   *spool, ball*
Petruchio. Proceed.
Tailor. "With a small compassed° cape."   *circular*

Grumio. I confess the cape.   140

Tailor. "With a trunk° sleeve."   *tapering from shoulder to wrist*

Grumio. I confess two sleeves.

Tailor. "The sleeves curiously° cut."   *ornately*

Petruchio. Ay, there's the villainy.

Grumio. Error i'th' bill,° sir, error i'th' bill!   *the note; bill of indictment*
  I commanded the sleeves should be cut out, and sewed up again,
  and that I'll prove upon thee,° though thy little   *establish by fighting you*
  finger be armed in a thimble.   148

Tailor. This is true that I say, and° I had thee in place   *if*
  where,° thou shouldst know it.   *the right spot*

Grumio. I am for thee straight.° Take thou the bill,°   *ready to fight now / note*
  give me thy mete-yard,° and spare not me.   *pike, measuring yard*

Hortensio. God-a-mercy, Grumio, then he shall have
  no odds.°   *no one will bet on him*

Petruchio. Well, sir, in brief, the gown is not for me.

Grumio. You are i'th' right, sir; 'tis for my mistress.

Petruchio. Go, take it up unto thy master's use.

Grumio. Villain, not for thy life. Take up my mistress's gown for
  thy master's use?[86]   159

Petruchio. Why, sir, what's your conceit° in that?   *idea, innuendo*

Grumio. O, sir, the conceit is deeper than you think for. "Take up
  my mistress' gown to his master's use." O, fie, fie, fie.

Petruchio. [Aside] Hortensio, say thou wilt see the tailor paid—
  Go take it hence; be gone, and say no more.

Hortensio. [Aside] Tailor, I'll pay thee for thy gown tomorrow;
  Take no unkindness of° his hasty words.   *no offense at*
  Away, I say; commend me to thy master. *Exit tailor.*

Petruchio. Well, come, my Kate; we will unto your father's
  Even in these honest mean habiliments;°   *poor clothes*
  Our purses shall be proud, our garments poor;   170
  For 'tis the mind that makes the body rich;
  And as the sun breaks through the darkest clouds,
  So honor peereth in° the meanest habit.   *peeps out through*
  What, is the jay more precious than the lark
  Because his feathers are more beautiful?
  Or is the adder better than the eel

86. Grumio's interpretation of his master's simple command is that he should
raise his mistress' gown so that his master can have sexual enjoyment from her.
"Deeper" and "use" in the next lines take on sexual meanings.

Because his painted° skin contents the eye?   *richly colored*
O, no, good Kate; neither art thou the worse
For this poor furniture° and mean° array.   *clothing / inferior*
If thou accountest it shame, lay it on° me;   *blame*
And therefore frolic. We will hence forthwith   181
To feast and sport us at thy father's house.
Go, call my men, and let us straight to him.
And bring our horses unto Long-lane end;
There will we mount, and thither walk on foot.
Let's see; I think 'tis now some° seven o'clock,   *about*
And well we may come there by dinner-
    time.°   *(between eleven o'clock and noon)*

Katherina. I dare assure you, sir, 'tis almost two,
    And 'twill be supper-time° ere you   *(between half-past five and half-past six)*
    come there.

Petruchio. It shall be seven ere I go to horse.   190
    Look what I speak, or do, or think to do,
    You are still crossing° it. Sirs, let 't   *always contradicting*
    alone:°   *take no further action*
    I will not go today; and ere I do,
    It shall be what o'clock I say it is.

Hortensio. Why, so this gallant will command the sun.   *Exeunt.*

[ACT 4, SCENE 2]

Enter Tranio [as Lucentio], and the pedant dressed
like Vincentio (booted and bare-headed).[87]

Tranio. Sir, this is the house; please it you° that I call?   *may it please you*
Pedant. Ay, what else. And, but I be° deceived,   *unless I am*
    Signor Baptista may remember me
    Near twenty years ago in Genoa,
Tranio.[88] Where we were lodgers at the Pegasus.°   *(name of an inn)*

87. This description of the pedant is printed in F1 as part of the stage direction
that appears after Tranio's line at 4.2.18.

88. F1 assigns this line to Tranio. Editors since Theobald have given the line to
the pedant and started Tranio's speech at the next line. It is plausible that Tranio
could join in rehearsing the backstory that he has given the pedant to convince
Baptista of his identity as Vincentio.

'Tis well; and hold your own,° in any case,   *play your part well*
With such austerity as longeth° to a father.   *belongs*

Enter Biondello.

Pedant. I warrant you. But, sir, here comes your boy;
   'Twere good he were schooled.°   *instructed in his part*
Tranio. Fear you not him. Sirrah Biondello,   10
   Now do your duty throughly,° I advise° you.   *thoroughly / instruct*
   Imagine 'twere° the right Vincentio.   *that this man is*
Biondello. Tut, fear not me.
Tranio. But hast thou done thy errand to Baptista?
Biondello. I told him that your father was at Venice,
   And that you looked for him this day in Padua.
Tranio. Th'art a tall° fellow; hold thee that to   *fine*
   drink.°   *use that to buy a drink*
   Here comes Baptista. *[To pedant]* Set your
   countenance,° sir.   *expression*

Enter Baptista and Lucentio [as Cambio].

Signor Baptista, you are happily met.
Sir, this is the gentleman I told you of;   20
I pray you, stand° good father to me now;   *show yourself*
Give me Bianca for my patrimony.
Pedant. Soft,° son. Sir, by your leave: having   *gently*
   come° to Padua   *I having come*
To gather in some debts, my son Lucentio
Made me acquainted with a weighty cause°   *serious matter*
Of love between your daughter and himself;
And, for° the good report I hear of you,   *because of*
And for the love he beareth to your daughter,
And she to him, to stay him° not too long,   *keep him waiting*
I am content, in a good father's care,   30
To have him matched. And, if you please to like
No worse than I,° upon some agreement   *if you are no less satisfied than I*
Me shall you find ready and willing
With one consent° to have her so bestowed;   *in entire agreement*
For curious° I cannot be with you,   *overly particular*
Signor Baptista, of whom I hear so well.
Baptista. Sir, pardon me in what I have to say.
   Your plainness and your shortness please me well.

Right true it is your son Lucentio here
Doth love my daughter, and she loveth him,   40
Or both dissemble deeply their affections;
And therefore, if you say no more than this,
That like a father you will deal with him,
And pass° my daughter a sufficient dower,   *settle upon*
The match is made, and all is done.
Your son shall have my daughter with consent.
Tranio. I thank you, sir. Where then do you know best
  We be affied,° and such assurance° ta'en   *betrothed / legal arrangements*
  As shall with either part's agreement stand.°   *be agreeable to both parties*
Baptista. Not in my house, Lucentio, for you know   50
  "Pitchers have ears,"° and I have many   *there may be listeners (proverb)*
    servants;
  Besides, old Gremio is heark'ning still,°   *constantly on the watch*
  And happily° we might be interrupted.   *perhaps*
Tranio. Then at my lodging, an it like° you.   *if it please*
  There doth my father lie,° and there this night   *lodge*
  We'll pass the business privately and well.
  Send for your daughter by your servant here;
  My boy shall fetch the scrivener° presently.   *scribe, notary*
  The worst is this, that at so slender° warning   *little*
  You are like to have a thin and slender
    pittance.°   *insufficient fare (for celebrating)*
Baptista. It likes me well. Cambio, hie you home,°   *hurry off*
  And bid Bianca make her ready straight;°   *immediately*
  And, if you will, tell what hath happened: 63
  Lucentio's father is arrived in Padua,
  And how she's like° to be Lucentio's wife.   *probably*
      [Exit Lucentio.]
Biondello. I pray the gods she may, with all my heart.
Tranio. Dally not with the gods, but get thee gone. *Exit [Biondello].*

     Enter [servingman] Peter.[89]

Signor Baptista, shall I lead the way?

---

89. This entrance is strange, as the servingman does not speak in the four lines
left in the scene. Nor should this Peter be connected to Petruchio's servant Peter.
Oliver and Thompson omit the stage direction completely.

Welcome. One mess is like to be your
    cheer;°   *one dish is likely to be your fare*
Come, sir; we will better it in Pisa.   70
Baptista. I follow you. *Exeunt.*

[ACT 4, SCENE 3]

Enter Lucentio [as Cambio] and Biondello.

Biondello. Cambio.
Lucentio. What say'st thou, Biondello?
Biondello. You saw my master wink and laugh upon you?
Lucentio. Biondello, what of that?
Biondello. Faith, nothing; but 'has° left me here behind to   *he has*
    expound the meaning or moral of his signs and tokens.
Lucentio. I pray thee moralize° them.   *explain the meaning of*
Biondello. Then thus: Baptista is safe, talking with the deceiving
    father of a deceitful son.
Lucentio. And what of him?   10
Biondello. His daughter is to be brought by you to the supper.
Lucentio. And then?
Biondello. The old priest at Saint Luke's church is at your command
    at all hours.
Lucentio. And what of all this?
Biondello. I cannot tell, except they are busied about a counterfeit
    assurance.° Take your assurance of her, *cum*   *(i.e., the papers drawn up)*
    privilegio ad imprimendum solum;[90] to th' church take the priest,
    clerk, and some sufficient° honest witnesses.   *the required number of*
    If this be not that you look for, I have no more to say,   20
    But bid Bianca farewell for ever and a day.
Lucentio. Hear'st thou, Biondello?
Biondello. I cannot tarry. I knew a wench married in an afternoon
    as she went to the garden for parsley to stuff a rabbit. And

---

90. "With the privilege for printing only." This inscription was often found on
the title pages of books of the period. It came to mean, "with the sole right to
print." Biondello is comparing "copyright" to the exclusive rights bestowed to
a husband through marriage: the right to procreate, "to stamp one's own image
on a person by getting her with child" (Oliver 209).

so may you, sir; and so adieu, sir. My master hath appointed
me to go to Saint Luke's to bid the priest be ready to come
against you come° with your   *in preparation for your coming*
appendix.°   *an addition; a person attached to someone*

Exit.

Lucentio. I may and will, if she be so contented.
　　She will be pleased; then wherefore should I doubt?　　　　30
　　Hap what hap may,° I'll roundly go about   *come what may*
　　　her;°   *approach her directly*
　　It shall go hard if Cambio go without her.°   *lose her*

Exit.

[ACT 4, SCENE 4]

Enter Petruchio, Kate, Hortensio.

Petruchio. Come on, a God's name; once more toward our father's.
　　Good Lord, how bright and goodly shines the moon.
Katherina. The moon? The sun. It is not moonlight now.
Petruchio. I say it is the moon that shines so bright.
Katherina. I know it is the sun that shines so bright.
Petruchio. Now by my mother's son, and that's myself,
　　It shall be moon, or star, or what I list,°   *choose, please*
　　Or ere° I journey to your father's house.   *before*
　　Go on and fetch our horses back again.
　　Evermore crossed° and crossed, nothing but crossed.   *contradicted*
Hortensio. Say as he says, or we shall never go.   11
Katherina. Forward, I pray, since we have come so far,
　　And be it moon, or sun, or what you please.
　　And if you please to call it a rush-candle,[91]
　　Henceforth I vow it shall be so for me.
Petruchio. I say it is the moon.
Katherina. I know it is the moon.
Petruchio. Nay, then you lie; it is the blessèd sun.
Katherina. Then, God be blessed, it is the blessèd sun;
　　But sun it is not, when you say it is not;   20
　　And the moon changes even as your mind.

91. A candle of feeble power made by dipping a rush in tallow or grease.

What you will have it named, even that it is,
    And so it shall be so for Katherine.
Hortensio. Petruchio, go thy ways;° the field is won.   *carry on*
Petruchio. Well, forward, forward. Thus the bowl should run,
    And not unluckily against the bias.[92]
    But, soft, company is coming here.

Enter Vincentio.

Good-morrow, gentle mistress; where away?
    Tell me, sweet Kate, and tell me truly, too,
    Hast thou beheld a fresher° gentlewoman: *more youthful*
    Such war of white and red within her cheeks;   31
    What stars do spangle° heaven with such beauty   *brightly adorn*
    As those two eyes become° that heavenly face?   *adorn*
    Fair lovely maid, once more good day to thee.
    Sweet Kate, embrace her for her beauty's sake.
Hortensio. 'A° will make the man mad, to make the woman of him.   *he*
Katherina. Young budding virgin, fair and fresh and sweet,
    Whither away,° or whither is thy abode?   *where are you going*
    Happy the parents of so fair a child;
    Happier the man whom favorable stars   40
    Allots thee for his lovely bedfellow.
Petruchio. Why, how now, Kate, I hope thou art not mad.
    This is a man, old, wrinkled, faded, withered,
    And not a maiden, as thou sayst he is.
Katherina. Pardon, old father,° my mistaking eyes,   *venerable man*
    That have been so bedazzled with the sun
    That everything I look on seemeth green;°   *fresh, youthful*
    Now I perceive thou art a reverend father.
    Pardon, I pray thee, for my mad mistaking.
Petruchio. Do, good old grandsire, and withal make known   50
    Which way thou travelest. If along with us,
    We shall be joyful of thy company.
Vincentio. Fair sir, and you my merry mistress,
    That with your strange encounter° much amazed me,   *greeting*
    My name is called Vincentio, my dwelling Pisa,
    And bound I am to Padua, there to visit
    A son of mine, which long I have not seen.

---

92. In the game of bowls, the wood ball ("bowl") has a weight ("bias") that
makes it swerve from a straight path when rolled.

Petruchio. What is his name?

Vincentio. Lucentio, gentle sir.

Petruchio. Happily met; the happier for thy son.   60
> And now by law, as well as reverend
>   age,°   *(An old man could be addressed as "father.")*
> I may entitle thee my loving father:°   *(i.e., father-in-law)*
> The sister to my wife, this gentlewoman,
> Thy son by this hath married.[93] Wonder not,
> Nor be not grieved; she is of good esteem,°   *reputation*
> Her dowry wealthy, and of worthy birth;
> Beside, so qualified° as may beseem°   *possessing good qualities / befit*
> The spouse of any noble gentleman.
> Let me embrace with old Vincentio;
> And wander we to see thy honest son,   70
> Who will of thy arrival be full joyous.

Vincentio. But is this true; or is it else your pleasure,
> Like pleasant° travelers, to break a jest°   *merry / play a practical joke*
> Upon the company you overtake?

Hortensio. I do assure thee, father, so it is.

Petruchio. Come, go along, and see the truth hereof;
> For our first merriment hath made thee jealous.°   *suspicious*
>   *Exeunt [all but Hortensio].*

Hortensio. Well, Petruchio, this has put me in heart.°   *encouraged me*
> Have to° my widow; and if she froward,°   *I'll confront / be perverse*
> Then hast thou taught Hortensio to be untoward.°   *unruly*
>   *Exit.*

[ACT 4, SCENE 5]

Enter Biondello, Lucentio, and Bianca; Gremio
is out before.°   *enters first*

Biondello. Softly and swiftly, sir, for the priest is ready.

93. Neither Petruchio nor Hortensio know of the real Lucentio's marriage plans. Petruchio expects that Bianca will wed "Lucentio" (Tranio), but Hortensio believes that "Lucentio" (Tranio) renounced his claim to Bianca. Hortensio does not offer a correction to Petruchio here. He may be the more committed to his widow after witnessing Bianca's favoring of Cambio, or he may think that if Petruchio is right that the marriage to "Lucentio" is going forward anyway, he is even more safely committed to his widow.

Lucentio. I fly, Biondello; but they may chance to need thee at
   home; therefore, leave us. *Exit [with Bianca].*
Biondello. Nay, faith, I'll see the church a' your back,[94] and then
   come back to my master as soon as I can. *[Exit.]*
Gremio. I marvel Cambio comes not all this while.

Enter Petruchio, Katherina, Vincentio, Grumio, with attendants.

Petruchio. Sir, here's the door; this is Lucentio's house;
   My father's bears more toward° the market-place;   *closer to*
   Thither must I, and here I leave you, sir.   9
Vincentio. You shall not choose but° drink before you go;   *you must*
   I think I shall command your welcome° here,   *a welcome for you*
   And by all likelihood some cheer is toward.°   *expected*
                        Knock.
Gremio. They're busy within; you were best knock louder.

Pedant looks out of the window.

Pedant. What's he that knocks as he would beat down the gate?
Vincentio. Is Signor Lucentio within, sir?
Pedant. He's within, sir, but not to be spoken withal.°   *with*
Vincentio. What if a man bring him a hundred pound or two to make
   merry withal?
Pedant. Keep your hundred pounds to yourself; he shall need none so
   long as I live.   20
Petruchio. Nay, I told you your son was well beloved in Padua. Do
   you hear, sir, to leave frivolous circumstances,° I pray   *trivial matters*
   you tell Signor Lucentio that his father is come from Pisa, and
   is here at the door to speak with him.
Pedant. Thou liest; his father is come from Padua, and here looking
   out at the window.
Vincentio. Art thou his father?
Pedant. Ay, sir, so his mother says, if I may believe her.
Petruchio. Why, how now, gentleman. Why, this is flat°   *downright*
   knavery to take upon you another man's name.   30
Pedant. Lay hands on the villain; I believe 'a° means to cozen°   *he / cheat*
   somebody in this city under my countenance.°   *by pretending to be me*

---

94. Biondello's comment means that he will wait to see Lucentio leaving the
church—with his bride Bianca and safely married—so he follows Lucentio and
Bianca.

Enter Biondello.

Biondello. I have seen them in the church together. God send 'em
    good shipping.° But who is here? Mine old   *grant them a good voyage*
    master, Vincentio. Now we are undone° and brought   *ruined*
    to nothing.
Vincentio. Come hither, crack-hemp.°   *rogue deserving to be hanged*
Biondello. I hope I may choose, sir.°   *I hope I can go my way, sir.*
Vincentio. Come hither, you rogue. What, have you forgot me?
Biondello. Forgot you, no, sir. I could not forget you, for I never   40
    saw you before in all my life.
Vincentio. What, you notorious villain, didst thou never see thy
    master's father, Vincentio?
Biondello. What, my old worshipful old master? Yes, marry, sir; see
    where he looks out of the window.
Vincentio. Is't so, indeed? *He beats Biondello.*
Biondello. Help, help, help. Here's a madman will murder me. *[Exit.]*
Pedant. Help, son, help, Signor Baptista. *[Exit from window.]*
Petruchio. Prithee, Kate, let's stand aside and see the end of this
    controversy.   50

Enter [below] pedant with servants, Baptista, Tranio [as Lucentio].

Tranio. Sir, what are you that offer° to beat my servant?   *dare*
Vincentio. What am I, sir? Nay, what are you, sir? O, immortal
    gods! O, fine villain. A silken doublet, a velvet hose, a scarlet
    cloak, and a copatain hat.° O, I am undone, I am   *conical hat*
    undone. While I play the good husband° at   *careful economic manager*
    home, my son and my servant spend all at the university.
Tranio. How now! What's the matter?
Baptista. What, is the man lunatic?
Tranio. Sir, you seem a sober ancient gentleman by your habit,°   *clothes*
    but your words show you a madman. Why, sir, what 'cerns it   60
    you° if I wear pearl and gold? I thank my   *what business is it of yours*
    good father, I am able to maintain it.
Vincentio. Thy father. O villain, he is a sailmaker in Bergamo.[95]

95. Vincentio may be implying Tranio is a bastard, since the city Bergamo
is landlocked and unlikely to have a sailmaker, thus Tranio has no father. Or
Shakespeare may be confused about Bergamo, thinking it a port as he does
Padua at 1.2.182.

Baptista. You mistake, sir; you mistake, sir. Pray, what do you
    think is his name?
Vincentio. His name, as if I knew not his name. I have brought him
    up ever since he was three years old, and his name is Tranio.
Pedant. Away, away, mad ass. His name is Lucentio; and he is mine
    only son, and heir to the lands of me, Signor Vicentio.
Vincentio. Lucentio? O, he hath murd'red his master. Lay hold on   70
    him, I charge you, in the Duke's name. O, my son, my son. Tell
    me, thou villain, where is my son, Lucentio?
Tranio. Call forth an officer.

[Enter officer.]

Carry this mad knave to the jail. Father Baptista, I charge you
    see that he be forthcoming.°   *ready to stand trial when required*
Vincentio. Carry me to the jail?
Gremio. Stay, officer, he shall not go to prison.
Baptista. Talk not, Signor Gremio. I say he shall go to prison.
Gremio. Take heed, Signor Baptista, lest you be cony-catched°   *swindled*
    in this business. I dare swear this is the right Vincentio.   80
Pedant. Swear if thou dar'st.
Gremio. Nay, I dare not swear it.
Tranio. Then thou wert best say that I am not Lucentio.
Gremio. Yes, I know thee to be Signor Lucentio.
Baptista. Away with the dotard;° to the jail with him.   *silly old fool*

Enter Biondello, Lucentio, and Bianca.

Vincentio. Thus strangers may be haled° and abused.   *dragged about*
    O, monstrous villain.
Biondello. O, we are spoiled,° and yonder he is. Deny him,   *ruined*
    forswear him, or else we are all undone.

Exeunt Biondello, Tranio, and pedant, as fast as may be.

Lucentio. Pardon, sweet father. *Kneel.*
Vincentio. Lives my sweet son?   91
Bianca. Pardon, dear father.
Baptista. How hast thou offended? Where is Lucentio?
Lucentio. Here's Lucentio, right son to the right Vincentio,
    That have by marriage made thy daughter mine,

While counterfeit supposes[96] bleared thine eyne.°   *deceived your eyes*
Gremio. Here's packing° with a witness to deceive us all.   *plotting*
Vincentio. Where is that damned villain, Tranio,
    That faced and braved° me in this matter so?   *defied; threatened*
Baptista. Why, tell me, is not this my Cambio?   100
Bianca. Cambio is changed into Lucentio.
Lucentio. Love wrought these miracles. Bianca's love
    Made me exchange my state with Tranio,
    While he did bear my countenance in the town;
    And happily I have arrivèd at the last
    Unto the wishèd haven of my bliss.
    What Tranio did, myself enforced him to;
    Then pardon him, sweet father, for my sake.
Vincentio. I'll slit the villain's nose° that would have   *(a form of revenge)*
    sent me to the jail.   110
Baptista. But do you hear, sir? Have you married my daughter
    without asking my good will?
Vincentio. Fear not, Baptista; we will content you, go to;°   *don't worry*
    but I will in to be revenged for this villainy. *Exit.*
Baptista. And I to sound° the depth of this knavery.   *take the measure of*
                      Exit.
Lucentio. Look not pale, Bianca; thy father will not frown.
             Exeunt [Lucentio and Bianca].
Gremio. My cake is dough,° but I'll in   *I have failed*
    among° the rest;   *go in with*
    Out of hope of all° but my share of the feast.   *with no hope of anything*
                  Exit.
Katherina. Husband, let's follow to see the end of this ado.
Petruchio. First, kiss me, Kate, and we will.   120
Katherina. What, in the midst of the street?
Petruchio. What, art thou ashamed of me?
Katherina. No, sir; God forbid; but ashamed to kiss.
Petruchio. Why, then, let's home again. Come, sirrah, let's away.
Katherina. Nay, I will give thee a kiss; now pray thee, love, stay.
Petruchio. Is not this well? Come, my sweet Kate:
    Better once than never, for never too late.[97] *Exeunt.*

---

96. "False suppositions caused by the exchange of identities." The word "supposes" alludes to Shakespeare's source for the Bianca intrigue, George Gascoigne's *Supposes* (1566).

97. Petruchio blends two proverbs: "Better late than never" (Tilley L85) and "It is never too late to mend" (Tilley M875).

ACT 5, [SCENE 1]

Enter Baptista, Vincentio, Gremio, the pedant, Lucentio, and Bianca.
Tranio, [Petruchio, Katherina, Hortensio,] and widow. The servingmen with
Tranio [Biondello, and Grumio], bringing in a banquet.

Lucentio. At last, though long,° our jarring notes agree,°   *late / harmonize*
    And time it is when raging war is done
    To smile at 'scapes° and perils overblown.°   *escapes / dispelled*
    My fair Bianca, bid my father welcome,
    While I with self-same kindness° welcome thine.   *affection, kinship*
    Brother Petruchio, sister Katherina,
    And thou, Hortensio, with thy loving widow,
    Feast with the best, and welcome to my house.
    My banquet° is to close our stomachs   *dessert of fruits, sweets, wine*
      up°   *finish the meal*
    After our great good cheer. Pray you, sit down;   10
    For now we sit to chat as well as eat.
Petruchio. Nothing but sit and sit, and eat and eat.
Baptista. Padua affords this kindness, son Petruchio.
Petruchio. Padua affords nothing but what is kind.
Hortensio. For both our sakes I would that word were true.
Petruchio. Now, for my life, Hortensio fears° his   *is afraid of; make her fear*
    widow.
Widow. Then never trust me if I be afeared.°   *I am afraid*
Petruchio. You are very sensible,° and yet you miss my sense: *intelligent*
    I mean Hortensio is afeard of you.
Widow. He that is giddy thinks the world turns round.   20
Petruchio. Roundly° replied.   *plainly, glibly*
Katherina. Mistress, how mean you that?
Widow. Thus I conceive by him.°   *that is what I imagine his condition to be*
Petruchio. Conceives° by me. How likes Hortensio that?   *is impregnated*
Hortensio. My widow says thus she conceives her
    tale.°   *understands her remark*
Petruchio. Very well mended. Kiss him for that, good widow.
Katherina. "He that is giddy thinks the world turns round."
    I pray you tell me what you meant by that.
Widow. Your husband, being troubled with a shrew,
    Measures my husband's sorrow by his woe: 30
    And now you know my meaning.
Katherina. A very mean° meaning.   *petty*

Widow. Right, I mean you.

Katherina. And I am mean indeed, respecting
　　　you.°　　　　　　　　　　　*I behave moderately compared to you*

Petruchio. To her, Kate.

Hortensio. To her, widow.

Petruchio. A hundred marks, my Kate does put her down.°　　*defeat her*

Hortensio. That's my office.

Petruchio. Spoke like an officer.° Ha' to　　　　*one who does his duty*
　　　thee,° lad.　　　　　　　　　　*go for it; I drink to you*

Drinks to Hortensio.

Baptista. How likes Gremio these quick-witted folks?　　　40

Gremio. Believe me, sir, they butt together well.

Bianca. Head and butt°—an hasty-witted　　　　*tail, buttock*
　　　body°　　　　　　　　　　　*quick-witted person*
　　　Would say your head and butt were head and horn.[98]

Vincentio. Ay, mistress bride, hath that awakened you?

Bianca. Ay, but not frighted me; therefore, I'll sleep again.

Petruchio. Nay, that you shall not since you have begun.
　　　Have at you for a better jest or two.

Bianca. Am I your bird? I mean to shift my bush,
　　　And then pursue me as you draw your bow.[99]　　　49
　　　You are welcome all. *Exeunt Bianca, [Katherina, and widow].*

Petruchio. She hath prevented° me. Here, Signor　*kept me from taking a shot*
　　　Tranio,
　　　This bird you aimed at, though you hit her not;
　　　Therefore a health to all that shot and missed.

Tranio. O, sir, Lucentio slipped° me like his greyhound,　　*unleashed*
　　　Which runs himself, and catches for his master.

Petruchio. A good swift° simile, but something　　　*quick-witted*
　　　currish.°　　　　　　　　　　　　*dog-like*

Tranio. 'Tis well, sir, that you hunted for yourself;
　　　'Tis thought your deer does hold you at a bay.[100]

Baptista. O, O, Petruchio, Tranio hits you now.

98. A reference to the horns that were supposed to grow out of the forehead of a cuckold, a man whose wife is unfaithful to him.

99. Birds were hunted with bows, but when the bird moved to another bush, the hunter would have to move as well.

100. The stag was said to be "at bay" when it turned on the hounds and started fighting with its horns. Tranio suggests that Petruchio's deer (dear) has turned on him.

Lucentio. I thank thee for that gird,° good Tranio.   *taunt, gibe*

Hortensio. Confess, confess; hath he not hit you here?   61

Petruchio. 'A° has a little galled me,° I confess;   *he / made me a little sore*

    And, as the jest did glance away from° me,   *ricocheted off*

    'Tis ten to one it maimed you two outright.

Baptista. Now, in good sadness,° son Petruchio,   *in all seriousness*

    I think thou hast the veriest° shrew of all.   *truest, most accurately named*

Petruchio. Well, I say no; and therefore, for assurance,°   *to put it to a test*

    Let's each one send unto his wife,

    And he whose wife is most obedient,

    To come at first when he doth send for her,   70

    Shall win the wager which we will propose.

Hortensio. Content. What's the wager?

Lucentio. Twenty crowns.°   *five pounds sterling*

Petruchio. Twenty crowns.

    I'll venture so much of my hawk or hound,

    But twenty times so much upon my wife.

Lucentio. A hundred then.

Hortensio. Content.

Petruchio. A match. 'Tis done.

Hortensio. Who shall begin?   80

Lucentio. That will I.

    Go, Biondello, bid your mistress come to me.

Biondello. I go. *Exit.*

Baptista. Son, I'll be your half° Bianca comes.   *go half-shares with you*

Lucentio. I'll have no halves; I'll bear it all myself.

              Enter Biondello.

    How now! What news?

Biondello. Sir, my mistress sends you word

    That she is busy and she cannot come.

Petruchio. How?° She's busy, and she cannot come.   *Really?*

    Is that an answer?   90

Gremio. Ay, and a kind one too.

    Pray God, sir, your wife send you not a worse.

Petruchio. I hope better.

Hortensio. Sirrah Biondello, go and entreat my wife

    To come to me forthwith. *Exit Biondello.*

Petruchio. Oh-ho, "entreat" her.

    Nay, then she must needs come.

Hortensio. I am afraid, sir,
  Do what you can, yours will not be entreated.

                    Enter Biondello.

  Now, where's my wife?   100
Biondello. She says you have some goodly jest in hand.
  She will not come; she bids you come to her.
Petruchio. Worse and worse; she will not come.
  O, vile, intolerable, not to be endured.
  Sirrah Grumio, go to your mistress;
  Say I command her come to me. *Exit [Grumio].*
Hortensio. I know her answer.
Petruchio. What?
Hortensio. She will not.   109
Petruchio. The fouler fortune mine, and there an
  end.°   *The worse my luck and that's that.*

                    Enter Katherina.

Baptista. Now, by my holidame,° here comes Katherina.   *all I hold sacred*
Katherina. What is your will, sir, that you send for me?
Petruchio. Where is your sister, and Hortensio's wife?
Katherina. They sit conferring° by the parlor fire.   *conversing*
Petruchio. Go, fetch them hither. If they deny° to come,   *refuse*
  Swinge me° them soundly forth unto their husbands. *thrash (see n. 27)*
  Away, I say, and bring them hither straight. *[Exit Katherina.]*
Lucentio. Here is a wonder,° if you talk of a wonder.   *marvel*
Hortensio. And so it is. I wonder what it bodes.°   *portends*
Petruchio. Marry, peace it bodes, and love, and quiet life,   120
  An awful° rule, and right supremacy;   *commanding due respect*
  And, to be short, what not that's sweet and happy.
Baptista. Now fair befall thee,° good Petruchio,   *good luck to you*
  The wager thou hast won. And I will add
  Unto their losses twenty thousand crowns;
  Another dowry to another daughter,
  For she is changed, as° she had never been.   *as if*
Petruchio. Nay, I will win my wager better yet,
  And show more sign of her obedience,
  Her new-built virtue and obedience.   130

          Enter Katherina, Bianca, and widow.

See where she comes and brings your froward wives
As prisoners to her womanly persuasion.
Katherine, that cap of yours becomes you not:°   *does not suit you*
Off with that bauble, throw it underfoot. *[Katherina obeys.]*
Widow. Lord, let me never have a cause to sigh
'Til I be brought to such a silly pass.
Bianca. Fie, what a foolish duty call you this?
Lucentio. I would your duty were as foolish, too.
The wisdom of your duty, fair Bianca,
Hath cost me five hundred crowns since supper-time.   140
Bianca. The more fool you for laying° on my duty.   *wagering*
Petruchio. Katherine, I charge thee, tell these headstrong women
what duty they do owe their lords and husbands.
Widow. Come, come, you're mocking; we will have no telling.
Petruchio. Come on, I say, and first begin with her.
Widow. She shall not.
Petruchio. I say she shall. And first begin with her.
Katherina. Fie, fie, unknit that threatening
      unknit° brow,   *harsh; against nature*
And dart not scornful glances from those eyes
To wound thy lord, thy king, thy governor.   150
It blots° thy beauty as frosts do bite the meads,°   *disfigures / meadows*
Confounds thy fame° as whirlwinds shake fair   *destroys your reputation*
      buds,
And in no sense is meet° or amiable.   *appropriate*
A woman moved° is like a fountain troubled: *stirred to anger*
Muddy, ill-seeming, thick,° bereft° of beauty;   *muddy / robbed*
And while it is so, none° so dry or thirsty   *no one*
Will deign to sip or touch one drop of it.
Thy husband is thy lord, thy life, thy keeper,
Thy head, thy sovereign; one that cares for thee;
And for thy maintenance;° commits his body   *to provide your needs*
To painful labor both by sea and land,   161
To watch° the night in storms, the day in cold,   *be on guard through*
Whilst thou liest warm at home, secure and safe;
And craves no other tribute at thy hands
But love, fair looks, and true obedience:
Too little payment for so great a debt.
Such duty as the subject owes the prince,
Even such a woman oweth to her husband;
And when she is froward,° peevish, sullen, sour,   *perverse*
And not obedient to his honest will,   170

What is she but a foul° contending rebel   *wicked*
And graceless° traitor to her loving lord?   *sinful*
I am ashamed that women are so simple°   *foolish*
To offer war where they should kneel for peace;
Or seek for rule, supremacy, and sway,
When they are bound to serve, love, and obey.
Why are our bodies soft and weak and smooth,
Unapt to° toil and trouble in the world,   *unfit for*
But that° our soft conditions° and our   *except to show that / qualities*
    hearts
Should well agree with our external parts?   180
Come, come, you froward and unable° worms.   *weak*
My mind hath been as big as one of yours,
My heart° as great, my reason haply° more,   *courage / perhaps*
To bandy° word for word and frown for frown;   *exchange*
But now I see our lances are but straws,
Our strength as weak, our weakness past compare,
That seeming to be most which we indeed least are.
Then vail° your stomachs,° for it is no   *lower / valor; pride*
    boot,°   *of no avail*
And place your hands below your husband's foot;
In token of which duty, if he please,   190
My hand is ready, may it do him ease.
Petruchio. Why, there's a wench. Come on, and kiss me, Kate.
Lucentio. Well, go thy ways,° old lad, for thou shalt   *well done*
    ha't.°   *have your wish*
Vincentio. 'Tis a good hearing° when children are   *a nice thing to hear*
    toward.°   *obedient*
Lucentio. But a harsh hearing when women are froward.°   *perverse, obstinate*
Petruchio. Come, Kate, we'll to bed.
We three are married, but you two are sped.°   *defeated*
'Twas I won the wager, though you hit the white,[101]
And being a winner, God give you good night! *Exeunt Petruchio*
    [and Katherina].
Hortensio. Now go thy ways; thou hast tamed a curst shrew.   200
Lucentio. 'Tis a wonder, by your leave, she will be tamed so. *[Exeunt.]*

FINIS.

101. The white ring in the center of the target with a pun on the derivation of
the name "Bianca."

THE WOMAN'S PRIZE,
OR
THE TAMER TAMED

JOHN FLETCHER

[The Names of All the Characters

PETRONIUS, father to Maria and Livia
MOROSO, an old rich citizen, suitor to Livia
PETRUCHIO, husband to Maria
ROWLAND, a young man, in love with Livia
MARIA, new wife of Petruchio
LIVIA, sister of Maria
BYANCA, cousin of Maria
SOPHOCLES, friend of Petruchio
TRANIO, an old friend of Petruchio
JAQUES, servant to Petruchio
PEDRO, servant to Petruchio
A DOCTOR
AN APOTHECARY
Watchmen, porters, servants, city wives, country wives, maids]

THE WOMAN'S PRIZE, OR THE TAMER TAMED

PROLOGUE[1]

Ladies, to you, in whose defense and right	
Fletcher's brave muse prepared herself to fight	
A battle without blood, 'twas well fought, too,	
(The victory's yours though got with much ado)	
We do present this comedy, in which	
A rivulet° of pure wit flows, strong and rich	*small stream*
In fancy,° language, and all parts that may	*imagination*
Add grace and ornament to a merry play,	
Which this may prove. Yet not to go too far	
In promises from this our female war,	10
We do entreat the angry men would not	
Expect the mazes° of a subtle plot,	*intricacies*
Set speeches, high expressions; and what's worse,	
In a true comedy, politic° discourse.	*political*
The end we aim at is to make you sport;°	*divert you*
Yet neither gall° the City, nor the Court.	*irritate*
Hear and observe his comic strain and when	
Y'are sick of melancholy, see't again.	
'Tis no dear physic,° since 'twill quit° the	*expensive medicine / repay*
cost,	
Or his intentions, with our pains, are lost.	20

ACT 1, SCENE 1

*Enter Moroso, Sophocles, and Tranio with rosemary[2]
as from a wedding.*

Moroso. God give 'em joy.
Tranio. Amen.

---

1. In the Beaumont and Fletcher first folio of 1647 (hereafter F1) the "Prologue" is printed with the "Epilogue" after the text of the play.
2. An evergreen shrub used at weddings as a token of remembrance.

Sophocles. Amen, say I, too.
    The pudding's now i'th' proof.[3] Alas, poor
      wench,°   *lass (affectionate slang)*
    Through what a mine° of patience must thou work   *vast quantity*
    Ere° thou know'st good hour more.°   *before / another happy moment*
Tranio. 'Tis too true. Certain,°   *certainly*
    Methinks her father has dealt harshly with her,
    Exceeding harshly, and not like a father,
    To match her to this dragon. I protest°   *declare*
    I pity the poor gentlewoman.   11
Moroso. Methinks now
    He's not so terrible as people think him.
Sophocles. [*To Tranio*] This old thief° flatters out of mere   *scoundrel*
      devotion°   *intent*
    To please the father for his second daughter.
Tranio. [*To Sophocles*] But shall he have her?
Sophocles. [*To Tranio*] Yes, when I have Rome.
    And yet the father's for him.
Moroso. I'll assure ye,
    I hold° him a good man.   *consider*
Sophocles. Yes, sure, a wealthy,   21
    But whether a good woman's man is doubtful.
Tranio. Would 'twere no worse.
Moroso. What though° his other wife,°   *so what if / (i.e., Katherina)*
    Out of her most abundant stubbornness,
    Out of her daily hue and cries° upon him,   *outcries*
    (For sure she was a rebel) turned his temper°   *temperament*
    And forced him blow as high° as she? Does't   *storm as emphatically*
      follow
    He must retain° that long since buried tempest   *continue, remember*
    To this soft maid?   30
Sophocles. I fear it.
Tranio. So do I, too,
    And so far that if God had made me woman
    And his wife that must be—
Moroso. What would you do, sir?
Tranio. I would learn to eat coals with an angry cat

---

3. A humorous inversion of the proverb "The proof of the pudding is in the eating" (Tilley P608).

And spit fire at him.[4] I would (to prevent° him)   *anticipate*
Do all the ramping, roaring° tricks a whore,   *extravagant raging, riotous*
Being drunk and tumbling ripe,° would   *ready to fall down (or have sex)*
   tremble at.
There is no safety else,° nor moral wisdom,   *otherwise*
To be a wife, and his.   41
Sophocles. So I should think, too.
Tranio. For yet the bare remembrance of his first wife
   (I tell ye on my knowledge, and a truth, too)
   Will make him start° in's sleep, and very often   *awake suddenly*
   Cry out for cudgels, cowl-staffs,°   *clubs, stout poles used as weapons*
      anything,
   Hiding his breeches out of fear her ghost
   Should walk and wear 'em yet.[5] Since his first marriage,
   He is no more the still° Petruchio   *quiet, steady*
   Than I am Babylon.[6]   50
Sophocles. He's a good fellow,
   And on my word I love him. But to think
   A fit match for this tender soul—
Tranio. His very frown, if she but say her prayers
   Louder than men talk treason, makes him
      tinder.°   *ready to flame up, as from a "match"*
   The motion of a dial,° when he's testy,   *clock*
   Is the same trouble to him as a
      waterwork.°   *noisy machinery used to distribute water*
   She must do nothing of herself:° not eat,   *(by her own volition)*

4. The meaning of this colorful comparison is not clear. Fletcher used the image in *The Tragedy of Bonduca* where the First Daughter says, "they are cowards, and eat coals like compell'd cats" (4.4.117). In Sir Robert Stapylton's play *The Slighted Maid* (1663), a character refers to "a cat to spit Fire" (5.1.8–9). Ferguson notes, "The line seems to be no more than figurative—angry cats hiss as if they have coals in their mouths" (191).

5. "Breeches," pants reaching below the knee, are, for boys, a symbol of attaining manhood. Breeches are also a symbol of the husband's authority in the home. A woman wearing breeches was, at the time, seen as an inversion of the natural order and an assault on patriarchy. "She wears the Breeches" is proverbial (Tilley B645).

6. The vicious murderer in the medieval ballad "Babylon." After killing two sisters, the third tells him that their brother "Baby Lon" will seek revenge. The killer realizes that he is that brother and takes his own life.

Drink, say "sir, how do ye," make her ready, unready,
Unless he bid her.   60
Sophocles. He will bury her,
Ten pound to twenty shillings,° within these three   *(ten to one odds)*
weeks.
Tranio. I'll be your half.°   *go half-shares on the bet*

Enter Jaques with a pot of wine.

Moroso. He loves her most extremely,
And so long 'twill be honeymoon. Now, Jaques,
You are a busy man I am sure.
Jaques. Yes certain,
This old sport must have eggs.°   *(as an aphrodisiac)*
Sophocles. Not yet this ten days.
Jaques. Sweet gentlemen, with muscatel.[7]   70
Tranio. That's right, sir.
Moroso. This fellow broods° his master. Speed ye, Jaques.   *nurses*
Sophocles. We shall be for you presently.
Jaques. Your worships°   *honorable sirs*
Shall have it° rich and neat° and, o' my   *(i.e., the wine) / undiluted*
conscience,
As welcome as Our Lady Day.°   *a celebration of the Virgin Mary (New Year's*
O, my old sir,   *Day until 1751)*
When shall we see your worship run at ring?[8]
That hour, a standing° were worth money.   *observation post; an erection*
Moroso. So, sir.
Jaques. Upon my little honesty, your mistress,   80
If I have any speculation, must think
This single thrumming of a fiddle
Without a bow,° but ev'n poor sport.   *(i.e., having sex without an erection)*
Moroso. You're merry.
Jaques. Would I were wise, too. So, God bless your worships. *Exit*
Jaques.
Tranio. The fellow tells you true.

7. It was traditional at the conclusion of a wedding that the bride and groom and
attendees shared a cup of "muscatel," a strong, sweet wine, with cakes in it.

8. To "run at ring" was a competition where men ran their horses toward a post
that held a ring, trying to catch the ring on their lances. The term also suggests
marriage or sexual activity.

Sophocles. When is the day, man?
    Come, come, you'll steal a marriage.°   *elope*
Moroso. Nay believe me.
    But when her father pleases I am ready,   90
    And all my friends shall know it.
Tranio. Why not now?
    One charge had served for both.°   *combined weddings would have been cheaper*
Moroso. There's reason in't.
Sophocles. Called Rowland.°   *(his rival for Livia)*
Moroso. Will ye walk?
    They'll think we are lost. Come, gentlemen.
Tranio. You have wiped° him now.   *bettered, defeated*
Sophocles. So will he never the wench,[9] I hope.   99
Tranio. I wish it. *Exeunt.*

[ACT 1], SCENE 2

Enter Rowland and Livia.

Rowland. Now, Livia, if you'll go away tonight,
    If your affections be not made of words—
Livia. I love you, and you know how dearly, Rowland—
    Is there none near us?—My affections ever
    Have been your servants. With what superstition
    I have ever sainted you°—   *made you an object of worship*
Rowland. Why then take this way.°   *(i.e., elope)*
Livia. 'Twill be a childish and a less prosperous course
    Than his that knows not care.° Why should we do   *is completely careless*
    Our honest and our hearty° love such wrong   *courageous*
    To overrun° our fortunes?   *destroy*
Rowland. Then you flatter.   12
Livia. Alas, you know I cannot.
Rowland. What hope's left else
    But flying° to enjoy ye?   *fleeing, eloping*
Livia. None so far,
    For let it be admitted we have time,
    And all things now in other expectation,

9. Sophocles is using "wipe" in the sense of having intercourse (Williams 89).

> My father's bent against us. What but ruin
> Can such a by-way° bring us? If your fears   *indirect route*
> Would let you look with my eyes, I would show you,   21
> And certain, how our staying here would win us
> A course, though somewhat longer,° yet far surer.   *more delayed*

Rowland. And then Moroso has ye.

Livia. No such matter,

> For hold this certain: begging, stealing, whoring,
> Selling (which is a sin unpardonable)
> Of counterfeit cods,° or musty English   *civet or musk (perfume) bags*
>   cracus,°   *tobacco*
> Switches, or stones[10] for th' toothache sooner
>   finds me°   *will sooner occupy me*
> Than that drawn fox[11] Moroso.   30

Rowland. But his money!

> If wealth may win you—

Livia. If a hog may be

> High Priest among the Jews![12] His money, Rowland?
> O love, forgive me, what a faith hast thou?
> Why, can his money kiss me?

Rowland. Yes.

Livia. Behind,°   *on the posterior*

> Laid out upon a petticoat. Or grasp me   39
> While I cry "O good, thank you"?—O' my
>   troth,°   *on my word (emphatic assertion)*
> Thou mak'st me merry with thy fear—or lie° with me   *have sex*
> As you may do? Alas, what fools you men are.
> His moldy° money? Half a dozen riders[13]   *decaying, dirty*
> That cannot sit° but stamped fast to their saddles?   *ride*

---

10. Although this is a list of cures for toothache, it also may be best to assume that almost every speech of this play can be interpreted in some sexual way. A "switch" could be a whip or false hair. One meaning of "stone" is "testicle," and Daileader and Taylor suggest that some animal testicles are "used for medicinal purposes," although we find no connection to toothache. Coral is a "stone" that was given to teething babies in that era to ease their discomfort.

11. A fox thin from anxiety. Shakespeare uses the term in *Henry 4, Part 1*, 3.3.114.

12. Jews had been expelled from England in 1290; nevertheless, they continued to be characterized by their religious avoidance of pork. Thus the phrase means "never."

13. Gold coins with a horseman stamped on the observe.

No, Rowland, no man shall make use of me.°   *use me sexually*
  My beauty was born free, and free I'll give it
  To him that loves, not buys, me. You yet doubt me.
Rowland. I cannot say I doubt ye.
Livia. Go thy ways,   49
  Thou art the prettiest puling° piece of passion.   *whining like a child*
  I'faith,° I will not fail thee.   *in faith (mild oath)*
Rowland. I had rather feel it.
Livia. Prithee, believe me, if I do not carry it°   *bring it off*
  For both our goods—
Rowland. But—
Livia. What "but"?
Rowland. I would tell you.
Livia. I know all you can tell me. All's but this:
  You would have me and lie with me. Is't not so?
Rowland. Yes.   60
Livia. Why, you shall. Will that content you? Go.
Rowland. I am very loath° to go.   *unwilling*

Enter Byanca and Maria.

Livia. Now, o' my conscience,°   *I swear (on my conscience)*
  Thou art an honest fellow. Here's my sister.
  Go, prithee, go. This kiss, and credit° me,   *believe*
  Ere° I am three nights older, I am for thee.   *before*
  You shall hear what I do.
Rowland. I had rather feel it.
Livia. Farewell.   69
Rowland. Farewell. *Exit Rowland.*
Livia. Alas poor fool, how it° looks,   *he (diminutive, used about children)*
  It would ev'n hang itself, should I but cross° it.   *oppose*
  For pure love to the matter I must hatch it.°   *come up with a plan*
Byanca. Nay, never look for merry hour, Maria,
  If now you make it not.° Let not your blushes,   *devise a plan*
  Your modesty and tenderness of spirit,
  Make you continual anvil° to his   *iron block on which his anger can beat*
    anger.
  Believe me, since his first wife set him going,
  Nothing can bind his rage. Take your own counsel:
  You shall not say that I persuaded you.   80
  But if you suffer him—
Maria. Stay, shall I do it?

Byanca. Have you a stomach to't?°   *courage to do it*
Maria. I never showed it.
Byanca. 'Twill show the rarer and the stranger in you.
    But do not say I urged you.
Maria. I am perfect,°   *resolved*
    Like Curtius, to redeem my country have I
    Leaped into this gulf of marriage, and I'll do it.[14]
    Farewell all poorer thoughts but spite and anger   90
    'Til I have wrought a miracle. Now, cousin,
    I am no more the gentle, tame Maria.
    Mistake me not. I have a new soul in me
    Made of a north wind, nothing but tempest,
    And like a tempest shall it make all ruins
    'Til I have run my will out.°   *gotten my way*
Byanca. This is brave° now   *courageous, fine*
    If you continue it; but your own will lead you.
Maria. Adieu° all tenderness, I dare continue.   *farewell*
    Maids that are made of fears and modest blushes,   100
    View me and love example.°   *embrace my example*
Byanca. Here is your sister.
Maria. Here is the brave° old man's love.   *finely attired; courageous (ironic)*
Byanca. That loves the young man.
Maria. Ay, and hold thee there, wench. What a grief of heart is't
    When Paphos'[15] revels should up-rouse old Night
    To sweat against a cork, to lie and tell
    The clock o'th' lungs, to rise sport-starved?[16]
Livia. Dear sister,
    Where have you been you talk thus?   110

---

14. According to legend, in the fourth century B.C.E., the ground once opened
in the middle of the Roman Forum. An oracle said that the chasm would close
only if they threw their most prized possession into it. Marcus Curtius armed
himself and rode into the abyss, sacrificing himself for his country. The ground
closed behind him. A "gulf" is also a vagina (as in 2.4.53) (Williams 629–30).

15. Paphos was a town in Cyprus with a famous temple to the Goddess of
Love.

16. This passage is filled with puns. Maria complains about a night of lovemaking ("Paphos' revels") that should arouse "old Night" (primordial darkness or
old Moroso). Instead the woman "sweats" (labors) against a "cork" (cylindrical
stopper or penis) to "lie" (recline or have sex) and "tell" (count) the hours by
coughs ("clock o'th' lungs") to rise "sport-starved" (sexually unfulfilled). Livia's
response acknowledges the bawdiness.

Maria. Why at church, wench,
    Where I am tied° to talk thus: I am a wife now.   *have been bound*
Livia. It seems so, and a modest.
Maria. You are an ass.
    When thou art married once, thy modesty
    Will never buy thee pins.°   *will be worthless*
Livia. Bless me.
Maria. From what?
Byanca. From such a tame fool as our cousin Livia?
Livia. You are not mad?°   *insane; angry*
Maria. Yes, wench, and so must you be   121
    Or° none of our acquaintance—mark me, Livia—   *or be*
    Or indeed fit for our sex. 'Tis bedtime.
    Pardon me, yellow Hymen, that I mean
    Thine off'rings to protract,° or to keep   *delay*
        fasting°   *denying food (sex) to*
    My valiant bridegroom.[17]
Livia. Whither will this woman?°   *Where is this woman going with this argument?*
Byanca. You may perceive her end.
Livia. Or rather fear it.
Maria. Dare you be partner in't?   130
Livia. Leave it, Maria.
    I fear I have marked° too much. For goodness leave it.   *heard*
    Devest° you with obedient hands to bed.   *unclothe*
Maria. To bed? No, Livia, there are comets° hang   *(considered omens)*
    Prodigious° over that yet. There's a   *comets will appear before that happens*
        fellow
    Must yet, before I know that heat° (ne'er   *sexual pleasure*
        start,° wench),   *be startled*
    Be made a man, for yet he is a monster.
    Here° must his head be, Livia.   *(gesture will clarify)*
Livia. Never hope it.
    'Tis as easy with a sieve to scoop the ocean° as   *(proverbial)*
    To tame Petruchio.   141
Maria. Stay. Lucina° hear me,   *goddess of childbirth*
    Never unlock the treasure of my womb

17. Hymen, the god of marriage, was often described as dressed in yellow. His name was adopted for the vaginal membrane that was considered the sign of virginity. Maria will delay offering her maidenhead to the god of marriage; Petruchio must go without the "food" husbands expect.

For human fruit° to make it capable,   *(i.e., children)*
Nor never with thy secret hand make brief
A mother's labor to me, if I do
Give way unto my married husband's will,
Or be a wife in anything but hopes,
'Til I have made him easy° as a child   *tractable*
And tame as fear.° He shall not win a smile   *some fearful creature*
Or a pleased look from this austerity,   151
Though it would pull another jointure°   *the estate the groom gives the bride*
   from him
And make him every day another man.
And when I kiss him, 'til I have my
   will,°   *what I want (in general and sexual terms)*
May I be barren of delights and know
Only what pleasures are in dreams and guesses.

Livia. A strange exordium.°   *beginning*
Byanca. All the several° wrongs   *various*
   Done by imperious husbands to their wives
   These thousand years and upwards, strengthen thee;   160
   Thou hast a brave cause.
Maria. And I'll do it bravely,
   Or may I knit my life out ever after.
Livia. In what part of the world got she this spirit?
   Yet pray, Maria, look before you truly:°   *at your future*
   Besides the disobedience of a wife,
   Which you will find a heavy imputation,°   *accusation*
   Which yet I cannot think your own, it shows
   So distant from your sweetness.
Maria. 'Tis, I swear.   170
Livia. Weigh but the person and the hopes you have
   To work this desperate cure.
Maria. A weaker subject
   Would shame the end I aim at—disobedience.
   You talk too tamely. By the faith I have
   In mine own noble will, that childish woman
   That lives a prisoner to her husband's pleasure
   Has lost her making° and becomes a beast,   *human shape*
   Created for his use, not fellowship.
Livia. His first wife said as much.   180
Maria. She was a fool
   And took a scurvy° course. Let her be named   *worthless*
   'Mongst those that wish for things but dare not do 'em.

I have a new dance for him, and a mad one.
Livia. Are you of this faith?
Byanca. Yes, truly, and will die in't.
Livia. Why, then, let's all wear breeches.°   *(see n. 5)*
Byanca. That's a good wench.
Maria. Now thou com'st near the nature of a woman.
    Hang these tame-hearted eyases° that no sooner   *young hawks*
    See the lure out and hear their husband's holla   191
    But cry like kites° upon 'em. The free   *birds of prey*
       haggard°   *wild female hawk*
    (Which is that woman that hath wing and knows it,
    Spirit and plume) will make an hundred checks°   *turns, tricks*
    To show her freedom, sail in every air
    And look out every pleasure, not regarding
    Lure nor quarry, 'til her pitch command
    What she desires, making her foundered° keeper   *disabled*
    Be glad to fling out trains, and golden ones,
    To take her down again.[18]   200
Livia. You arc learnèd, sister,
    Yet I say still, take heed.
Maria. A witty saying.
    I'll tell thee, Livia, had this fellow tired
    As many wives as horses under him
    With spurring of their patience, had he got
    A patent with an office to reclaim us
    Confirmed by Parliament, had he all the malice
    And subtlety of devils, or of us,
    Or anything that's worse than both—   210
Livia. Hey, hey, boys, this is excellent.
Maria. Or could he
    Cast° his wives new again like bells to make   *reshape (as molten metal)*
      'em
    Sound° to his will, or had the fearful name°   *ring / fearsome reputation*
    Of the first breaker of wild women, yet,

18. This speech compares the process of a husband taming his wife to a falconer training new, young hawks ("eyases"). He prepares a "lure" of feathers for the hawk to come to at his command ("holla"). Maria pictures herself as a "haggard," a wild female hawk in her full adult plumage that flies free, making "checks," false stoops where the hawk avoids the target. She soars to her "pitch," the highest point of flight, and ignores the "lure" or "quarry," making her master use "trains," birds on a line, to try and recover her.

Yet would I undertake this man, thus single,°   *by myself*
And spite of all the freedom he has reached to,
Turn him and bend him as I list,° and mold him   *wish*
Into a babe again, that° aged women,   *so that*
Wanting° both teeth and spleen,° may master   *lacking / peevish temper*
    him.
Byanca. Thou wilt be chronicled.°   *recorded in history*
Maria. That's all I aim at.   222
Livia. I must confess, I do with all my heart
    Hate an imperious husband, and in time
    Might be so wrought upon°—   *persuaded*
Byanca. To make him cuckold?°   *man whose wife is unfaithful*
Maria. If he deserve it.
Livia. Then I'll leave ye, ladies.
Byanca. Thou hast not so much noble anger in thee.
Maria. Go sleep, go sleep. What we intend to do   230
    Lies not for such starved° souls as thou hast,   *anemic; lacking courage*
        Livia.
Livia. Good night. The bridegroom will be with you presently.
Maria. That's more than you know.
Livia. If ye work upon him
    As you have promised, ye may give° example,   *set an*
    Which no doubt will be followed.
Maria. So.
Byanca. Good night. We'll trouble you no further.
Maria. If you intend no good, pray do no harm.   239
Livia. None but pray for you.   *Exit Livia.*
Byanca. Cheer,° wench!   *good cheer*
Maria. Now, Byanca,
    Those wits we have let's wind 'em to the height.
    My rest is up,° wench, and I   *I am venturing my final hope or stake*
        pull° for that°   *draw a card / something that*
    Will make me ever famous. They that lay
    Foundations are half-builders, all men say.

Enter Jaques.

Jaques. My master, forsooth°—   *in truth*
Maria. O how does thy master? Prithee commend me to him.
Jaques. How's this? My master stays,° forsooth—   *waits*
Maria. Why, let him stay. Who hinders him, forsooth?   250
Jaques. The revel's° ended now—to visit you.   *celebration has*

Maria. I am not sick.°   *(assumes "visit" implies she is sick)*

Jaques. I mean to see his chamber, forsooth.

Maria. Am I his groom?° Where lay he last night, forsooth?   *serving man*

Jaques. In the low-matted parlor.°   *downstairs or inferior room laid with mats*

Maria. There lies his way, by the long gallery.°   *corridor*

Jaques. I mean your chamber. You're very merry, mistress.

Maria. 'Tis a good sign I am sound-hearted, Jaques.   *have a healthy heart*

     But if you'll know where I lie, follow me,

     And what thou see'st, deliver to thy master.   260

Byanca. Do, gentle Jaques. *Exeunt Maria and Byanca.*

Jaques. Ha, is the wind in that

         door?°   *"Is that the way the wind is blowing?" (proverb)*

     By'rlady,° we shall have foul weather then.   *by our lady (Virgin Mary)*

     I do not like the shuffling° of these   *shifty conduct; moving together*

         women.

     They are mad beasts when they knock their heads together.

     I have observed them all this day: their whispers,

     One in another's ear; their signs and pinches;

     And breaking often into violent laughters

     As if the end they purposed were their

         own.°   *keeping something to themselves*

     Call you this weddings? Sure this is a knavery,   270

     A very trick, and dainty° knavery,   *delicate*

     Marvelous finely carried,° that's the comfort.   *pulled off*

     What would these women do in ways of

         honor°   *if they had behaved properly*

     That are such masters this way? Well, my sir°   *master*

     Has been as good at finding out these toys°   *tricks*

     As any living; if he lose it now,

     At his own peril be it. I must follow. *Exit.*

[ACT 1], SCENE 3

Enter servants with lights,° Petruchio,   *(indicating night)*
Petronius, Moroso, Tranio, and Sophocles.

Petruchio. You that are married, gentlemen, have at ye°   *I challenge you*

     For a round° wager now.   *considerable*

Sophocles. Of this night's stage?°   *performance (sexual)*

Petruchio. Yes.

Sophocles. I am your first man: a pair of gloves of twenty shillings.

Petruchio. Done. Who takes me up next? I am for all bets.

Moroso. Well, Lusty Lawrence,[19] were but my night°   *(i.e., wedding night)*
    now,
    Old as I am, I would make you clap on spurs,°   *(for sexual riding)*
    But I would reach you and bring you to your trot, too.
    I would, gallants.   10

Petruchio. Well said, Good-will. But where's the staff°   *crutch; erection*
    boy, ha?
    Old father time, your hourglass is empty.

Tranio. A good tough train° would break thee all to pieces;   *gait of a horse*
    Thou hast not breath enough to say thy prayers.°   *you will be winded*

Petronius. See how these boys despise us. Will you to bed, son?
    This pride will have a fall.[20]

Petruchio. Upon your daughter.
    But I shall rise again, if there be truth
    In eggs and buttered parsnips.

Petronius. Will you to bed, son, and leave talking?   20
    Tomorrow morning we shall have you look
    For all your great words, like St. George at Kingston,[21]
    Running a-footback° from the furious dragon,   *on foot*
    That with her angry tail belabors him
    For being lazy.

Sophocles. His war-like lance°   *long shaft used in jousting; penis*

---

19. "Lusty Lawrence," proverbially a Lancashire man (see 1.3.173 later in this scene), was known for his sexual prowess. In a ballad he was said to have "had seventeen bastards in one year." Fletcher used the term again in *The Captain* (4.3.66) with the same meaning.

20. After Petronius quotes the well-known proverb, "Pride will have a fall" (Tilley P581; "pride" being a word used to refer to the penis, particularly when erect), Petruchio points out that he will "fall" on Maria, but he will be able to "rise" (become erect) again if the aphrodisiacs he took ("eggs and buttered parsnips") work as they are supposed. But there may be another proverb that applies to the situation: "Fair words butter no parsnips" (Tilley W791).

21. Petronius appears to be referring to a painted sign in Kingston, a village west of London. St. George, the patron saint of England, is usually depicted conquering the dragon; here, St. George is described as retreating on foot from the dragon. The suggestion is that tomorrow morning Petruchio will be fleeing from Maria whose "tail" (genitalia) is "angry" (sexually unsatisfied) because he was "lazy" (didn't work hard enough) in his lovemaking. The following speeches have sexual overtones.

Bent like a crossbow lath,° alas the while.   *bending part of crossbow*

Tranio. His courage° quenched, and so far quenched—   *bravery; sexual vigor*

Petruchio. 'Tis well,° sir.   *enough*

Tranio. That any privy saint, even small Saint Davy,   30
    May lash him with a leek.²²

Petruchio. What then?

Sophocles. "Fly, fly," quoth then the fearful dwarf,
    "Here is no place for living man."²³

Petruchio. Well, my masters, if I do sink under my business, as I find 'tis
    very possible, I am not the first that has miscarried. So that's my
    comfort: what may be done without impeach° or   *damage, injury*
    waste, I can and will do.

Enter Jaques.

How now, is my fair bride abed?

Jaques. No truly, sir.   40

Petronius. Not abed yet? Body o'me,²⁴ we'll up and rifle° her.   *search*
    Here's a coil° with a maidenhead: 'tis not   *fuss*
    entailed,° is it?   *legally untransferrable (with pun on "tail")*

Petruchio. If it be, I'll try all the law i'th' land but I'll cut it
    off.° Let's up, let's up, come.   *break the legal obstacle*

Jaques. That you cannot neither.

Petruchio. Why?

Jaques. Unless you'll drop through the chimney like a daw,°   *small bird*
    or force a breach i'th' windows. You may untile°   *strip the roof of tiles*
    the house; 'tis possible.   50

Petruchio. What dost thou mean?

Jaques. A moral,° sir. The ballad will express it: *practical lesson*
    [Sings] "The wind and the rain has turned you back again,
    And you cannot be lodged there."²⁵ The truth is all the doors

---

22. "Privy" means private or relating to sexual activity. St. Davy is the patron
saint of Wales. St. Davy's Day is celebrated by men wearing leeks. The British
tend to make fun of the Welsh, as indicated by the adjective "small."

23. A quotation, slightly garbled, from Edmund Spenser's *Faerie Queene*
(1.1.13.8–9).

24. A mild oath, originally "Body of Christ."

25. A portion of the popular renaissance ballad "Go from My Window," which
was arranged and printed in many forms. It also appears in several other plays,
including Beaumont's *Knight of the Burning Pestle* (1607) and Middleton's *Blurt,
Master Constable* (1602). See Claude Simpson (257–59).

are barricadoed: not a cat-hole° but holds a   *hole for a cat to enter*
murd'rer° in't. She's victualled° for this   *small cannon / provisioned*
month.

Petruchio. Art not thou drunk?

Sophocles. He's drunk, he's drunk; come, come, let's up.

Jaques. Yes, yes, I am drunk. Ye may go up, ye may, gentlemen,   60
but take heed to your heads. I say no more.

Sophocles. I'll try° that.   *test*

Exit Sophocles.

Petronius. How dost thou say? The door fast locked, fellow?

Jaques. Yes truly, sir, 'tis locked and guarded, too. And two as
desperate tongues planted behind it as ere yet battered: they
stand upon their honors and will not give up without strange
composition,° I'll assure you; marching away with   *contract*
their pieces° cocked, and bullets in their mouths will   *handguns*
not satisfy them.   69

Petruchio. How's this? How's this "they" are? Is there another with her?

Jaques. Yes, marry, is there, and an engineer.°   *military designer*

Moroso. Who's that, for heaven's sake?

Jaques. Colonel Byanca, she commands the works; Spinola's[26]
but a ditcher° to her. There's a half-moon—   *ditch-digger*
I am but a poor man, but if you'll give me leave, I'll venture a
year's wages, draw° all your force before it, and mount   *if you draw*
your ablest piece of battery, you shall not enter in't these three
nights yet.

Enter Sophocles.

Petruchio. I should laugh at that, good Jaques.

Sophocles. Beat back again. She's fortified forever.   80

Jaques. Am I drunk now, sir?

Sophocles. He that dares most, go up now and be cooled. I have
'scaped a pretty scouring.°   *escaped a considerable beating*

---

26. In the bloodiest battle of the Eighty Years' War between Dutch provinces
and the Spanish (Hapsburg) Empire, the city of Ostend (see also 1.3.99) was
under siege for three years. Under the command of Ambrogio Spinola, a self-
taught military engineer and leader from Italy, the Spanish forces took the
ruins of Ostend in 1604. The remainder of the speeches use terms from siege
warfare: "half-moon" is a crescent-shaped fortification (and a cuckold); "piece
of battery" is a siege gun.

Petruchio. What, are they mad? Have we another Bedlam?[27]
    They do not talk, I hope.
Sophocles. O terribly, extremely fearful; the noise at London Bridge
    is nothing near° her.   *equal to*
Petruchio. How got she tongue?
Sophocles. As you got tail:° she was born to't.   *a penis*
Petruchio. Locked out o' doors, and on my wedding night?   90
    Nay, and I suffer° this, I may go graze.°   *if I tolerate / be put to pasture*
    Come, gentlemen, I'll batter. Are these virtues?
Sophocles. Do, and be beaten off with shame as I was. I went up,
    came to th' door, knocked; nobody answered. Knocked louder,
    yet heard nothing. Would have broke in by force when
    suddenly a waterwork° flew from the window   *apparently a chamber pot*
    with such violence that had I not ducked° quickly like a   *bowed*
    friar, *caetera quis nescit?*[28] The chamber's nothing but a mere
    Ostend:° in every window pewter cannons°   *(see n. 26) / chamber pots*
    mounted. You'll quickly find with what° they are   *(i.e., human waste)*
    charged, sir.   101
Petruchio. Why then tantara° for us.   *flourish of trumpets*
Sophocles. And all the lower works° lined sure with   *fortifications, windows*
    small shot,° long tongues with firelocks that at   *musket bullets*
    twelve-score blank° hit to the heart. Now, and°   *a range of 240 feet / if*
    ye dare, go up.

                 Enter Maria and Byanca above.

Moroso. The window opens—beat a parley° first.   *beat drums for a meeting*
    I am so amazed my very hair stands.
Petronius. Why, how now, daughter? What, entrenched?
Maria. A little guarded for my safety, sir.   110
Petruchio. For your safety, sweetheart? Why, who offends you?
    I come not to use violence.
Maria. I think you cannot, sir; I am better fortified.
Petruchio. I know your end;° you would fain reprieve   *purpose, objective*
    your maidenhead° a night or two.   *maintain your virginity*
Maria. Yes, or ten, or twenty, or, say, an hundred; or, indeed,
    'til I list° lie with you.   *wish to*

---

27. St. Mary of Bethlehem was the hospital for the insane. It became known
as Bedlam.
28. "Who can't guess what follows?"—a quote from Ovid's *Amores* (1.5.25).

Sophocles. That's a shrewd° saying; from this present   shrewish, ill-tempered
  hour I never will believe a "silent woman."²⁹ When they
  break out they are bonfires.   120
Petronius. 'Til you list lie with him? Why, who are you, madam?
Byanca. That trim° gentleman's wife, sir.   fine
Petruchio. Cry you mercy, do you command, too?
Maria. Yes, marry, does she, and in chief.
Byanca. I do command, and you shall go without. (I mean your
  wife for this night.)
Maria. And for the next, too, wench, and so as't
  follows.°   works out, proceeds
Petronius. Thou wilt not, wilt 'a?°   will you
Maria. Yes, indeed, dear father,   130
  And 'til he seal to° what I shall set down,   put his seal to, accept
  For anything I know, forever.
Sophocles. Indeed, these are bug-words.°   words meant to frighten
Tranio. You hear, sir, she can talk, God be thanked.
Petruchio. I would I heard it not, sir.
Sophocles. I find that all the pity bestowed upon this woman
  Makes but an anagram of "an ill wife,"³⁰
  For she was never virtuous.
Petruchio. You'll let me in, I hope, for all this jesting.
Maria. Hope still,° sir.   forever
Petronius. You will come down I am sure.   141
Maria. I am sure I will not.
Petronius. I'll fetch you then.
Byanca. The power of the whole county cannot, sir,
  Unless we please to yield, which yet I think
  We shall not. Charge when you please, you shall
  Hear quickly from us.
Moroso. Bless me from a chicken of thy
  hatching.°   protect me from a child of yours
  Is this wiving?°   What marriage is?

29. A complaint against women at the time was that they talked too much. "The Silent Woman" is the alternate title of *Epicoene,* a play by Ben Jonson (performed 1609), in which the title character, apparently a woman, seems "epicoene" or of uncertain gender because she speaks little and softly.

30. The reference is to the rearrangement of "a fine will" into "an ill wife" where "fine" means "egregious, artful" and "will" is "volition and sexual appetite" (OED). Thus a woman with "a fine will" makes "an ill wife."

Petruchio. Prithee, Maria, tell me what's the reason,   150
     And do it freely; you deal thus strangely with me?
     You were not forced to marry; your consent
     Went equally with mine, if not before it.
     I hope you do not doubt I want that mettle°   *vigor*
     A man should have to keep a woman
        waking.°   *from sleeping in bed (i.e., sexually engaged)*
     I would be sorry to be such a saint yet.
     My person,° as it is not excellent,   *appearance, body*
     So 'tis not old, nor lame, nor weak with physic,°   *medications, treatments*
     But well enough to please an honest° woman   *trustworthy, chaste*
     That keeps her house and loves her husband.   160
Maria. 'Tis so.
Petruchio. My means and my conditions° are no shamers   *qualities*
     Of him that owes° 'em—all the world knows that—   *owns*
     And my friends° no reliers on my fortunes.   *family*
Maria. All this I believe, and none of all these parcels°   *particulars*
     I dare except against.° Nay, more, so far   *take exception to*
     I am from making these the ends I aim at,
     These idle outward things, these women's fears,
     That were I yet unmarried, free to choose
     Through all the tribes of man, I'd take Petruchio   170
     In's shirt,° with one ten groats[31] to pay the priest,   *with just his shirt*
     Before the best man living or the ablest
     That e'er leaped out of Lancashire,[32] and they are
        right° ones.   *excellent*
Petronius. Why do you play the fool then and stand prating
     Out of the window like a broken° miller?[33]   *bankrupt*
Petruchio. If you will have me credit° you, Maria,   *believe, trust*
     Come down and let your love confirm it.
Maria. Stay there, sir; that bargain's yet to make.
Byanca. Play sure, wench, the pack's° in thine own hand.   *deck of cards is*
Sophocles. Let me die lousy° if these two wenches   *infested with lice*
     Be not brewing knavery to stock a kingdom.   181
Petruchio. Why, this is a riddle: I love you and I love you not.

---

31. A groat is equal to four pence.

32. See n. 19 for the proverbial sexual powers of Lancashire men.

33. A miller had to develop a loud voice to be heard over the noise of the mill machinery.

Maria. It is so.

> And 'til your own experience do untie it,
> This distance I must keep.

Petruchio. If you talk more, I am angry, very angry.

Maria. I am glad on't, and I will talk.

Petruchio. Prithee° peace.   *I pray thee*

> Let me not think thou art mad. I tell thee woman,
> If thou goest forward I am still Petruchio.   190

Maria. And I am worse, a woman that can fear

> Neither Petruchio Furious[34] nor his fame,°   *reputation*
> Nor anything that tends to our
>   allegiance.°   *pertains to our loyalty to the cause*
> There's a short method° for you—now you know me.   *set of procedures*

Petruchio. If you can carry't° so, 'tis very well.   *bring it about*

Byanca. No, you shall carry it,° sir.   *put up with it*

Petruchio. Peace, gentle low-bell.°   *cowbell*

Petronius. Use no more words, but come down instantly—

> I charge thee by the duty of a child.

Petruchio. Prithee come, Maria. I forgive all.   200

Maria. Stay there. That duty that you° charge me by   *(i.e., Petronius)*

> (If you consider truly what you say)
> Is now another man's. You gave't away
> I'th' church, if you remember, to my husband.
> So all you can exact now is no more
> But only a due reverence to your person,
> Which thus I pay: your blessing, and I am gone
> To bed for this night.

Petronius. This is monstrous.

> That blessing that St. Dunstan gave the devil,[35]   210
> If I were near thee, I would give thee—
> Pull thee down by th' nose.

Byanca. Saints should not rave, sir.

> A little rhubarb° now were excellent.   *(a laxative)*

---

34. A humorous name for Petruchio modeled on the hero of Ariosto's epic poem *Orlando Furioso* (1532).

35. Tenth-century St. Dunstan was a talented metalworker. Legend has it that the Devil approached him in the form of a beautiful young woman. Dunstan was working at his forge, and when he recognized his visitor, he took a large pair of red-hot tongs and clamped them hard on the Devil's nose.

Petruchio. Then by that duty you owe to me, Maria,
    Open the door and be obedient. I am quiet yet.
Maria. I do confess that duty—make your best on't.
Petruchio. Why, give me leave, I will.
Byanca. Sir, there's no learning°   *teaching*
    An old stiff jade° to trot—you know   *(i.e., teach an old horse new tricks)*
    the moral.
Maria. Yet as I take it, sir, I owe no more   221
    Than you owe back again.
Petruchio. You will not article?°   *stipulate particulars as in a treaty*
    All I owe, presently, let me but up, I'll pay.
Maria. You're too hot, and such prove jades° at length.   *worn-out horses*
    You do confess a duty or respect to me from you again,
    That's very near, or full° the same, with mine?   *equally*
Petruchio. Yes.
Maria. Then by that duty, or respect, or what
    You please to have it, go to bed and leave me   230
    And trouble me no longer with your fooling.
    For know, I am not for you.
Petruchio. Well, what remedy?
Petronius. A fine, smart cudgel.° O that I were near thee—   *club*
Byanca. If you had teeth now, what a case° were we in?   *predicament*
Moroso. These are the most authentic rebels, next° Tyrone,[36]   *most like*
    I ever read of.
Maria. A week hence, or a fortnight, as you bear you,°   *behave yourself*
    And as I find my will observed, I may
    With intercession° of some friends be brought   *mediation*
    Maybe to kiss you; and so quarterly   241
    To pay a little rent by composition.°   *in portions*
    You understand me?
Sophocles. Thou boy, thou.
Petruchio. Well, there are more maids than Maudlin,° that's   *woman's name*
    my comfort.
Maria. Yes, and more men than Michael.
Petruchio. I must not to bed with this stomach° and no   *appetite; desire*
    meat,° lady.   *food; sex*
Maria. Feed where you will, so it be sound and wholesome.°   *healthy*
    Else live at livery,° for I'll none with ye.   *on allowance*

---

36. Hugh O'Neill, 2nd Earl of Tyrone (c. 1550–1616), leader of the Irish resistance to English rule.

Byanca. You had best back° one of the dairymaids; they'll carry.   *mount*
    But take heed to your girths;° you'll get a   *straps holding saddle on*
      bruise else.
Petruchio. Now, if thou would'st come down and tender me   252
    All the delights due to a marriage bed,
    Study such kisses as would melt a man,
    And turn thyself into a thousand
      figures°   *sexual positions; seductive persuasion*
    To add new flames unto me, I would stand
    Thus heavy,° thus regardless,° thus despising   *severe; unmoved / indifferent*
    Thee and thy best allurings. All thy beauty
    That's laid upon your bodies, mark me well,
    For without doubt your minds are miserable.   260
    You have no masks for them. All this rare beauty,
    Lay but the painter and the silkworm
      by,°   *put aside beauticians and fine clothes*
    The doctor with his diets and the tailor,
    And you appear like flayed° cats, not so handsome.   *skinned*
Maria. And we appear, like her that sent us hither,
    That only excellent and beauteous Nature,
    Truly ourselves for men to wonder at,
    But too divine to handle. We are gold,
    In our own natures pure, but, when we suffer   269
    The husband's stamp upon us, allays;°   *alloys*
    And base° ones of you men are mingled with us   *(metals)*
    And make us blush like copper.°   *(elemental copper is red)*
Petruchio. Then, and never
    'Til then, are women to be spoken of,
    For 'til that time you have no souls, I take it.
    Good night. Come, gentlemen. I'll fast for this night,
    But by this hand—well, I shall come up yet!
Maria. No.
Petruchio. There will I watch thee like a withered
      Jewry:°   *decayed Jewish ghetto*
    Thou shalt neither have meat, fire, nor candle,   280
    Nor anything that's easy. Do you rebel so soon?
    Yet take mercy.
Byanca. Put up your pipes.° To bed, sir. I'll assure   *give it a rest (proverbial)*
    you
    A month's siege will not shake us.
Moroso. Well said, Colonel.

Maria. To bed, to bed, Petruchio. Good night, gentlemen.
 You'll make my father sick with sitting up.
 Here you shall find us any time these ten days,
 Unless we may march off with our contentment.°   *satisfied*
Petruchio. I'll hang first.   290
Maria. And I'll quarter° if I do not.   *be cut in quarters*
      (traitors were "hanged, drawn, and quartered")
 I'll make you know and fear a wife, Petruchio.
 There my cause lies.
 You have been famous for a woman-tamer
 And bear the feared name of a brave wife-breaker.
 A woman now shall take those honors off
 And tame you. Nay, never look so big.° She shall, *threatening*
  believe me,
 And I am she. What think ye? Good night to all.
 You shall find sentinels.   299
Byanca. If ye dare sally.°   *venture out to attack*
      Exeunt above.
Petronius. The devil's in 'em, even the very devil, the downright devil.
Petruchio. I'll devil 'em. By these ten bones,° I will. I'll *fingers (two hands)*
 bring it to the old proverb: "no sport,° no pie"— *sex; recreation*
 taken down i'th top of all my speed. This is fine dancing
 Gentlemen, stick to me. You see our freehold's° *status as husbands is*
 touched,° and by this light, we will beleaguer 'em *endangered*
 and either starve 'em out, or make 'em
 recreant.°   *vanquished, false to their cause*
Petronius. I'll see all passages stopped but those about 'em.
 If the good women of the town dare succor 'em, 310
 We shall have wars indeed.
Sophocles. I'll stand perdu° upon 'em.   *guard*
Moroso. My regiment shall lie before.
Jaques. I think so: 'tis grown too old to stand.° *(i.e., stand erect)*
Petruchio. Let's in, and each provide his tackle.° *weapons*
 We'll fire 'em out or make 'em take their pardons—
 Hear what I say—on their bare knees.
 Am I Petruchio, feared, and spoken of,
 And on my wedding night am I thus jaded?° *tricked, made a fool of*
     Exeunt omnes.

[ACT 1], SCENE 4

Enter Rowland and Pedro, at several doors.

Rowland. Now, Pedro?

Pedro. Very busy, Master Rowland.

Rowland. What haste, man?

Pedro. I beseech you pardon me,

    I am not mine own man.°   *at another's command*

Rowland. Thou art not mad?

Pedro. No, but believe me, as hasty.

Rowland. The cause, good Pedro?

Pedro. There be a thousand, sir; you are not married?

Rowland. Not yet.   10

Pedro. Keep yourself quiet then.

Rowland. Why?

Pedro. You'll find a fiddle

    That never will be tuned else: from all such women deliver me.

      Exit.

Rowland. What ails the fellow, trow?°   *I wonder*

Enter Jaques.

    Jaques?

Jaques. Your friend, sir. But very full of business.

Rowland. Nothing but business? Prithee the reason. Is there any

      dying?

Jaques. I would there were, sir.

Rowland. But thy business?   20

Jaques. I'll tell you in a word: I am sent to lay

    An imposition upon souse° and   *an injunction against pickled food*

      puddings,

    Pasties,° and penny   *meat pies, baked without a dish*

      custards,° that the women   *baked dishes*

    May not relieve yon rebels. Fare ye well, sir.

Rowland. How does my mistress?

Jaques. Like a resty jade.° She's spoiled for riding.   *worn-out horse*

      Exit Jaques.

    What a devil ail they?

    Custards, and penny pasties, fools° and fiddles,   *clotted cream trifle*

    What's this to th' purpose?

Enter Sophocles.

O, well met.   30
Sophocles. Now, Rowland, I cannot stay to talk long.
Rowland. What's the matter? (Here's stirring, but to what end?)
    Whither go you?
Sophocles. To view the works.°   *military ditches of fortification; vaginas*
Rowland. What works?
Sophocles. The women's trenches.
Rowland. Trenches? Are such to see?
Sophocles. I do not jest, sir.
Rowland. I cannot understand you.
Sophocles. Do not you hear   40
    In what a state of quarrel the new bride
    Stands with her husband?
Rowland. Let him stand with her° and there's an   *be erect and ready for sex*
    end.
Sophocles. It should be, but by'rlady
    She holds him out at pike's end, and defies him,
    And now is fortified. Such a regiment of
        rutters°   *cavaliers; men in periodic sexual excitement*
    Never defied men braver. I am sent
    To view their preparation.
Rowland. This is news
    Stranger than armies in the air.[37] You saw not   50
    My gentle mistress?
Sophocles. Yes, and meditating
    Upon some secret business. When she had found it,
    She leapt for joy and laughed, and straight retired
    To shun Moroso.
Rowland. This may be for me.
Sophocles. Will you along?
Rowland. No.
Sophocles. Farewell. *Exit Sophocles.*
Rowland. Farewell, sir.   60
    What should her musing mean, and what her joy in't,
    If not for my advantage? Stay ye;°   *hold on, on second thought*
        may not
    That bobtail° jade° Moroso, with his gold,   *contemptible / worn-out horse*

---

37. The phrase suggests a menacing omen. Fletcher uses the idea again in *Wit without Money*: "fiery battles / Seen in the air" (2.4.53–54).

His gewgaws,° and the hope she has to send him   *baubles*
Quickly to dust,° excite this? Here she comes,   *that he will not live long*

    Enter Livia at one door and Moroso at another, harkening.

And yonder walks the stallion° to   *the (old) lady's man (i.e., Moroso)*
   discover.°   *listen in*
Yet I'll salute° her. Save you,° beauteous   *address / God save you*
   mistress.
Livia. The fox is kenneled° for me. Save you, sir.   *Moroso is hiding*
Rowland. Why do you look so strange?   69
Livia. I use° to look, sir,   *am accustomed*
   Without examination.°   *being scrutinized*
Moroso. Twenty spur-royals[38] for that
   word.°   *what she just said is worth much to me*
Rowland. Belike then
   The object° discontents you?   *what you are looking at*
Livia. Yes it does.
Rowland. Is't come to this? You know me, do you not?
Livia. Yes, as I may know many, by repentance.°   *to my sorrow*
Rowland. Why do you break your faith?
Livia. I'll tell you that, too.
   You are under age,° and no band°   *too young to inherit / bond, contract*
   holds upon you.
Moroso. Excellent wench.   81
Livia. Sue out° your understanding   *institute legal proceedings*
   And get more hair to cover your bare
     knuckle°   *(i.e., body hair), manliness*
   (For boys were made for nothing but dry° kisses)   *lacking passion*
   And if you can, more manners.
Moroso. Better still.
Livia. And then if I want Spanish gloves, or stockings,
   A ten-pound waistcoat, or a nag to hunt on,°   *horse to ride in hunts*
   It may be I shall grace° you to accept° 'em.   *favor / by accepting*
Rowland. Farewell, and when I credit women more,   90
   May I to Smithfield° and there buy a   *(market known for the sale of horses)*
     jade°   *inferior horse*
   (And know him to be so) that breaks my neck.

---

38. "A gold coin of the value of fifteen shillings, chiefly coined in the reign of James I; so called from having on its reverse the form of the sun with rays, resembling a spur-rowel" (*OED*).

Livia. Because I have known you, I'll be thus kind to you:
    Farewell, and be a man, and I'll provide you,
    Because I see you're desperate, some staid° chambermaid   *steady*
    That may relieve your youth with wholesome
        doctrine.°   *healthy teachings; sex*
Moroso. She's mine from all the world. Ha,° wench?   *so you say*
Livia. Ha, chicken? *Gives him a box o'th' ear and exits.*
Moroso. How's this? I do not love these favors. Save you.
Rowland. The devil take thee— *Wrings him by th' nose.*   100
Moroso. O!
Rowland. There's a love token for you. Thank me now. *Exit.*
Moroso. I'll think on some of ye, and if I live,
    My nose alone shall not° be played withal.   *something besides my nose will*
        Exit.

ACT 2, SCENE 1

Enter Petronius and Moroso.

Petronius. A box o'th' ear, do you say?
Moroso. Yes, sure, a sound one,
    Beside my nose blown to my hand.[39] If Cupid
    Shoot arrows of that weight, I'll swear devoutly,
    He's sued his livery° and is no more a boy.   *(an indication he is of legal age)*
Petronius. You gave her some ill language?
Moroso. Not a word.
Petronius. Or might be you were fumbling°?   *groping*
Moroso. Would I had, sir.   9
    I had been aforehand° then. But to be   *made the first move*
        baffled°   *disgraced*
    And have no feeling° of the cause°—   *sense / reason*

---

39. This phrase refers to Rowland's wringing of Moroso's nose in the previous scene. Its meaning may be clarified by this quotation from Fletcher's portion of *The Woman Hater* (1607). The misogynist is afraid of coming under a woman's control: "to ha' my hair curled by an idle finger, / My cheeks turned tabors and played upon, / Mine eyes looked babies in [images reflected in another's eyes, see n. 96], / And my nose blowed to my hand" (3.1.95–97). The phrase appears to mean "blow my nose with another's assistance," a description of what Rowland did to him. At 4.1.12, Petronius warns Moroso that a "wench" will "blow thy nose and buss [kiss] thee."

Petronius. Be patient,
    I have a medicine, clapped° to her back, will cure her.   *applied*
Moroso. No, sure, it must be afore,° sir.   *on the front (Moroso is thinking of sex)*
Petronius. O' my conscience,
    When I got° these two wenches (who 'til now   *begot*
    Ne'er showed their riding°) I was drunk with   *ability to carry a mount*
      bastard,°   *sweet wine*
    Whose nature is to form things like itself:
    Heady and monstrous. Did she slight him,° too?   *(i.e., Rowland)*
Moroso. That's all my comfort. A mere hobbyhorse°   *foolish fellow*
    She made child Rowland.[40] 'Sfoot,° she would   *by God's foot (oath)*
      not know him,
    Not give him a free look, not reckon him   22
    Among her thoughts, which I held more than wonder,
    I having seen her within's° three days kiss him   *within these*
    With such an appetite as though she would eat him.
Petronius. There is some trick in this. How did he take it?
Moroso. Ready to cry, he ran away.
Petronius. I fear° her.   *suspect*
    And yet I tell you, ever to my anger,
    She is as tame as innocency. It may be   30
    This blow was but a favor.°   *she hit you to show her regard for you*
Moroso. I'll be sworn
    'Twas well tied on° then.   *administered*
Petronius. Go to. Pray, forget it.
    I have bespoke° a priest, and within's two hours   *ordered*
    I'll have ye married. Will that please you?
Moroso. Yes.
Petronius. I'll see it done myself, and give the lady
    Such a sound exhortation° for this knavery,   *admonishing*
    I'll warrant you, shall make her smell this month
      on't.°   *stink for a month*
Moroso. Nay, good sir, be not violent.   41
Petronius. Neither—
Moroso. It may be
    Out of her earnest love there grew a longing
    (As you know women have such toys°) in kindness   *whims*
    To give me a box o'th' ear or so.

---

40. This is a mocking comparison of Rowland to Childe Roland, whose heroic quest is celebrated in fairy tales and ballads.

Petronius. It may be.

Moroso. I reckon for the best still. This night, then
    I shall enjoy her.

Petronius. You shall handsel° her.   *be the first to try her*

Moroso. Old as I am, I'll give her one blow for't   51
    Shall make her groan this twelvemonth!

Petronius. Where's your jointure?°   *marriage settlement*

Moroso. I have a jointure[41] for her.

Petronius. Have your counsel°   *legal representatives*
    Perused it yet?

Moroso. No counsel but the night, and your sweet daughter,
    Shall e'er peruse that jointure.

Petronius. Very well, sir.

Moroso. I'll no demurrers° on't nor no rejoinders.°   *legal objections / rebuttals*
    The other's ready sealed.   61

Petronius. Come then, let's comfort
    My son Petruchio. He's like little children
    That lose their baubles,° crying ripe.°   *toys / ready to cry*

Moroso. Pray, tell me,
    Is this stern woman still upon the flaunt
    Of bold defiance?°   *Is Maria still making her display of defiance?*

Petronius. Still, and still she shall be
    'Til she be starved out. You shall see such justice
    That women shall be glad, after this tempest,   70
    To tie their husband's shoes and walk their horses.

Moroso. That were a merry world. Do you hear the rumor?
    They say the women are in insurrection
    And mean to make a—[42]

Petronius. They'll sooner
    Draw upon walls as we do.[43] Let 'em, let 'em,
    We'll ship 'em out in cuck-stools;[44] there they'll sail

41. Following Rubinstein's suggestion that "to join" can be "to copulate" and "joint" is a term for genitals or penis, the possibility of sexual punning here makes sense.

42. Something unspeakable that was censored. Some sort of "nation of women" seems warranted here, although it must have been expressed in censored language as is the case in other dashes in F1 that have readings in F2 or the MS.

43. "Make designs on walls with our flow of urine as we men may do."

44. A cucking-stool was "An instrument of punishment formerly in use for scolds, disorderly women, etc., consisting of a chair in which the offender was

As brave Columbus did, 'til they discover
The happy islands of obedience.
We stay too long. Come.   80
Moroso. Now, Saint George be with us. *Exeunt.*

[ACT 2], SCENE 2

Enter Livia alone.

Livia. Now, if I can but get in° handsomely,   *into (the women's stronghold)*
    Father, I shall deceive you, and this night,
    For all your private plotting, I'll no wedlock.°   *I'll have no wedding*
    I have shifted sail° and find my sister's   *changed directions*
        safety°   *stronghold*
    A sure retirement.° Pray to heaven that Rowland   *shelter*
    Do not believe too far what I said to him,
    For yon old fox-case° forced me; that's my fear.   *skin of a fox (Moroso)*
    Stay,° let me see. This   *hold on*
        quarter° fierce Petruchio   *part of the house (as battlefield)*
    Keeps with his Myrmidons.[45] I must be sudden:
    If he seize on me, I can look for nothing   10
    But martial law.° To this place have I   *(when civil rights are suspended)*
        'scaped him.
    Above there.

Enter Maria and Byanca above.

Maria. Qui va la?°   *"Who goes there?"*
Livia. A friend.
Byanca. Who are you?
Livia. Look out and know.
Maria. Alas, poor wench, who sent thee?
    What weak fool made thy tongue his orator?
    I know you come to parley.°   *negotiate*

---

fastened and exposed to the jeers of the bystanders, or conveyed to a pond or
river and ducked" (*OED*).
45. "Followers," named for the warriors Achilles led to the siege of Troy.

Livia. You're deceived.   20
    Urged by the goodness of your cause, I come
    To do as you do.
Maria. You're too weak, too foolish,
    To cheat us with your smoothness.° Do not we   *simulated friendliness*
      know
    Thou hast been kept up tame?
Livia. Believe me!
Maria. No, prithee, good Livia.
    Utter° thy eloquence somewhere else.   *speak, sell*
Byanca. Good cousin,
    Put up your pipes.° We are not for your   *"give it a rest" (proverbial)*
      palate.°   *taste, liking*
    Alas, we know who sent you.   31
Livia. O° my word—   *on, upon*
Byanca. Stay° there. You must not think "your word,"   *stop*
    Or "by your maidenhead," or such
      Sunday° oaths   *(i.e., suitable for Sunday), best*
    Sworn after evensong,° can inveigle° us   *service held at sunset / deceive*
    To loose our handfast. Did their wisdoms think   *agreement*
    That sent you hither, we would be so foolish
    To entertain our gentle sister Sinon,[46]
    And give her credit,° while the wooden jade°   *trust her / worthless horse*
    Petruchio stole upon us? No, good sister.   40
    Go home and tell the merry Greeks° that sent you   *(proverbial)*
    Ilium shall burn, and I, as did Aeneas,
    Will on my back, spite of the Myrmidons,
    Carry this warlike lady, and through seas
    Unknown and unbelieved, seek out a land
    Where, like a race of noble Amazons,°   *female warriors*
    We'll root ourselves, and to our endless glory
    Live and despise base men.
Livia. I'll second° ye.   *support, assist*
Byanca. How long have you been thus?   50

---

46. Byanca embarks on an elaborate comparison of the women's stronghold to Troy ("Ilium"). Sinon is the Greek who persuaded the Trojans to take the "wooden jade" (horse) into the town. At the destruction of Troy, Aeneas carried his father Anchises on his back out of the flames. They set sail west to found Rome, as Byanca hopes to found a land where women (Amazons) rule, having escaped men ("the merry Greeks").

Livia. That's all one,° cousin.   *all the same (doesn't matter)*
  I stand for freedom now.
Byanca. Take heed° of lying,   *beware*
  For, by this light, if we do credit° you   *believe*
  And find you tripping,° his infliction   *making a false step*
  That killed the Prince of Orange[47] will be sport
  To what we purpose.
Livia. Let me feel the heaviest.
Maria. Swear by thy sweetheart Rowland (for by your maidenhead
  I fear 'twill be too late to swear) you mean   60
  Nothing but fair and safe and honorable
  To us, and to yourself.
Livia. I swear.
Byanca. Stay yet.
  Swear as you hate Moroso, that's the surest,
  And as you have a certain° fear to find him   *fixed*
  Worse than a poor dried jack,° full of more   *cheap dried fish*
   aches°   *pains*
  Than autumn has, more knavery, and usury,
  And foolery, and brokery,° than Dog's   *rascally dealing*
   Ditch;°   *Houndsditch in London*
  As you do constantly believe he's nothing   70
  But an old empty bag with a grey beard,
  And that beard such a bobtail° that it looks   *shortened tail (contemptible)*
  Worse than a mare's tail eaten off with fillies;°   *by young mares*
  As you acknowledge that young handsome wench
  That lies by such a bilbo blade[48] that bends
  With ev'ry pass he makes to th' hilts, most miserable,
  A dry nurse to his coughs, a fewterer°   *attendant*
  To such a nasty fellow, a robbed thing°   *someone robbed*
  Of all delights youth looks for; and to end,
  One cast away on coarse beef,° born to brush   *(i.e., a vulgar old man)*

---

47. Dutch William I, Prince of Orange, was assassinated by Balthasar Gérard in
1584. Gérard acted at the behest of Phillip II of Spain. The list of tortures that
Gérard underwent is both gruesome and long. The manner of his death will
suffice: he was disemboweled and quartered alive, his heart torn from his chest
and flung in his face, and his head then chopped off.

48. A "bilbo" is a sword known for the elasticity of its blade. That elasticity is
applied to Moroso's penis, which "bends" "to th' hilts" every time he makes a
sexual "pass." Compare Fletcher's *Wild Goose Chase:* "This bilbo-lord shall reap
that maidenhead / That was my due" (3.1.416; Williams 106).

That everlasting cassock that has worn   81
As many servants out as the north-east passage
Has consumed sailors. If you swear this, and truly
Without the reservation° of a gown   *holding back*
Or any meritorious petticoat,
'Tis like° we shall believe you.   *likely*
Livia. I do swear it.
Maria. Stay yet a little. Came this wholesome motion°   *beneficial move*
  (Deal truly, sister) from your own opinion
  Or some suggestion of the foe?   90
Livia. Ne'er fear me,
  For by that little faith I have in husbands,
  And the great zeal I bear your cause, I come
  Full of that liberty you stand for, sister.
Maria. If we believe, and you prove recreant,° Livia,   *traitor*
  Think what a maim° you give the noble cause   *wound*
  We now stand up for. Think what women shall
  An hundred year hence speak° thee, when examples   *say about*
  Are looked for, and so great ones, whose relations°   *stories*
  Spoke° as we do° 'em, wench, shall make new customs. *told / perform*
Byanca. If you be false, repent, go home, and pray,   101
  And to the serious° women of the city   *solemn*
  Confess yourself. Bring not a sin so heinous°   *serious; mortal*
  To load thy soul to this place. Mark me, Livia,
  If thou be'st double,° and betray'st our honors,   *duplicitous*
  And we fail in our purpose, get thee where
  There is no woman living, nor no hope
  There ever shall be.
Maria. If a mother's daughter
  That ever heard the name of stubborn husband   110
  Found thee and know thy sin—
Byanca. Nay, if old age,
  One that has worn away the name of woman,
  And no more left to know her by but railing,
  No teeth, nor eyes, nor legs but wooden ones,
  Come but i'th' windward of thee, for sure she'll smell thee,
  Thou'lt be so rank:° she'll ride thee like a   *foul-smelling*
    nightmare°   *a female spirit haunting a sleeping person*
  And say her prayers backward° to undo thee.   *as in casting a spell*
  She'll curse thy meat and drink. And when thou marriest, 119
  Clap° a sound spell forever on thy pleasures.   *impose*

Maria. Children of five year old, like little fairies,
    Will pinch thee into motley.° All   *enough colors to resemble a fool's outfit*
      that ever
    Shall live, and hear of thee—I mean all women—
    Will (like so many Furies°) shake their keys   *avenging spirits*
    And toss their flaming distaffs° o'er their heads,   *spinning staffs*
    Crying, "Revenge." Take heed: 'tis hideous.
    O, 'tis a fearful office.° If thou had'st   *service*
    (Though thou be'st perfect now) when thou cam'st hither,
    A false imagination,° get thee gone   *treacherous idea*
    And, as my learnèd cousin said, repent.   130
    This place is sought° by soundness.°   *desired / constancy*
Livia. So I seek it,
    Or let me be a most despised example.
Maria. I do believe thee; be thou worthy of it.
    You come not empty?°   *(i.e., empty-handed)*
Livia. No, here's cakes, and cold meat,
    And tripe° of proof;° behold,   *dish of cow stomach / quality*
      here's wine, and beer.
    Be sudden—I shall be surprised° else.   *captured*
Maria. Meet at the low° parlor door; there lies a close   *downstairs*
      way.°   *secret passage*
    What fond° obedience you have living in you,   *foolish*
    Or duty to a man, before you enter,   141
    Fling it away. 'Twill but defile our off'rings.
Byanca. Be wary as you come.
Livia. I warrant ye. *Exeunt.*

[ACT 2, SCENE 3]

    Enter Rowland and Tranio at several° doors.   *separate*

Tranio. Now, Rowland?
Rowland. How do you?
Tranio. How dost thou, man?
    Thou look'st ill.
Rowland. Yes. Pray, can you tell me, Tranio,
    Who knew the devil first?
Tranio. A woman.
Rowland. So, were they not well acquainted?

Tranio. Maybe so,
    For they had certain dialogues together.   10
Rowland. He sold her fruit,° I take it?   *(an apple in Eden)*
Tranio. Yes, and cheese°   *(which accompanies fruit at dessert)*
    That choked all mankind after.
Rowland. Canst thou tell me
    Whether that woman ever had a faith°   *was loyal to anything*
    After she had eaten?
Tranio. That's a school question.°   *question for philosophers*
Rowland. No,
    'Tis no question, for believe me, Tranio,
    That cold fruit after eating bred nought in her   20
    But windy promises and colic° vows   *relating to intestinal discomfort*
    That broke out both ways.° Thou hast heard, I   *as flatulence and belching*
      am sure,
    Of Aesculapius,° a far-famed surgeon,   *Greek god of medicine and healing*
    One that could set together quartered
      traitors°   *heal traitors who are cut in quarters*
    And make 'em honest men.
Tranio. How dost thou,° Rowland?   *What do you mean?*
Rowland. Let him but take (if he dare do a cure
    Shall get him fame indeed) a faithless woman.
    There will be credit° for him; that will   *reputation*
      speak° him.   *proclaim*
    A broken° woman, Tranio, a base woman,   *vow-breaking*
    And if he can cure such a rack° of honor,   *ruin*
    Let him come here and practice.   32
Tranio. Now, for heaven's sake,
    Why, what ail'st thou, Rowland?
Rowland. I am ridden, Tranio,
    And spur-galled° to the life° of patience   *irritated by spurs / extent*
    (Heaven keep my wits together) by a thing
    Our worst thoughts are too noble for—a woman.
Tranio. Your mistress has a little frowned, it may be?
Rowland. She was my mistress.   40
Tranio. Is she not?
Rowland. No, Tranio.
    She has done me such disgrace, so spitefully,
    So like a woman bent to my undoing,
    That henceforth a good horse shall be my mistress,
    A good sword, or a book. And if you see her,
    Tell her, I do beseech you, even for love's sake—

Tranio. I will, Rowland.

Rowland. She may sooner

    Count the good I have thought her,   50

    Our old love and our friendship,

    Shed one true tear, mean one hour constantly,°   *be faithful one hour*

    Be old and honest, married and a maid,

    Than make me see her more or more believe her.

    And, now I have met a messenger, farewell, sir. *Exit.*

Tranio. Alas, poor Rowland, I will do it for thee.

    This is that dog Moroso, but I hope

    To see him cold i'th'

        mouth° first ere he enjoy her.   *having lost the scent (i.e., defeated or dead)*

    I'll watch this young man; desperate thoughts may seize him,   59

    And if my purse or counsel can, I'll ease him. *Exit.*

[ACT 2, SCENE 4]

Enter Petruchio, Petronius, Moroso, and Sophocles.

Petruchio. For look you, gentlemen, say that I grant her,

    Out of my free and liberal love, a pardon,

    Which you and all men else know she deserves not—

    Teneatis amici°—can all the world   *"Grasp this, friends"*

        leave° laughing?   *stop*

Petronius. I think not.

Petruchio. No, by this hand, they cannot.

    For pray, consider, have you ever read,

    Or heard of, or can any man imagine

    So stiff° a tomboy,° of so set a malice   *stubborn / bold or immodest woman*

    And such a brazen resolution,   10

    As this young crab-tree?° And then   *(i.e., crooked), sour apple tree*

        answer me,

    And mark but this too, friends, without a cause,

    Not a foul word comes 'cross her,° not a   *I said nothing unkind to her*

        fear

    She justly can take hold on. And do you think

    I must sleep out my anger and endure it,

    Sew pillows to her ease and lull° her mischief?   *soothe*

    Give me a spindle° first. No, no,   *implement to twist fibers into thread*

        my masters,   *(i.e., a sign of woman's work)*

Were she as fair as Nell o' Greece,° and housewife   *Helen of Troy*
As good as the wise sailor's wife,° and   *Penelope, wife of Ulysses*
   young still,
Never above fifteen, and these tricks to it,°   *and played such tricks*
She should ride the wild mare[49] once a week—she should,   21
Believe me, friends, she should—I would tabor° her   *beat, as on a drum*
'Til all the legions° that are crept into her   *(of devils)*
Flew out with fire i'th' tails.°   *(like devils)*
Sophocles. Methinks you err now,
   For to me seems° a little sufferance°   *it seems to me / patience*
   Were a far surer cure.
Petruchio. Yes, I can suffer—
   Where I see promises of peace and amendment.
Moroso. Give her a few conditions.   30
Petruchio. I'll be hanged first.
Petronius. Give her a crab-tree cudgel.°   *club*
Petruchio. So I will;
   And after it a flock-bed° for her bones,   *an uncomfortable bed*
   And hard eggs,° 'til they brace her   *hard-boiled egg, considered constipating*
   like a drum.
   She shall be pampered with—
   She shall not know a stool° in ten months,   *move her bowels*
   gentlemen.
Sophocles. This must not be.

Enter Jaques.

Jaques. Arm, arm, out with your weapons,   39
   For all the women in the kingdom's on° ye.   *attacking*

Enter Pedro.

They swarm like wasps, and nothing can destroy 'em
But stopping of their hive and smothering of 'em.
Pedro. Stand to your guard, sir. All the devils extant
   Are broke upon us, like a cloud of thunder;
   There are more women marching hitherward,
   In rescue of my mistress, than ere turned tail°   *had sex*

---

49. "A wooden frame on which soldiers were made to 'ride' as punishment" (*OED*).

At Sturbridge Fair°—and, I   *a two-week fair held north of Cambridge*
    believe, as fiery.°   *having venereal disease*
Jaques. The forlorn hope's° led by a tanner's   *troops selected to begin an attack*
    wife—
I know her by her hide—a desperate woman.   49
She flayed° her husband in her youth and made   *skinned*
Reins of his hide to ride the parish. Her
    placket°   *slit in a woman's skirt or underskirt; vagina*
Looks like the straits of Gibraltar, still wider
Down to the gulf.° All sunburned   *(i.e., her vagina)*
    Barbary°   *dark-skinned North African*
Lies in her breech.° Take 'em all together,   *buttocks; pants*
They are a genealogy of jennets,°   *a race of small Spanish horses*
    gotten°   *begotten*
And born° thus: by the   *given birth; borne, endured*
    boisterous° breath of husbands.   *rough*
They serve, sure,° and are swift to catch occasion   *steadfastly*
(I mean their foes, or husbands) by the forelocks,[50]
And there they hang like
    favors.° Cry they can,   *tokens of affection like ribbons or jewelry*
But more for noble spite than fear; and crying   60
Like the old Giants that were foes to heaven,[51]
They heave ye[52] stool on stool, and fling main° pot-lids   *heavy; large*
Like massy rocks, dart° ladles, tossing   *throw like spears*
    irons°   *cooking utensils (for toasting?)*
And tongs like thunderbolts, 'til overlade,°   *overburdened*
They fall beneath the weight. Yet still aspiring
At those imperious codsheads° that would   *godheads; boneheads*
    tame 'em.
There's ne'er a one of these (the worst and weakest—
Choose where you will) but dare attempt the raising

50. The personification of "occasion" or opportunity is pictorially portrayed as a woman having a single growth of hair coming from the front of her head ("forelock") and otherwise bald, suggesting the need to seize her when she approaches, since there is nothing to grab when she is past.

51. In Greek myth the Giants were "enormous beings of invincible strength and terrifying appearance" (Grimal 171) who rebelled against the gods.

52. In early modern English, a pronoun can follow a verb to stress that the antecedent has a special interest in the action of the verb. This grammatical form is called the ethical dative (ethical in the sense of adding emphasis).

Against the sovereign peace of Puritans,   69
A maypole and a morris,[53] maugre° mainly   *despite*
Their zeal and dudgeon-daggers.° And   *daggers with wooden handles*
    yet more,
Dares plant a stand° of batt'ring ale against 'em°   *station / (the Puritans)*
And drink 'em out o'th' parish.

Pedro. There's one brought in the bears,° against the   *(for bear-baiting)*
    canons°   *laws*
Of two church wardens, made it good,° and   *justified the act*
    fought 'em,
And in the churchyard after evensong.

Jaques. Another, to her everlasting fame, erected   77
Two alehouses of ease,° the quarter-   *taverns; brothels*
    sessions°   *quarterly court sessions*
Running against her roundly;° in which   *trying to shut her down*
    business
Two of the disannullers° lost their   *those who would close the brothel*
    nightcaps.[54]
A third stood excommunicate by the cudgel.°   *was persuaded by violence?*
The constable, to her° eternal glory,   *(i.e., the rebellious woman's)*
Drunk hard and was converted, and she victor.

Pedro. Then are they victualed° with pies and puddings   *provided with food*
(The trappings° of good stomachs), noble ale,   *decorations*
The true defender,° sausages (and smoked ones),   *(it gives courage)*
If need be, such as serve for pikes,°   *smoked fish; pointed wooden shafts*
    and pork
(Better the Jews never hated°), here and there   *(see n. 12)*
A bottle of metheglin,° a stout Britain   *spiced mead*
That will stand to 'em.° What else they want they   *stand by them*
    war for.

Sophocles. Lo, you fierce Petruchio, this comes of your impatience.   91
Petruchio. Come, to council.
Sophocles. Now, you must grant conditions or the kingdom
    Will have no other talk but this.

53. Puritans were against dances like the "maypole" or the "morris." Fletcher describes their displeasure in *Women Pleased* (4.1).

54. While this passage is difficult to follow, it appears that two of those who wanted to close the brothel were made cuckolds (their wives slept with other men). The "nightcap" is associated with cuckoldry, as in *Othello* where Iago says, "I fear Cassio with my nightcap too" (2.1.306). Compare Fletcher's use of "nightcaps" in 4.1.10.

Petronius. Away then, and let's advise the best.
Sophocles. [To Moroso] Why do you tremble?
Moroso. Have I lived thus long to be knocked o'th' head
    With half a washing-beetle?°   *a wooden bat used to beat clothes in washing*
        Pray, be wise, sir.
Petruchio. Come, something I'll do, but what it is I know not.
Sophocles. To counsel then, and let's avoid their follies.   100
    Guard all the doors, or we shall not have a cloak left. *Exeunt.*

[ACT 2, SCENE 5]

Enter three maids at several doors.

1 Maid. How goes your business, girls?
2 Maid. Afoot° and fair.   *on the move*
3 Maid. If fortune favor us. Away to your strength.°   *fortification*
    The country forces are arrived. Be gone.
    We are discovered else.°   *betrayed otherwise*
1 Maid. Arm and be valiant.   6
2 Maid. Think of our cause.
3 Maid. Our justice.
1 Maid. 'Tis sufficient. *Exeunt.*

[ACT 2, SCENE 6]

Enter Petronius, Petruchio, Moroso, Sophocles, and Tranio.

Petronius. I am indifferent, though I must confess
    I had rather see her carted.[55]
Tranio. No more of that, sir.
Sophocles. Are ye resolved to give her fair conditions?
    'Twill be the safest way.
Petruchio. I am distracted.
    Would I had run my head into a halter°   *strap by which horses are led; noose*

---

55. "Carting," carrying through the streets on display in a cart, was a punishment.

When I first wooed her. If I offer peace,
She'll urge her own conditions, that's the
   devil.°   *(an expression of vexation)*

Sophocles. Why, say° she do.   *suppose*

Petruchio. Say I am made an ass then;   11
   I know her aim. May I with reputation
   (Answer me this) with safety of mine honor
   (After the mighty manage of my first wife—
   Which was indeed a fury to this filly—
   After my twelve strong labors to reclaim her,
   Which would have made Don Hercules[56] horn
      mad,°   *enraged as a horned beast or cuckold*
   And hid him in his hide) suffer this
      Cicely,°   *woman's name, associated with lower classes*
   Ere she have warmed my sheets, ere grappled°   *wrestled (sexually)*
      with me,
   This pink,[57] this painted foist, this cockle-boat,   20
   To hang her fights out and defy me, friends,
   A well-known man-of-war? If this be equal,°   *just*
   And I may suffer,° say,° and I have
      done.°   *must endure / just say so*
                               am finished

Petronius. I do not think you may.

Tranio. You'll make it worse, sir.

Sophocles. Pray, hear me, good Petruchio. But ev'n now,
   You were contented to give all conditions,
   To try how far she would carry.° 'Tis a folly   *pursue this*
   (And you will find it so) to clap the
      curb° on   *put on the chain used to check a horse*
   Ere you be sure it proves a natural wildness,   30
   And not a forced. Give her conditions,
   For on my life this trick is put into her°—   *she was put up to this*

Petronius. I should believe so, too—

56. Hercules is the ancient hero who performed twelve great labors. His first labor was to slay the Nemean lion and return with its skin. He was rewarded with the lion's "hide," which made him invincible when he wore it.

57. Petruchio begins a series of maritime references, perhaps suggested by "grapple," which also means "to seize a ship." "Pink" is a small fishing boat; "foist" a small barge and a rogue; "cockle-boat" a small boat; "fights" "a kind of screen used during a naval engagement to conceal and protect the crew of the vessel" (*OED*); and "man-of-war" a vessel equipped for war. The terms also have sexual connotations (Williams 1034).

Sophocles. And not her own.

Tranio. You'll find it so.

Sophocles. Then, if she flounder° with you,   *stumble, rear (as of a horse)*
    Clap spurs on, and in this you'll deal with temperance,
    Avoid the hurry° of the world—   *agitation*

Tranio. And lose— *Music above.*

Moroso. No honor, on my life, sir.   40

Petruchio. I will do it.

Petronius. It seems they are very merry.

          Enter Jaques.

Petruchio. Why, God hold it.

Moroso. Now, Jaques?

Jaques. They are i'th' flaunt,° sir.   *flaunting themselves*

Sophocles. Yes, we hear 'em.

Jaques. They have got a stick of fiddles, and they
       firk it°   *frisk about (with sexual suggestions)*
    In wond'rous ways. The two grand capitanos°   *captains*
    (They brought the auxiliary regiments)   49
    Dance with their coats° tucked up to their bare   *skirts*
       breeches°   *buttocks*
    And bid the kingdom kiss 'em—that's the burden.°   *chorus, refrain*
    They have got metheglin° and   *spiced mead*
       audacious° ale   *inspiring boldness*
    And talk like tyrants.

Petronius. How knowest thou?

Jaques. I peeped in
    At a loose lansket.°   *door latch*

Tranio. Hark.

Petronius. A song—pray, silence!

          Song[58]

      A health for all this day
    To the woman that bears the sway   60
      And wears the breeches.
      Let it come, let it come.

58. Although both F1 and MS have stage directions calling for a song, they do not include it. The text of the song is taken from F2.

Let this health be a seal,
For the good of the commonweal.
The woman shall wear the breeches.
Let's drink then and laugh it.
And merrily merrily quaff it,
And tipple° and tipple a round.   *drink freely or hard*
Here's to thy fool°   *husband, lover?*
And to my fool.   70
Come, to all fools,
Though it cost us, wench, many a pound.

*All the women [Maria, Byanca, a city wife, a
country wife, and three maids] above.*

Moroso. They look out.
Petruchio. Good ev'n, ladies.
Maria. Good you good ev'n, sir.
Petruchio. How have you slept tonight?
Maria. Exceeding well, sir.
Petruchio. Did you not wish me with you?
Maria. No, believe me, I never thought upon you.
Country wife. Is that he?   80
Byanca. Yes.
Country wife. Sir!
Sophocles. She has drunk hard—mark her
      hood.°   *cap (sarcastically as academic or cleric)*
Country wife. You are—
Sophocles. Learnedly drunk—I'll hang else! Let her utter.
Country wife. And I must tell you, *viva voce,*°   *"orally" (as academic exams)*
      friend,
   A very foolish fellow.
Tranio. There's an ale-figure.°   *rhetoric inspired by drink*
Petruchio. I thank you, Susan Brotes.°   *(unidentified)*
City wife. Forward, sister.   90
Country wife. You have espoused here a hearty° woman,   *bold*
   A comely° and courageous.   *beautiful*
Petruchio. Well, I have so.
Country wife. And to the comfort of distressed damsels,
   Women outworn in wedlock and such vessels,°   *receptacles (i.e., women)*
   This woman has defied you.
Petruchio. It should seem so.
Country wife. And why?

Petruchio. Yes, can you tell?

Country wife. For thirteen causes.   100

Petruchio. Pray, by your patience,° mistress.   *permission (spare me the details)*

City wife. Forward, sister.

Petruchio. Do you mean to treat of° all these?   *deal with*

City wife. Who shall let° her?   *stop*

Petronius. Do you hear, velvet-hood,[59] we come not now
  To hear your doctrine.

Country wife. For the first,° I take it,   *(cause)*
  It doth divide itself into seven branches.

Petruchio. Hark you, good Maria,   109
  Have you got a catechizer° here?   *one who teaches by question and answer*

Tranio. Good zeal.°   *fervor (a term associated with Puritans)*

Sophocles. Good three-piled predication,° will   *triple-thick (as velvet) speech*
  you peace°   *be quiet*
  And hear the cause we come for?

Country wife. Yes, bobtails,°   *contemptible ones*
  We know the cause you come for. Here's the cause,°   *(i.e., Maria)*
  But never hope to carry° her, never dream   *prevail with*
  Or flatter your opinions with a thought
  Of base repentance in her.

City wife. Give me sack.°   *sweet white wine*
  By this, and next strong ale—   120

Country wife. Swear forward,° sister.   *go ahead and swear*

City wife. By all that's cordial,° in this place we'll bury   *cheering (as liquor)*
  Our bones, fames,° tongues, our triumphs and then all   *reputations*
  That ever yet was chronicled of woman,
  But° this brave wench, this excellent despiser,   *unless*
  This bane° of dull obedience shall inherit°   *destroyer / come into possession*
  Her liberal will° and march off with conditions   *volition, sexual desire*
  Noble and worth herself.

Country wife. She shall, Tom Tylers,[60]
  And brave ones, too. My hood shall make a hearse-cloth,   130
  And I lie under it like Joan o'
    Gaunt,°   *female equivalent of John of Gaunt, important nobleman*

---

59. See 2.6.83 above.

60. A reference to the protagonist of the anonymous early interlude *Tom Tyler and His Wife* (c. 1551, author unknown), where Tom has a shrewish wife, named only "Strife," who remains untamed. "Tom Tyler" became generic for a henpecked husband.

Ere I go° less. My distaff stuck up by me   *settle for*
For the eternal trophy of my conquests,
And loud fame at my head, with two main bottles,
Shall fill to all the world° the glorious fall   *tell the complete story of?*
Of old Don Gillian.°   *woman's name, lower class*

City wife. Yet a little further:
We have taken arms in rescue of this lady,
Most just and noble. If ye beat us off°   *defeat us*
Without conditions, and we recant,°   *renounce our cause*
Use us as we deserve: and first degrade us   141
Of all our ancient chamb'ring;° next that   *effeminacy; lewdness*
The symbols of our secrecy, silk stockings,
Hew off our heels; our petticoats of
   arms°   *(female version of "coats of arms")*
Tear off our bod'ces;° and our   *bodices*
   bodkins° break   *daggers, needles, hairpins*
Over our coward heads.

Country wife. And ever after
To make the tainture° most notorious,   *defilement*
At all our crests, *videlicet*° our   *"that is to say"*
   plackets,°   *slits in skirts and underskirts*
Let laces hang,° and we return again   *be unlaced*
Into our former titles—dairymaids.   151

Petruchio. No more wars, puissant° ladies. Show   *powerful*
   conditions°   *stipulations*
And freely I accept 'em.

Maria. Call in Livia—
She's in the treaty, too.

                    Enter Livia above.

Moroso. How, Livia?

Maria. Hear you that, sir?
There's the conditions for ye; pray, peruse 'em. *[Throws down a
   paper to Petruchio.]*

Petronius. Yes, there she is. 'T had° been no right° rebellion   *it had / true*
Had she held off. What think you, man?   160

Moroso. Nay, nothing.
I have enough o'th prospect.°   *what can be expected*
   O° my conscience,   *on*
The world's end and the goodness of a woman

Will come
   together.°   *the end of the world and a good woman will appear at the same time*
Petronius. Are you there, sweet lady?
Livia. Cry you mercy, sir, I saw you not. Your blessing.
Petronius. Yes, when I bless a jade that stumbles with
   me.°   *a horse that falls with me*
   How are the articles?
Livia. This is for you, sir, and I shall think upon't. *[Throws down a*
   paper to Moroso.]
Moroso. You have used me finely.   170
Livia. There's no other use of thee now extant
   But to be hung up, cassock, cap, and all,
   For some strange monster at apothecaries.[61]
Petronius. I hear you, whore.
Livia. It must be his° then, sir,   *the "whore" must be Moroso's*
   For need will then compel me.°   *(were I forced to marry him)*
City wife. Blessing on thee.
Livia. He will undo me in mere° pans of coals   *ordinary*
   To make him lusty.[62]
Petronius. There's no talking to 'em.   180
   How are they, sir?
Petruchio. *[Reads]* As I expected. Liberty and clothes
   When, and in what way she will; continual moneys,
   Company, and all the house at her dispose;°   *disposal*
   No tongue to say, "Why is this?" or "Whither
     will it?"°   *Where will it (she) go?*
   New coaches and some buildings she appoints° here,   *stipulates*
   Hangings° and hunting horses; and for   *wall hangings, tapestries*
     plate°   *gold or silver vessels and utensils*
   And jewels—for her private use, I take it—
   Two thousand pound° in   *(a huge sum)*
     present;° then for music,   *ready money*
   And women to read° French—   *teach*
Petronius. This must not be.   191
Petruchio. And at the latter end a clause put in

---

61. Apothecaries, such as the character who sells poison to Romeo in Shakespeare's *Romeo and Juliet,* were known to hang stuffed and skinned exotic creatures in their shops. Moroso would be so displayed.

62. "The cost of the 'pans of coals,' used to provide warmth or to burn sweet perfumes to enflame Moroso's lust, will bankrupt me."

That Livia shall by no man be
    importuned°—   *troubled, subjected to persuasion*
This whole month yet—to marry.

Petronius. This is monstrous.

Petruchio. This shall be done. I'll humor her° awhile.   *go along with her whims*
    If nothing but repentance and undoing
    Can win her love, I'll make a shift for one.°   *give it a try*

Sophocles. When ye are once abed, all these conditions
    Lie under your own
      seal.°   *stamp of agreement as intercourse would be*

Maria. Do you like 'em?   201

Petruchio. Yes.
    And by that faith° I gave you fore° the priest   *marriage oath / in front of*
    I'll ratify 'em.

Country wife. Stay, what pledges?°   *surety*

Maria. No, I'll take that oath,
    But have a care you keep it.

City wife. "'Tis not now
    As when Andrea lived."[63]

Country wife. If you do juggle,°   *deceive, trick*
    Or alter but a letter of these articles,   211
    We have set down, the selfsame persecution—

Maria. Mistrust him not.

Petruchio. By all my honesty—

Maria. Enough. I yield.

Petronius. What's this inserted here?

Sophocles. That the two valiant women that command here
    Shall have a supper made 'em,° and a large one,   *for them*
    And liberal entertainment without grudging,
    And pay for all their soldiers.   220

Petruchio. That shall be, too.
    And if a tun° of wine will serve to pay 'em,   *barrel*
    They shall have justice. I ordain° ye all   *deputize*
    Paymasters,° gentlemen.   *to join in the payment*

Tranio. Then we shall have sport, boys.

Maria. We'll meet you in the parlor. *[Exeunt all the women above.]*

Petruchio. Ne'er look sad, sir, for I will do it.

Sophocles. There's no danger in't.

---

63. A quotation from the ever-popular Elizabethan play *The Spanish Tragedy* by
Thomas Kyd (3.14.111); i.e., "Times have changed."

Petruchio. For Livia's article, you shall observe it.
   I have tied° myself.   *obligated, pledged*
Petronius. I will.   231
Petruchio. Along then. Now
   Either I break, or this stiff plant must bow.   *Exeunt.*

ACT 3, SCENE 1

Enter Tranio and Rowland.

Tranio. Come, you shall take my counsel.
Rowland. I shall hang first.
   I'll no more love, that's certain. 'Tis a bane,°   *poison*
   Next that they poison rats with, the most mortal.[64]
   No, I thank heaven, I have got my sleep again,
   And now begin to write sense. I can walk ye°   *(see n. 52)*
   A long hour in my chamber like a man,
   And think of something that may better me,
   Some serious point of learning or my state.°   *condition, status*
   No more "Ay me's" and "*Misereres*,"[65] Tranio,   10
   Come near my brain. I'll tell thee, had the devil
   But any essence in him of a man
   And could be brought to love, and love a woman,
   'Twould make his head ache worser than his horns do,
   And firk° him with a fire he never felt yet;   *drive; beat*
   Would make him dance. I tell thee, there is nothing—
   It may be thy case, Tranio, therefore hear me—
   Under the sun (reckon° the mass of follies   *count*
   Crept into th' world with man) so desperate,
   So mad, so senseless, poor and base, so wretched,   20
   Roguey and scurvy—
Tranio. Whither wilt thou,° Rowland?   *Where are you going with this?*
Rowland. As 'tis to be in love.
Tranio. And why, for virtue sake?
Rowland. "And why, for virtue's sake?" Dost thou not
   conceive° me?   *understand*

---

64. "Love is a poison almost as deadly as that used to kill rats."
65. "Have mercy," the opening of Psalm 51. The term is used again at 5.2.32.
See n. 99.

Tranio. No, by my troth.

Rowland. Pray, then, and heartily,
    For fear thou fall into't. I'll tell thee why, too,
    For I have hope to save thee. When thou lov'st,
    And first begin'st to worship the gilt calf[66]   30
    Imprimis,° thou hast lost thy gentry°   *"first item"* / *qualities of a gentleman*
    And, like a prentice,° flung away thy freedom.   *apprentice*
    Forthwith° thou art a slave.   *immediately*

Tranio. That's a new doctrine.

Rowland. Next, thou art no more a man.

Tranio. What, then?

Rowland. A frippery.°   *a display of cast-off clothes*
    Nothing but braided hair and penny ribbon,
    Glove, garter, ring, rose;° or, at best,   *ornamental ribbon knot*
    a swabber.°   *mop for cleaning ovens*
    If thou canst love so near to keep thy
       making,°   *in a way that more or less preserves your shape*
    Yet thou wilt lose thy language.   41

Tranio. Why?

Rowland. O Tranio,
    Those things° in love ne'er talk   *creatures (who have lost their manhood)*
    as we do.

Tranio. No?

Rowland. No, without doubt. They sigh and shake the head
    And sometimes whistle dolefully.°   *mournfully*

Tranio. No tongue?°   *language*

Rowland. Yes, Tranio, but no truth in't, nor no reason.   49
    And when they cant° (for 'tis a kind of canting),   *speak in jargon*
    Ye shall hear, if you reach° to understand 'em   *strive*
    (Which you must be a fool first, or you cannot),
    Such gibberish, such "believe me, I protest, sweet,"
    And "O dear heavens," in which such constellations
    Reign at the births of lovers, this is too well,
    And "deign° me, lady, deign me, I beseech ye,   *condescend to think of*
    Your poor unworthy lump." And then she licks[67] him.

Tranio. A pox on't,° this is nothing.   *(an exclamation of impatience)*

---

66. The Golden Calf, the idol that the Children of Israel misguidedly constructed and worshipped while Moses was on Mount Sinai (Exodus 32).

67. It was believed that a newborn bear cub was an unformed mass ("lump") that the mother bear "licked" into the shape of a bear.

Rowland. Thou hast hit it.°   *you've figured it out*
  Then talks she ten times worse, and wries° and wriggles   *twists*
  As though she had the itch;° and so it may be.   *skin disease*
Tranio. Of what religion are they?   62
Rowland. Good old Catholics.
  They deal by intercession° all.   *praying to saints to intercede for them to God*
   They keep
  A kind of household gods, called chambermaids,
  Which, being prayed to, and their off'rings brought
  (Which are in gold; yet some observe the old law
  And give 'em flesh),° *probatum est,°* you   *meat; sex / "it is proven"*
   shall have
  As good love for your money, and as tidy,°   *opportune, healthy*
  As e'er you turned your leg o'er;° and, that ended—   *mounted*
Tranio. Why, thou art grown a strange discoverer.°   *explorer, informer*
Rowland. Of mine own follies, Tranio.   72
Tranio. Wilt thou, Rowland, certain° ne'er love again?   *certainly*
Rowland. I think so, certain.
  And if I be not dead drunk, I shall keep it.
Tranio. Tell me but this: what dost thou think of women?
Rowland. Why, as I think of fiddles. They delight me
  'Til their strings break.
Tranio. What strings?
Rowland. Their modesties,   80
  Faiths, vows, and maidenheads—for they are like kits,°   *small fiddles*
  They have but four strings to 'em.
Tranio. What wilt thou
  Give me for ten pound now, when thou next lov'st,
  And the same woman still?
Rowland. Give me the money. A hundred,° and   *(i.e., ten-to-one odds)*
   my bond for't.
Tranio. But, pray, hear me:
  I'll work all means° I can to reconcile ye.   *do everything*
Rowland. Do, do. Give me the money.
Tranio. *[Giving money]* There.   90
Rowland. Work, Tranio.
Tranio. You shall go sometimes where she is.
Rowland. Yes, straight.°   *directly*
  This° is the first good I e'er got by   *(i.e., a wager which is a sure thing)*
  woman.
Tranio. You would think it strange now, if another beauty
  As good as hers, say better—

Rowland. Well?

Tranio. Conceive me, this is no point o'th' wager.°   *not what we bet on*

Rowland. That's all one.°   *all the same (doesn't matter)*

Tranio. Love you as much, or more, than she now hates you.   100

Rowland. 'Tis a good hearing.° Let 'em love. Ten pound more   *report*
    I never love that woman.

Tranio. *[Giving money]* There it is. And so a hundred, if ye lose.

Rowland. 'Tis done. Have ye another to put in?

Tranio. No, no, sir.

Rowland. I am very sorry. Now will I erect°   *start*
    A new game,° and go hate for th'   *competition*
        bell.° I am sure   *hate women for the prize*
    I am in excellent case° to win.   *position*

Tranio. I must have leave
    To tell ye, and tell truth too, what she is   110
    And how she suffers for you.

Rowland. Ten pound more I never believe ye.

Tranio. No, sir, I am stinted.°   *finished (out of money)*

Rowland. Well, take your best way,° then.   *be on your way*

Tranio. Let's walk, I am glad your sullen fever's off.°   *gloomy mood's over*

Rowland. Shalt see me, Tranio,
    A monstrous merry man now. Let's to the wedding.
    And as we go, tell me the general hurry°   *commotion*
    Of these mad wenches and their works.°   *activities, fortifications*

Tranio. I will.   120

Rowland. And do thy worst.

Tranio. Something I'll do.

Rowland. Do, Tranio. *Exeunt.*

[ACT 3], SCENE 2

Enter Pedro and Jaques.

Pedro. A pair of stocks bestride 'em.° Are they gone?   *may they sit in the stocks*

Jaques. Yes, they are gone, and all the pans i'th' town
    Beating before 'em. What strange admonitions
    They gave my master, and how fearfully
    They threatened, if he broke 'em!

Pedro. O° my conscience,   *on*
    He's found his full match now.

Jaques. That I believe, too.

Pedro. How did she entertain him?

Jaques. She looked on him.   10

Pedro. But scurvily?°   *meanly, sourly*

Jaques. Faith, with no great affection
　　That I saw, and I heard some say he kissed her,
　　But 'twas upon a treaty°—and some copies°   *contract / reports*
　　Say "but her cheek."

Pedro.　Faith, Jaques, what wouldst thou give
　　For such a wife now?

Jaques. Full as many prayers
　　As the most zealous Puritan conceives
　　(Out of the meditation of fat veal   20
　　Or birds of prey, crammed capons) against
　　　　players,°   *Puritans campaigned against theater*
　　And to as good a tune, too, but against her
　　That heaven would bless° me from her. Mark it, Pedro: *guard*
　　If this house be not turned° within this fortnight   *turned upside down*
　　With the foundation upward, I'll be
　　　　carted.°   *carried in a cart as punishment*
　　My comfort is yet that those Amorites[68]
　　That came to back her cause, those heathen whores,
　　Had their hoods hallowed with sack.

Pedro. How dev'lish drunk they were!

Jaques. And how they tumbled, Pedro. Didst thou mark   30
　　The country cavaliero?°   *soldier*

Pedro.　Out upon her. How she turned down the bragget.[69]

Jaques. Ay, that sunk her.

Pedro. That drink was well put to her. What a sobersault,°   *somersault*
　　When the chair fell, she fetched,° with her heels upward!   *made*

Jaques. And what a piece of landscape she
　　　　discovered!°   *quantity of country scenery she exposed*

Pedro. Didst mark her when her hood fell in the
　　　　posset?°   *hot milk curdled with ale*

Jaques. Yes, and there rode, like a Dutch hoy.°   *small vessel*
　　The tumbrel,°   *flat-bottomed boat*
　　When she had got her ballast°—   *material giving ship weight; balance*

---

68. One of the tribes living in Canaan before the Israelites arrived; *fig.,* heathens.

69. "Guzzled the drink of honey and ale fermented together."

Pedro. That I saw, too.   40

Jaques. How fain° she would have drawn on Sophocles   *willingly*

    To come aboard,° and how she simpered   *(i.e., have sex with her)*

      it.°   *smirked*

Pedro. I warrant her, she has been a worthy striker.°   *fornicator*

Jaques. I'th' heat of summer, there had been some hope on't,

    For then old women are cool cellars.

Pedro. Hang her.

Jaques. She offered him a Harry-groat,°   *groat (4 pence) with image of Henry VIII*

    and belched out

    (Her stomach being blown with ale) such courtship,

    Upon my life, has giv'n him twenty stools° since.   *bowel movements*

    Believe my calculation. These old women,   50

    When they are tippled° and a little heated,°   *drunk / (with drink)*

    Are like new wheels: they'll roar you° all the town o'er   *squeal*

    'Til they be greased.°   *lubricated (sexual)*

Pedro. The city cinquepace,°   *lively five-step dance, galliard; fast woman*

    Dame Toast-and-Butter, had her

      bob,° too?   *refrain of song; sexual encounter*

Jaques. Yes,

    But she was sullen drunk, and given to filching.°   *stealing*

    I see her offer at° a spoon—my master,   *make an attempt at*

    I do not like his look. I fear he's fasted°   *gone without (sex)*

    For° all this preparation. Let's steal° by him   *in spite of / sneak*

                 Exeunt.

[ACT 3], SCENE 3

Enter Petruchio and Sophocles.

Sophocles. Not let you touch her all this night?

Petruchio. Not touch her.

Sophocles. Where was your courage?

Petruchio. Where was her obedience?

    Never poor man was shamed so; never rascal

    That keeps a stud° of whores was used° so basely.   *stable / treated*

Sophocles. Pray you, tell me one thing truly: do you love her?

Petruchio. I would° I did not, upon that condition   *wish*

    I passed thee half my land.°   *I would give you half my land if I didn't (love her)*

Sophocles. It may be then   10
    Her modesty required a little violence?
    Some women love to struggle.
Petruchio. She had it,
    And so much that I sweat for't, so I did;
    But to no end.° I washed an Ethiop.[70]   *unsuccessfully*
    She swore my force might weary her, but win her
    I never could, nor should, 'til she consented;
    And I might take her body prisoner,
    But for her mind or appetite°—   *desire*
Sophocles. 'Tis strange.   20
    This woman is the first I ever read of
    Refused a warranted occasion,°   *legitimate (sexual) opportunity*
    And standing° on so fair terms.   *based*
Petruchio. I shall quit° her.   *requite, pay back*
Sophocles. Used you no more art?°   *craft, guile*
Petruchio. Yes, I swore unto her,
    And by no little ones,° if presently,   *oaths*
    Without more disputation on the matter,
    She grew not nearer to me and dispatched me
    Out of the pain I was (for I was nettled),°   *irritated*
    And willingly and eagerly and sweetly,   31
    I would to her chambermaid and, in her hearing,
    Begin her such a hunt's-up—[71]
Sophocles. Then she started?
Petruchio. No more than I do now. "Marry," she answered,
    If I "were so disposed," she "could not help it;
    But there was one called Jaques, a poor butler,
    One that might well content a single
      woman."°   *(she would do the same with the butler)*
Sophocles. And he should tilt her?°   *thrust at her (as in jousting); have sex with*
Petruchio. To that sense.° And last,   *(words) to that effect*
    She bade me yet these six nights look for nothing,   41
    Nor strive to purchase° it, but° fair "good night"   *obtain / nothing but*

70. An old European proverb for an impossible task: washing a black person white (Tilley E186).

71. "The Hunt Is Up" is an old tune sung or played to awaken huntsmen or newlyweds in the morning. Petruchio is threatening to go to Maria's chambermaid and (sexually) rouse her if Maria will not be his willing sex partner (Williams 699).

And so "good morrow," and a kiss or two
To close my stomach,° for her vow had   *(i.e., to stave off my appetite)*
   sealed it,
And she would keep it constant.°   *her word faithfully or constantly*
Sophocles. Stay ye,° stay ye.   *wait*
   Was she thus when you wooed her?
Petruchio. Nothing, Sophocles,
   More keenly eager. I was oft afraid
   She had been light and easy;° she would shower   *promiscuous*
   Her kisses so upon me.   51
Sophocles. Then I fear
   Another spoke's i'th' wheel.°   *(i.e., she is getting sex elsewhere)*
Petruchio. Now, thou hast found° me.   *you understand*
   There gnaws my devil,° Sophocles. O patience   *that's what worries me*
   Preserve me, that° I make her not example   *heaven help me if*
   By some unworthy way, as flaying° her,   *skinning*
   Boiling, or making verjuice,[72] drying her—
Sophocles. I hear her.   59
Petruchio. Mark her then, and see the heir°   *offspring*
   Of spite° and prodigality° She has studied   *frustration / wastefulness*
   A way to beggar's° both, and, by this hand,   *impoverish us*
   She shall be, if I live, a doxy.°   *prostitute*

     [Enter] Maria at the door, and servant and woman.

Sophocles. Fie, sir.
Maria. [To woman] I do not like that dressing;° 'tis too poor.   *outfit*
   Let me have six gold laces, broad and massy,°   *large and weighty*
   And betwixt ev'ry lace a rich embroidery.
   Line the gown through with plush° perfumed,   *rich fabric*
     and purfle°   *adorn the border*
   All the sleeves down with pearl.
Petruchio. What think you, Sophocles?   70
   In what point° stands my state° now?   *situation / estate, affairs*
Maria. [To servant] For those hangings,°   *tapestries*
   Let 'em be carried where I gave appointment;°   *I told you to*
   They are too base° for my use; and bespeak °   *cheap / order*

72. Sour fruit such as the crab-apple is crushed and the juice extracted and
formed into a liquor, "verjuice." Fletcher wrote in *The Island Princess* (c. 1620),
women "love a man that crushes 'em to verjuice" (3.2.45).

New pieces, of° the civil wars of France.   *representing*
Let 'em be large and lively, and all silk-work,
The borders gold.
Sophocles. Ay, marry, sir, this cuts it.°   *this is too much*
Maria. [To servant] That fourteen yards of satin, give my
    woman.°   *serving woman*
  I do not like the color; 'tis too civil.°   *sober, grave*
  There's too much silk i'th' lace, too. Tell the Dutchman   81
  That brought the mares, he must with all speed send me
  Another suit° of horses and, by all means,   *set*
  Ten cast° of hawks for th' river. I much care not   *pairs*
  What price they bear,° so° they be   *what they cost / as long as*
    sound° and flying,   *healthy*
  For the next winter I am for the country
  And mean to take my pleasure. Where's the horseman?
Petruchio. She means to ride a great-horse.°   *war horse, charger*
Sophocles. With a side-saddle?   89
Petruchio. Yes, and she'll run a-tilt° within this twelvemonth.   *joust*
Maria. [To servant] Tomorrow I'll begin to learn. But pray, sir,
  Have a great care he be an easy doer;°   *gentle, easy to ride*
  'Twill spoil a scholar° else.   *someone trying to learn*
Sophocles. An easy doer? Did you hear that?
Petruchio. Yes, I shall meet her morals°   *sink to her ethical behavior*
  Ere it be long, I fear not. *[Exeunt servant and woman.]*
Maria. [To Sophocles] O, good morrow.
Sophocles. Good morrow, lady. How is't now?
Maria. Faith, sickly.   99
  This house stands in an ill air°—   *is in a place with a bad atmosphere*
Petruchio. Yet more charges!°   *expenses*
Maria. Subject to rots and rheums.° Out on't.   *wasting diseases and colds*
    'Tis nothing
  But a tiled fog.°   *a fog covered with tiles*
Petruchio. What think you of the lodge° then?   *cottage*
Maria. I like the seat,° but 'tis too little. Sophocles,   *location*
  Let me have thy opinion; thou hast judgment.
Petruchio. 'Tis very well.
Maria. What if I pluck it down
  And build a square° upon it, with two courts° *quadrangle / enclosed areas*
  Still rising from° the entrance?   *elevated from the level of*
Petruchio. And i'th' midst   111
  A college for young scolds.°   *women of abusive speech*

Maria. And to the southward
    Take in a garden of some twenty acres
    And cast it of the Italian fashion, hanging?
Petruchio. And you could cast yourself so,°   *have a statue of yourself cast*
    too. Pray, lady,
    Will not this cost much money?
Maria. Some five thousand;
    Say six. I'll have it battled,° too.   *crenellated, decorated with a notched wall*
Petruchio. And gilt?° Maria,   *decorated with gold*
    This is a fearful course you take. Pray, think on't.   121
    You are a woman now, a wife, and his
    That must in honesty and justice look for
    Some due obedience from you.
Maria. That bare word
    Shall cost you many a pound more, build upon't.°   *count on it*
    Tell me of due obedience! What's a husband?
    What are we married for? To carry sumpters?°   *packs, saddlebags*
    Are we not one piece° with you, and as worthy   *equal; one flesh*
    Our own intentions as you yours?   130
Petruchio. Pray, hear me.
Maria. Take two small drops of water, equal weighed:
    Tell me which is the heaviest, and which ought
    First to descend in duty.
Petruchio. You mistake me.
    I urge not service from you, nor obedience
    In way of duty, but of love and credit.°   *trust*
    All I expect is but a noble care
    Of what I have brought you and of what I am
    And what our name° may be.   *reputation*
Maria. That's in my making.   141
Petruchio. 'Tis true, it is so.
Maria. Yes, it is, Petruchio,
    For there was never man, without our° molding,   *(i.e., women's)*
    Without our stamp upon him and our justice,
    Left anything three ages° after him   *generations*
    Good and his own.°   *maintained wealth or property for three generations*
Sophocles. Good lady, understand him.
Maria. I do too much, sweet Sophocles. He's one   149
    Of a most spiteful self-condition,°   *disposition*
    Never at peace with anything but age,°   *old age*
    That has no teeth left to return his anger.
    A bravery° dwells in his blood yet of abusing   *defiant boasting*

His first good wife; he's sooner fire° than
    powder,°   *quicker to burn than gunpowder*
And sooner mischief.°   *(than gunpowder)*
Petruchio. If I be so sudden,°   *rash, impetuous, explosive*
    Do not you fear me?
Maria. No, nor yet care for you
    And, if it may be lawful, I defy you.
Petruchio. Does this become you° now?   *do you credit*
Maria. It shall become me.   161
Petruchio. Thou disobedient, weak, vainglorious woman,
    Were I but half so willful as thou spiteful,
    I should now drag thee to thy duty.
Maria. Drag me?
Petruchio. But I am friends again. Take all your pleasure.
Maria. Now you perceive him,° Sophocles.   *see how he acts*
Petruchio. I love thee
    Above° thy vanity, thou faithless creature.   *despite*
Maria. [*To Sophocles*] Would I had been so happy, when I married,   170
    But to have met an honest man like thee
    (For I am sure thou art good, I know thou art honest),
    A handsome hurtless° man, a loving man,   *harmless*
    Though never a penny with him,° and these eyes,   *even if penniless*
    That face, and that true heart. Wear this for my sake. [*She gives
      him a ring.*]
    And, when thou think'st upon me, pity me.
    I am cast away.°   *discarded, wasted on a man like him*
              Exit Maria.
Sophocles. Why, how now, man?
Petruchio. Pray, leave me, and follow your advices.°   *plans*
Sophocles. The man's jealous.   180
Petruchio. I shall find a time, ere it be long, to ask you
    One or two foolish questions.
Sophocles. I shall answer
    As well as I am able, when you call me.
    [*Aside*] If she mean true, 'tis but° a little killing;   *only*
    And if I do not venture it's—Farewell, sir. *Exit Sophocles.*
Petruchio. Pray, farewell. Is there no keeping
    A wife to one man's use? No wintering
    These cattle without straying?° 'Tis hard dealing,   *(their straying)*

Very hard dealing, gentlemen,° strange   *(addressing the audience)*
   dealing.
Now, in the name of madness, what star[73] reigned,   191
What dog-star, bull or bear-star, when I married
This second wife, this whirlwind, that takes all
Within her compass?° Was I not well warned   *reach*
(I thought I had,° and I believe I know it)   *had been*
And beaten to repentance in the days
Of my first doting? Had I not wife enough
To turn my love to? Did I want° vexation   *lack*
Or any special care to kill my heart?
Had I not ev'ry morning a rare° breakfast   *special*
Mixed with a learnèd lecture of ill language   201
Louder than Tom o' Lincoln,[74] and at dinner
A diet of the same dish? Was there evening
That e'er passed over us without "thou knave"
Or "thou whore" for digestion? Had I ever
A pull° at this same poor sport° men run   *turn, attempt / (i.e., sex)*
   mad for
But like a cur° I was fain° to show my teeth first   *snappish dog / obliged*
And almost worry° her? And did   *seize by the throat with the teeth (as a dog)*
   heaven forgive me
And take this serpent from me? And am I
Keeping tame devils now again? My heart aches.   210
Something I must do speedily. I'll die,
If I can handsomely,° for that's the way   *in good style*
To make a rascal° of her. I am sick,   *knave*
And I'll go very near it, but I'll perish.°   *I'll come as close to it or die trying*
            Exit.

73. Petruchio refers to several constellations here. The star Sirius in the constellation of the Greater Dog is called the "dog-star," and was considered responsible for the "dog-days" of midsummer. Taurus and Ursa Major are the "bull" and "bear" constellations.

74. The great bell installed in Lincoln Cathedral in 1611. This portion of the play could not have been written earlier than that date. Fletcher also mentions "Tom o' Lincoln" in his play *The Night Walker*.

[ACT 3], SCENE 4

Enter Livia, Byanca, Tranio, and Rowland.

Livia. Then I must be content, sir, with my fortune.
Rowland. And I with mine.
Livia.   I did not think a look
    Or a poor word or two could have displanted°   *uprooted*
    Such a fixed constancy, and for your end,° too.   *on your behalf*
Rowland. Come, come, I know your courses. There's your
       gewgaws,°   *trinkets, baubles*
    Your rings and bracelets and the purse you gave me.
    The money's spent in entertaining you
    At plays and cherry gardens.
Livia. There's your chain, too.   10
    But, if you'll give me leave, I'll wear the hair° still;   *(in a locket)*
    I would yet remember you.
Byanca. Give him his love,° wench.   *love-gift?*
    The young man has employment for't.
Tranio. Fie, Rowland.
Rowland. You cannot "fie" me out a hundred pound
    With this poor plot. *[Aside]* Yet let me ne'er see day
      more°   *never see another day (die)*
    If something do not struggle strangely in me.
Byanca. Young man, let me talk with you.
Rowland. Well, young woman.   20
Byanca. This was your mistress once.
Rowland. Yes.
Byanca. Are ye honest? I see you are young and handsome.
Rowland. I am honest.
Byanca. Why, that's well said. And there's no doubt your judgment
    Is good enough and strong enough to tell you
    Who are your foes and friends. Why did you leave her?
Rowland. She made a puppy° of me.   *fool, inexperienced young man*
Byanca. Be that granted.
    She must do so sometimes, and oftentimes;   30
    Love were too serious else.°   *otherwise*
Rowland. A witty woman.
Byanca. Had you loved me—
Rowland. I would I had.

Byanca. —and dearly,
      And I had loved you so—you may love worse, sir.
      But that is not material.°   *to the point*
Rowland. [Aside] I shall lose.°   *(the bet not to fall in love again)*
Byanca. Some time or other, for variety,
      I should have called you fool or boy, or bid you   40
      Play with the pages,° but have   *young male servants, (i.e., sent you away)*
         loved you still,
      Out of all question, and extremely, too.
      You are a man made to be loved.
Rowland. [Aside] This woman
      Either abuses° me or loves me dearly.   *deceives*
Byanca. I'll tell you one thing: if I were to choose
      A husband to my own mind, I should think
      One of your mother's making would content me,
      For, o'° my conscience, she makes good ones.   *on*
Rowland. Lady,   50
      I'll leave you to your commendations.°   *compliments*
      [Aside] I am in° again. The devil take their tongues. *(falling for it)*
Byanca. You shall not go.
Rowland. I will. Yet thus far, Livia:
      Your sorrow may induce me to forgive ye,
      But never love again. *[Aside]* If I stay longer,
      I have lost two hundred pound.
Livia.   Good sir, but thus much—
Tranio. [To Rowland] Turn, if thou be'st a man.
Livia. [To Rowland] But one kiss of you,   60
      One parting kiss, and I am gone, too.
Rowland. Come.
      I shall kiss fifty pound away at this clap.°   *at this one stroke*
               [He kisses Livia.]
      We'll have one more, and then farewell. *[He kisses Livia again.]*
Livia. Farewell.
Byanca. [To Rowland] Well, go thy ways. Thou bear'st a kind
      heart with thee.
Tranio. He's made a stand.°   *held his ground; has an erection*
Byanca. A noble brave young fellow,
      Worthy a wench indeed.   70
Rowland. I will; I will not. *Exit Rowland.*
Tranio. [To Livia] He's gone, but shot° again. Play you   *(with Cupid's arrow)*
      but your part

And I will keep my promise. Forty angels[75]
In fair gold, lady. Wipe your eyes; he's yours,
If I have any wit.
Livia.   I'll pay the forfeit.°   *amount of the lost wager*
Byanca. Come then, let's see your sister, how she fares now
     After her skirmish, and be sure Moroso
     Be kept in good hand.° Then all's perfect, Livia.   *under control*
                    Exeunt.

[ACT 3], SCENE 5

Enter Jaques and Pedro.

Pedro. O, Jaques, Jaques, what becomes° of us?   *will become*
     O my sweet master.
Jaques. Run for a physician
     And a whole peck of 'pothecaries,° Pedro.   *medical practitioners*
     "He will die, diddle, diddle, die" if they come not quickly.
     And bring all empirics straight, and
          mountebanks,°   *(both terms used for quacks)*
     Skilful in lungs and livers. Raise the neighbors
     And all the aqua-vitae° bottles   *strong alcoholic liquor used as restorative*
          extant.
     And O, the parson, Pedro, O, the parson,   9
     A little of his comfort, never so little.°   *as much as can be*
     Twenty to one you find him at the Bush;°   *a tavern*
     There's the best ale.
Pedro. I fly. *Exit Pedro.*

Enter Maria and servants carrying out household stuff and trunks.

Maria. Out with the trunks, ho.
     Why are you idle? Sirrah, up to th' chamber
     And take the hangings down, and see the linen
     Packed up and sent away within this half hour.
     What, are the carts come yet? Some honest body°   *good person*

75. A gold coin worth half a pound sterling, so called because it was stamped
with the angel Michael battling a dragon.

Help down° the chests of plate, and some the wardrobe.   *carry down*
    Alas, we are undone else.   20
Jaques. Pray, forsooth,
    And I beseech ye, tell me, is he dead yet?
Maria. No, but 'is drawing on.° Out with the   *close to death*
    armor.°   *suits of armor*
Jaques. Then I'll go see him.
Maria. Thou art undone then, fellow.
    No man that has been near him come near me.

Enter Sophocles and Petronius.

Sophocles. Why, how now, lady, what means this?
Petronius. Now, daughter, how does my son?°   *son-in-law*
Maria. Save all ye can, for heaven's sake.

Enter Livia, Byanca, and Tranio.

Livia. Be of good comfort, sister.   30
Maria. O, my casket.°   *jewel box*
Petronius. How does thy husband, woman?
Maria. Get you gone, if you mean to save your lives.
    The sickness°—   *plague*
Petronius. Stand further off, I prithee.
Maria. Is i'th' house, sir; my husband has it now.
    Alas he is infected and raves extremely.
    Give me some counsel, friends.
Byanca. Why, lock the doors up
    And send him in a woman to attend him.   40
Maria. I have bespoke° two women, and the city   *engaged*
    Hath sent a watch° by this time. Meat° nor money   *watchman / food*
    He shall not want,° nor prayers.   *lack*
Petronius. How long is't° since it first took him?   *has it been*
Maria. But within this three hours.

Enter watch.°   *watchman, sentinel*

I am frighted from my wits, my friends. —O, here's the watch.
[To the watch] Pray, do your office. Lock the doors up, friends.
And patience be his angel.°   *ministering spirit*
                    They lock the door.

Tranio. This comes unlooked for.°   *unexpected*

Maria. I'll to the lodge.° Some, that are kind and love me,   *cottage*
    I know will visit me.   51

Petruchio. Do you hear, my masters? *Petruchio [from] within.*
    Ho, you that lock the doors up.

Petronius. 'Tis his voice.

Tranio. Hold,° and let's hear him.   *quiet, wait a minute*

Petruchio. Will ye starve me here? Am I a traitor or an heretic?
    Or am I grown infectious?

Petronius. Pray sir, pray.

Petruchio. I am as well as you are, goodman°   *(lower rank than "gentleman")*
    puppy.

Maria. Pray, have patience. You shall want° nothing, sir.   *lack*

Petruchio. I want a cudgel° and thee, thou wickedness.   *club*

Petronius. [*To Maria*] He speaks well enough.   62

Maria. 'Had° ever a strong heart, sir.   *he had*

Petruchio. Will ye hear me? First, be pleased
    To think I know ye all, and can distinguish
    Ev'ry man's several° voice. You that spoke first   *individual*
    I know my father-in-law; the other, Tranio;
    And I heard Sophocles; the last, pray mark me,
    Is my damned wife Maria. Gentlemen,
    If any man misdoubt° me for infected,   *have fear for*
        [*Petruchio thrusts out his arm.*]
    There is mine arm: let any man look on't.   71

            Enter doctor and pothecary.°   *apothecary, dispenser of*
                                                              medicine

Doctor. Save ye, gentlemen.

Petronius. O welcome, doctor,
    Ye come in happy time. Pray, your opinion:
    What think you of his pulse?

Doctor. It beats with busiest°   *very fast*
    And shows a general inflammation,
    Which is the symptom of a pestilent° fever.   *infectious*
    Take twenty ounces° from him.   *bleed twenty ounces from him*

Petruchio. Take a fool!   80
    Take an ounce from mine arm and, Doctor
        Deuce-ace,°   *an unlucky throw of the dice*

I'll make a close-stool° of your velvet costard.[76]   *chamber pot*
'Death,° gentlemen, do ye make a May°-   *God's death (oath) / May-day*
    game on° me?   *of*
I tell ye once again, I am as sound,°   *healthy*
As well, as wholesome, and as sensible
As any of ye all. Let me out quickly
Or, as I am a man, I'll beat the walls down,
And the first thing I light upon shall pay for't.   *Exit doctor and
    pothecary.*

Petronius. Nay, we'll go with you, doctor.
Maria. 'Tis the safest. I saw the tokens,° sir.   *spots indicating plague*
Petronius. Then there is but one way.   91
Petruchio. Will it please ye open?
Tranio. His fit grows stronger still.
Maria. Let's save ourselves, sir. He's past all worldly cure.
Petronius. [To the watch] Friends, do your office.°   *duty*
    And what he wants, if money, love, or labor,
    Or any way may win it, let him have it.
    Farewell, and pray, my honest friends—
                    Exeunt, Manent° watchmen.   *remain*
Petruchio. Why, rascals.
    Friends, gentlemen, thou beastly wife, Jaques.   100
    None hear me? Who's at the door there?
1 Watchman. Think, I pray, sir,
    Whither ye are going,° and prepare yourself.   *(i.e., after your death)*
2 Watchman. These idle thoughts disturb you. The good gentlewoman,
    Your wife, has taken care ye shall want° nothing.   *lack*
Petruchio. The blessing of her grandam Eve light on her.
    Nothing but thin fig leaves, to hide her knavery.
    Shall I come out in quiet? Answer me,
    Or shall I charge° a fowling-piece,° and make   *load / light gun*
    Mine own way? Two of ye I cannot miss,   110
    If °I miss three. Ye come here to assault me.   *even if*
1 Watchman. There's onions° roasting for your sore, sir.   *(for a poultice)*
Petruchio. People,
    I am as excellent well, I thank heav'n for't,
    And have as good a stomach° at this instant—   *appetite*
2 Watchman. That's an ill sign.

---

76. "Velvet cap." The College of Physicians prescribed a purple gown and velvet
cap for members.

1 Watchman. Ay, he draws on;° he's a dead man.   *is dying*
Petruchio. And sleep as soundly. Will ye look upon me?
1 Watchman. Do ye want pen and ink?° While ye have   *(for a will)*
    sense, sir,
    Settle your state.°   *estate*
Petruchio. Sirs, I am as well as you are, or any rascal living.   121
2 Watchman. Would ye were, sir.
Petruchio. Look to yourselves, and, if ye love your lives,
    Open the door and fly° me, for I shoot else.°   *run away from / if you don't*
    I swear I'll shoot, and presently,° chain-bullets;[77]   *without delay*
    And under four I will not kill.°   *I'll kill at least four*
1 Watchman. Let's quit° him,   *leave*
    It may be it is a trick; he's dangerous.   128
2 Watchman. "The devil take the hindmost," I cry! *Exit watch running.*
Petruchio. Have among ye.°   *here I come*
    The door shall open, too. I'll have a fair shoot.°   *shot*

      Enter Petruchio with a piece,° and forces the door open.   *gun*

    Are ye all gone? Tricks in my old days, crackers°   *lies*
    Put now upon me? And by Lady Greensleeves?[78]
    Am I grown so tame after all my triumphs?
    But that° I should be thought mad if I railed   *were it not that*
    As much as they deserve against these women,
    I would now rip up,° from the primitive°   *expose / original, first*
      cuckold,
    All their arch° villainies and all their doubles,°   *principal / evasions*
    Which are more than a hunted hare° e'er thought on.   *rabbit*
    When a man has the fairest and the sweetest   140
    Of all their sex and, as he thinks, the noblest,
    What has he then? And I'll speak
      modestly:°   *moderately, without exaggeration*
    He has a quartern-ague,° that shall shake *fever that returns every fourth day*
    All his estate to nothing, never cured,

---

77. "Chain-bullets," or "chain-shot," is "a kind of shot formed of two balls, or half-balls, connected by a chain" (*OED*).

78. The central figure in the well-known ballad who "cast [her lover] off discourteously." Petruchio is speaking of Maria.

Nor never dying, has a ship[79] to venture
His fame and credit in, which, if he man° not   *provide sailors for*
With more continual labor than a galley,
To make her tith,° either she grows a tumbrel,°   *tight / barge*
Not worth the cloth she wears, or springs more leaks   149
Than all the fame of his posterity°   *forebears*
Can ever stop again. Out on 'em,
    hedgehogs.°   *prickly beasts (i.e., regardless of others' feelings)*
He that shall touch 'em has a thousand thorns
Runs through his fingers. If I were unmarried,
I would do anything below° repentance,   *short of*
Any base dunghill slavery, be a hangman,
Ere I would be a husband. O the thousand,
Thousand, ten thousand ways they have to kill us!
Some fall with too much stringing of the fiddles,[80]   158
And those are fools; some, that they are not suffered,°   *allowed (sex)*
And those are maudlin° lovers; some, like scorpions,   *tearful*
They° poison with their tails,°   *women / genitals (with venereal disease)*
    and those are martyrs;°   *(burning with venereal disease)*
Some die with doing good, those benefactors,
And leave 'em land to leap away;°   *squander through frivolity or sexual activity*
    some few,
For those are rarest, they are said to kill
With kindness and fair usage; but what they are
My catalogue discovers not, only 'tis thought
They are buried in old walls,° with their heels   *unconsecrated ground*
    upward.
I could rail° twenty days together now.   *rant*
I'll seek 'em out, and, if I have not reason,
And very sensible, why this was done,   170
I'll go a-birding yet,° and some shall   *continue hunting (for women)*
    smart° for't.   *get hurt*

                         Exit.

---

79. In this complicated passage Petruchio compares a wife to a "ship" in which
he will "venture" (hazard) his reputation. A ship, which if he does not work
as hard as a galley slave to make "tith" (tight), becomes either a "tumbrel"
("flat-bottomed boat" but derogatory; see 3.2.38) or a leaky vessel that lets
(sexual) fluids in.

80. Another use of the "fiddle" (female sex organs) and "fiddle-stick" (male sex
organs). Here a man may be worn out by attending too much to the fiddle and
its strings (Williams 478–80). Cf. 1.1.82; 1.4.13; 2.6.47; 3.1.77; and 4.1.135.

ACT 4, SCENE 1

Enter Moroso and Petronius.

Moroso. That I do love her is without all question;
    And most extremely, dearly, most exactly;
    And that I would even now, this present Monday,
    Before all others—maids, wives, women, widows,
    Of what degree or calling—marry her,
    As certain, too. But to be made a whim-wham,°   *fantastic object, trifle*
    A gimcrack,° and a gentleman o'the first   *fop; trifle*
       house,°   *highest rank (ironic)*
    For all my kindness to her—
Petronius. How you take it!°   *carry on*
    Thou get a wench, thou get a dozen
      nightcaps.°   *(threats of cuckoldry, see n. 54)*
    Wouldst have her come and lick thee like a calf   11
    And blow thy nose and buss° thee?   *kiss*
Moroso. Not so, neither.
Petronius. What wouldst thou have her do?
Moroso. Do as she should do:
    Put on a clean smock,° and to church and marry,   *undergarment*
    And then to bed, a God's name. This is fair play,
    And keeps the king's peace.° Let her leave   *public law and order*
      her bobs°   *tricks (sexual)*
    (I have had too many of them) and her quillets.°   *quibbles*
    She is as nimble that way as an eel,   20
    But in the way she ought,° to me especially,   *duty she owes*
    A sow° of lead° is swifter. *female pig; ingot / (made of the heaviest metal)*
Petronius. Quote° your griefs down.   *write*
Moroso. Give fair quarter.° I am old and crazy° *treatment, conditions / impaired*
    And subject to much fumbling,° I confess it;   *clumsiness*
    Yet something I would have that's warm, to
      hatch me.°   *make me young again*
    But understand me, I would have it so°   *so that*
    I buy not more repentance° in the bargain   *regret*
    Than the ware's° worth I have. If you allow me   *stuff or commodity is*
    Worthy° your son-in-law and your allowance,   *of sufficient merit to be*
    Do it a way of credit,° let me show so,   *reputably*
    And not be troubled in my visitations   32
    With blows and bitterness and downright railings,
    As if we were to couple like two cats

With clawing and loud clamor.

Petronius. Thou fond° man,   *foolish*
　Hast thou forgot the ballad "Crabbèd Age"?[81]
　Can May and January° match together,   *(i.e., young woman and old man)*
　And never a storm between 'em? Say° she abuse° thee; *suppose / scolds*
　Put case° she do.   *say, for the sake of argument*

Moroso. Well?   41

Petronius. Nay, believe she does.

Moroso. I do believe she does.

Petronius. And devilishly. Art thou a whit° the worse?   *at all*

Moroso. That's not the matter.°   *point*
　I know, being old, 'tis fit° I am abused;   *appropriate, to be expected*
　I know 'tis handsome,° and I know moreover   *deemed right*
　I am to love her for't.

Petronius. Now you come to me.°   *make sense*

Moroso. Nay, more than this: I find, too, and find certain,   50
　What gold I have, pearl, bracelets, rings, or
　　'ooches,°   *brooches set with gems*
　Or what she can desire, gowns, petticoats,
　Waistcoats, embroidered stockings, scarves,
　　cauls,° feathers,   *hooded caps or headdresses*
　Hats, five-pound garters, muffs, masks, ruffs and ribbons,
　I am to give her for't.

Petronius. 'Tis right, you are so.

Moroso. But when I have done all this and think it duty,
　Is't requisite another bore my nostrils?°   *trick or swindle me*
　Riddle me° that.   *solve that one for me*

Petronius. Go, get you gone, and dream   60
　She's thine within these two days, for she is so.
　The boy's beside the saddle.° Get warm broths   *everything is ready*
　And feed apace.° Think not of worldly business;   *eat a lot quickly*
　It cools the blood. Leave off your tricks,° they are   *mannerisms*
　　hateful,
　And mere forerunners of the ancient measures.°   *dances in the past*
　Contrive your beard o' the top cut, like verdugos;[82]

---

81. A ballad that begins, "Crabbèd age and youth cannot live together."

82. This grooming advice is difficult to understand, because Petronius is suggesting that Moroso cut his beard to resemble "verdugos," hangmen or executioners in both English and Spanish. The title page woodcut from *The Confession of Richard Brandon,* the executioner who dispatched Charles I, suggests a modest moustache and goatee.

It shows you would be wise. And burn your nightcap;
It looks like half a winding sheet,° and urges   *shroud*
From a young wench nothing but cold repentance.
You may eat onions, so° you'll not be lavish.°   *provided / excessive*

Moroso. I am glad of that.   71

Petronius. They purge the blood and quicken.°   *enliven*
But, after 'em, conceive° me, sweep° your mouth   *understand / cleanse*
And, where there wants° a tooth, stick in a clove.   *lacks*

Moroso. Shall I hope once again? Say't?°   *Sayest, do you say?*

Petronius. You shall, sir.
And you shall have your hope.

Moroso. Why, there's a match, then.

Enter Byanca and Tranio.

Byanca. [To Tranio] You shall not find me wanting. Get you gone.
Here's the old man. He'll think you are plotting else   80
Something against his new son.   *Exit Tranio.*

Moroso. [To Petronius] Fare you well, sir.   *Exit Moroso.*

Byanca. [Sings] And every buck had his doe
And every cuckold° a bell at his toe,   *man whose wife is unfaithful*
O, what sport should we have then, then, boys, then,
O, what sport should we have then.

Petronius. This is the spirit that inspires 'em° all.   *(women)*

Byanca. Give you good ev'n.

Petronius. A word with you, sweet lady.

Byanca. I am very hasty,° sir.   *in a hurry*

Petronius. So you were ever.   91

Byanca. Well, what's your will?

Petronius. Was not your skilful hand
In this last stratagem?° Were not your mischiefs   *device*
Eking° the matter on?   *urging*

Byanca. In's° shutting up? Is that it?   *in his (Petruchio's)*

Petronius. Yes.

Byanca. I'll tell you.

Petronius. Do.

Byanca. And truly.   100
Good old man, I do grieve exceeding much;
I fear too much.

Petronius. I am sorry for your heaviness.°   *sadness*
Belike° you can repent, then?   *perhaps*

Byanca. There you are wide,° too.   *wide of the mark*
    Not that the thing was done (conceive me rightly)
    Does any way molest° me.   *upset, bother*
Petronius. What, then, lady?
Byanca. But that I was not in it, there's my sorrow, there.
    Now you understand me. For, I'll tell you,   110
    It was so sound a piece,° and so well carried,°   *plot / carried out*
    And, if you mark° the way, so handsomely,   *observe*
    Of such a height and excellence and art
    I have not known a braver;° for (conceive me)   *finer*
    When the gross fool her husband would be sick—
Petronius. Pray, stay.
Byanca. (Nay, good, your patience)—and no sense° for't,   *explanation*
    Then stepped your daughter in—
Petronius. By your appointment.°   *direction*
Byanca. I would it had, on that condition   120
    I had but one half-smock, I like it so well.[83]
    And, like an excellent cunning° woman, cured me   *(skilled in healing)*
    One madness with another, which was rare°   *uncommonly excellent*
    And, to our weak beliefs, a wonder.
Petronius. Hang ye.
    For surely, if your husband look not to ye,
    I know what will.
Byanca. I humbly thank your worship,
    And so I take my leave.
Petronius. You have a hand, I hear, too—   130
Byanca. I have two,° sir.   *(i.e., hands)*
Petronius. —In my young daughter's business.
Byanca. You will find there
    A fitter hand than mine to reach her frets
    And play down-diddle to her.°   *(see n. 80)*
Petronius. I shall watch ye.
Byanca. Do.
Petronius. And I shall have justice.
Byanca. Where?   139
Petronius. That's all one.°   *all the same (doesn't matter)*
    I shall be with you at a turn° henceforward.   *even with you*

---

83. "I wish it had. I would have given everything until I was left with half a chemise to have had a part in it."

Byanca. Get you a posset,° too. And so good   *hot milk curdled with ale*
    ev'n, sir.

              Exeunt [severally].

[ACT 4, SCENE 2]

Enter Petruchio, Jaques, and Pedro.

Jaques. And, as I told your worship, all the hangings,
    Brass, pewter, plate, ev'n to the very looking-glasses.
Pedro. And that that hung for our defense, the armor,
    And the March-beer° was going, too.   *strong beer brewed in spring*
      O, Jaques,
    What a sad sight was that.
Jaques. Even the two roundlets°   *casks*
    (The two that was our hope) of muscatel,
    Better, ne'er tongue tripped over, those two
      cannons°   *(figurative) casks of wine*
    To batter brawn° withal at Christmas, sir,   *to take on roast pig*
    Ev'n those two lovely twins, the enemy   10
    Had almost cut off° clean.   *finished*
Petruchio. Go trim the house up
    And put the things in order as they were.
    I shall find time for all this. *Exeunt Jaques and Pedro.*
      Could I find her
    But constant any way, I had done my business.
    Were she a whore directly,° or a scold,°   *overtly / an abusive woman*
    An unthrift,° or a woman made to hate me,   *spendthrift*
    I had my wish, and knew which way to rein° her.   *control*
    But while she shows all these, and all their
      losses,°   *she does and doesn't show these flaws*
    A kind of linsey-woolsey mingled mischief[84]   20
    Not to be guessed at, and whether true or borrowed
    Not certain neither. What a hap° had I,   *fortune, luck*

---

84. "Linsey-woolsey" is a textile woven from a mixture of wool and flax, hence, a strange combination. Maria appears likewise composed of mischief and virtue.

Enter Maria.

And what a tidy fortune, when my fate
Flung me upon this bear-whelp.° Here she   *newborn bear (see n. 67)*
  comes.
Now, if she have a color,° for the fault is   *excuse*
A cleanly° one, upon my conscience,   *chaste, decent*
I shall forgive her yet, and find a something
Certain I married for, her wit. I'll mark her.

Maria. *[As to herself]* Not let his wife come near him in his sickness,
Not come to comfort him? She that all laws   30
Of heaven and nations have ordained his second,°   *assistant*
Is she refused? And two old paradoxes,[85]
Pieces° of five-and-fifty, without faith,°   *women / religion*
Clapped in upon him?° H'as a little pet,°   *put in with him / peevishness*
That all young wives must follow necessary,°   *necessarily*
Having their maidenheads—

Petruchio. *[Aside]* This is an axiom° I never heard before.   *proposition*

Maria. —or say rebellion,   38
If we durst be so foul, which two fair words,   *dare to be so insolent*
Alas, win us from° in an hour, an instant,   *deter us from (the insolence)*
We are so easy,° made him so forgetful   *docile*
Both of his reason, honesty, and credit,
As to deny his wife a visitation?
His wife that, though she was a little foolish,
Loved him—O heaven, forgive her for't—nay, doted,
Nay, had run mad, had she not married him.

Petruchio. *[Aside]* Though I do know this falser than the devil,
  I cannot choose but love it.

Maria. What do I know   49
But° those that came to keep him might have killed him?   *but that*
In what a case° had I been then? I dare not   *situation*
Believe him such a base debauched companion
That one refusal of a tender maid
Would make him feign this sickness out of need,
And take a keeper to him of fourscore°   *eighty years old*

---

85. Maria is talking about old women. The *OED* defines a sense of "paradox" as "a person or thing whose life or behavior is characterized by paradox . . . *spec.* one that exhibits some contradiction or conflict with preconceived notions of what is reasonable or possible," using this passage as the first example.

To play at billiards, one that mewed content
And all her teeth together.[86] Not come near him?

Petruchio. [Aside] This woman would have made a most rare Jesuit.[87]

She can prevaricate° on anything.   *equivocate*

There was not to be thought a way to save her,   60

In all imagination, beside this.

Maria. His unkind dealing, which was worst of all,

In sending, who knows whither,° all the plate   *where*

And all the household stuff, had I not crossed it,°   *thwarted it*

By a great providence° and my friends'   *foresight; divine intervention*
    assistance,

Which he will thank me one day for. Alas,

I could have watched° as well as they, have served   *taken care of, nursed*
    him

In any use better and willinger.°   *more willingly*

The law commands me do it, love commands me,

And my own duty charges me.   70

Petruchio. [Aside] Heav'n bless me.

And, now I have said my prayers, I'll go to her.

[To Maria] Are you a wife for any man?

Maria. For you, sir,

If I were worse, I were better.° That you are well,   *(for you)*

At least that you appear so, I thank heaven.

Long may it hold. And that you are here, I am glad, too.

But that you have abused me wretchedly,

And such a way that shames the name of husband,   79

Such a malicious mangy° way, so mingled   *contemptible*

(Never look strangely° on me; I dare tell you)   *wonderingly*

With breach° of honesty, care, kindness, manners—   *violation*

Petruchio. Holla,° you kick° too fast.   *stop / show your temper*

Maria. Was I a stranger?

Or had I vowed perdition° to your person?   *harm*

Am I not married to you? Tell me that.

Petruchio. I would I could not tell you.

---

86. "A nurse of eighty to play billiards, one who lost her sense of pleasure (sexual?) at the same time that she lost all of her teeth."

87. Jesuits, members of the Roman Catholic Society of Jesus, were associated with equivocation, saying something that seems one thing and means another. The phrase means "a fine liar."

Maria. Is my presence,
     The stock I come of, which is worshipful°—   *honorable*
     If I should say "right worshipful," I lied not;   90
     My grandsire was a knight—
Petruchio. O'the shire?°   *representing a shire in parliament, not chosen for valor*
Maria. ˙A soldier,
     Which none of all thy family e'er heard of,°   *could boast of*
     But one conductor of thy name,° a grazier°   *ancestor / one who feeds cattle*
     That ran away wi'th' pay.° Or am I grown,   *with the payroll*
     (Because I have been a little peevish to you,
     Only to try° your temper) such a   *test*
          dog-leech°   *veterinarian; medical quack*
     I could not be admitted to your presence?
Petruchio. If I endure this, hang me.   100
Maria. And two death's heads,°   *skulls*
     Two Harry-groats that had their faces
          worn,°   *coins with the face of Henry VIII worn (i.e., the nurses)*
     Almost their names away, too.
Petruchio. Now, hear me, for I will stay no longer.
Maria. This you shall:°   *you shall stay and hear me out*
     However you shall think to flatter me
     For this offence, which no submission
     Can ever mediate° for, you'll find it so,   *atone*
     Whatever you shall do by intercession,°   *entreaty*
     What you can offer, what your land can purchase,   110
     What all your friends or families can win,
     Shall be but this: not to forswear° your knowledge,   *deny*
     But ever to forbear it.° Now, your will, sir.   *but never to do it anymore*
Petruchio. Thou art the subtlest° woman, I think, living;   *most cunning*
     I am sure, the lewdest.° Now be still, and   *most wicked, most lascivious*
          mark me.
     Were I but any way addicted° to the devil,   *devoted*
     I should now think I had met a playfellow
     To profit by, and that way° the most learnèd   *(i.e., in the way of evil)*
     That ever taught° to murmur. Tell me, thou,   *was trained*
     Thou most poor, paltry, spiteful whore—do you cry?   120
     I'll make you roar, before I leave.
Maria. Your pleasure.°   *as you wish*
Petruchio. Was it not sin enough, thou
          fruiterer°   *one who deals in fruit (as Eve did an apple)*
     Full of the fall thou eat'st, thou devil's broker,
     Thou seminary of all sedition,°   *begetter of the seed of all rebellion, strife*

Thou sword of vengeance with a thread hung o'er us,[88]
Was it not sin enough and wickedness
In full abundance, was it not vexation
At all points, *cap-à-pie?*° Nay, I shall   *"head to foot"*
    pinch° you   *blame; torment*
Thus like a rotten rascal to abuse   130
The name of heaven, the tie of marriage,
The honor of thy friends, the expectation
Of all that thought thee virtuous, with rebellion,
Childish and base rebellion? But continuing
After forgiveness, too, and worse, your mischief?
And against him, setting the hope of heaven by
And the dear reservation° of his honor,   *preservation*
Nothing above ground° could have won to hate thee?   *on earth*
Well, go thy ways.°   *go ahead in your ways*
Maria. [*Going*] Yes.   140
Petruchio. You shall hear me out first.
    What punishment mayst thou deserve, thou thing,
Thou idle thing of nothing, thou pulled° primrose   *plucked*
That two hours after art a weed and withered,
For this last flourish° on me? Am I one,   *embellishment of your trick*
Selected out of all the husbands living,
To be so ridden by a tit of ten-pence?°   *cheap whore*
Am I so blind and bed-rid? I was mad
And had the plague and no man must come near me?   149
I must be shut up, and my substance 'bezzled,° *possessions embezzled*
And an old woman watch me?
Maria. Well, sir, well,
    You may well glory° in't.   *gloat*
Petruchio. And when it comes to opening,° 'tis my   *revealing everything*
    plot.°   *plan*
I must undo° myself, forsooth. Dost hear me?   *explain*
If I should beat thee now as much may be,
Dost thou not well deserve it, o'° thy conscience?   *on, in*
Dost thou not cry "Come beat me"?

---

88. A reference to the legend of the Sword of Damocles. Damocles, a flatterer
of Dionysus II of Syracuse, noted how wonderful it must be to be the king.
Dionysus offered to trade places with Damocles, but when he did, Damocles
noticed, amid the luxury, a sword suspended over his head by a single horsehair.
Damocles then begged to return to his former position.

Maria. I defy you.

> And, my last loving tears, farewell. The first stroke,   160
> The very first you give me, if you dare strike—
> (Try me, and you shall find it so) for ever,
> Never to be recalled (I know you love me,
> Mad 'til you have enjoyed me) I do turn
> Utterly from you. And what man I meet first,
> That has but spirit to deserve a favor,
> Let him bear any shape, the worse the better,
> Shall kill you and enjoy me. What I have said
> About your foolish sickness, ere you have me
> As you would have me, you shall swear is certain,   170
> And challenge any man that dares deny it,
> And in all companies approve my actions.
> And so farewell for this time. *Exit Maria.*

Petruchio. Grief go with thee.

> If there be any witchcrafts, herbs, or potions,
> Saying my prayers backward,° fiends or fairies,   *as in casting a spell*
> That can again unlove me,° I am made.°   *make me fall out of love / a success*

Exit.

[ACT 4, SCENE 3]

Enter Byanca and Tranio.

Tranio. Mistress, you must do it.

Byanca. Are the writings ready I told you of?

Tranio. Yes, they are ready, but to what use I know not.

Byanca. You're an ass. You must have all things construed.°   *explained*

Tranio. Yes, and pierced,° too, or I find little   *understood (with sexual pun)*
     pleasure.

Byanca. Now, you are knavish. Go to.° Fetch   *(expression of impatience)*
     Rowland hither° presently.   *here*
   Your twenty pound° lies bleeding else.   *(i.e., Tranio's wager with Rowland)*
     She is married
   Within these twelve hours, if we cross° it not.   *thwart*
     And see the papers of one size.°   *see to it that the papers are all of the same size*

Tranio. I have° ye.   *understand*

Byanca. And for disposing of 'em—   11

Tranio. If I fail you, now I have found the way,° use   *figured out the plot*
    martial law
  And cut my head off with a hand-saw.
Byanca. Well, sir, Petronius and Moroso I'll see sent for.
    About your business, go.
Tranio. I am gone. *Exit Tranio.*
Byanca. Ho, Livia.

Enter Livia.

Livia. Who's that?
Byanca. A friend of yours. Lord, how you look now,
    As if you had lost a carrack.°   *large trading ship*
Livia.   O, Byanca, I am the most undone, unhappy woman.   21
Byanca. Be quiet, wench. Thou shalt be done and done
    And done and double done, or all shall split[89] for't.
    No more of these minced° passions; they are   *affected*
      mangy°   *contemptible*
    And ease° thee of nothing but a little wind;°   *relieve / fart*
    An apple will do more. Thou fear'st Moroso.
Livia. Even as I fear the gallows.
Byanca. Keep thee there still.°   *stay that way*
    And you love Rowland? Say.
Livia. If I say not, I am sure I lie.   30
Byanca. What wouldst thou give that woman,
    In spite of all his° anger and thy fear   *(Moroso's)*
    And all thy father's policy, that could
    Clap° ye within these two nights quietly   *put*
    Into a bed together?
Livia. How?
Byanca. Why, fairly,
    At half-sword,° man and wife. Now the red   *close quarters*
      blood° comes.   *blush*
    Ay, marry, now the matter's changed.
Livia. Byanca, methinks you should not mock me.   40

---

89. "Break open (as a ship)." Williams (1290) also calls "split" allusive to the violence of "the case of ruptured virginity." He provides this example, with parallel nautical imagery, from Henry Glapthorne's *Albertus Wallenstein* (1639): "The virgin lady's sometimes fearful; fears / A man of war shall board her, least his charge / Should make her keel split" (34).

Byanca. Mock a pudding,°   nonsense
    I speak good honest English, and good meaning.
Livia. I should not be ungrateful to that woman.
Byanca. I know thou wouldst not. Follow but my counsel
    And, if thou hast him not, despite of fortune,
    Let me never know a good night more. You must
    Be very sick o'th' instant.°   suddenly
Livia. Well, what follows?
Byanca. And in that sickness send for all your friends,
    Your father, and your fever,° old Moroso;   affliction
    And Rowland shall be there, too.   51
Livia. What of these?
Byanca. Do you not twitter° yet? Of this shall follow   tremble with excitement
    That which shall make thy heart leap and thy lips
    Venture as many kisses as the merchants
    Do dollars° to the East Indies. You   English name for peso, or piece of eight
        shall know all,
    But first walk in and practice. Pray, be sick.
Livia. I do believe you, and I am sick.
Byanca. So, to bed, then, come. I'll send away your servants,   59
    Post° for your fool° and father. And good fortune,   quickly / (Moroso)
    As we mean honestly, now strike an
        upshot.°   the last shot in archery, ending
                Exeunt.

[ACT 4, SCENE 4]

Enter Tranio and Rowland.

Tranio. Nay, o' my conscience, I have lost my money.
    But that's all one.° I'll never more persuade   all the same (doesn't matter)
        you.
    I see you are resolute, and I commend you.
Rowland. But did she send for me?
Tranio. You dare believe me?
Rowland. I cannot tell. You have your ways for profit
    Allowed you, Tranio, as well as I
    Have (to avoid 'em) fear.
Tranio. No, on my word, sir, I deal directly with you.

Enter servant [of Petronius].

Rowland. How now, fellow? Whither post you so fast?   10
Servant. O, sir, my master; pray, did you see my master?
Rowland. Why your master?
Servant. Sir, his jewel—
Rowland. With the gilded button?
Servant. My pretty mistress Livia—
Rowland. What of her?
Servant. Is fallen sick o'th' sudden—
Rowland. How, o'th' sullens?°   a state of gloomy ill humor (he mishears)
Servant. O'th' sudden, sir, I say, very sick.
Rowland. It seems she hath got the toothache with raw apples.   20
Servant. It seems you have got the headache. Fare you well, sir.
        You did not see my master?
Rowland. Who told you so?
Tranio. [*To servant*] No, no, he did not see him.
Rowland. [*To servant*] Farewell, blue-bottle.°   (reference to blue uniform)
                        Exit Servant.
        What should her sickness be?
Tranio. For you, it may be.
Rowland. Yes, when my brains are out, I may believe it;
        Never before, I am sure. Yet I may see her;
        'Twill be a point of honesty.°   decency, courtesy
Tranio. It will so.   31
Rowland. It may be not, too. You would fain be fing'ring
        This old sin-off'ring of two hundred,° Tranio.   (i.e., the wager)
        How daintily° and cunningly you drive me   neatly
        Up like a deer to th' toil.° Yet I may leap it°   net / leap over the net
        And what's the woodman° then?   hunter
Tranio. A loser, by you. Speak, will you go or not? To me 'tis equal.
Rowland. Come, what goes less?°   What about a smaller bet?
Tranio. Nay, not a penny, Rowland.
Rowland. Shall I have liberty of conscience   40
        Which, by interpretation, is ten kisses?
        Hang me if I affect° her. Yet it may be   love
        This whoreson manners° will require a   detestable courtesy
            struggling°   grappling
        Of two-and-twenty or, by'rlady, thirty.°   (kisses)
Tranio. By'rlady, I'll require my wager° then,   call in my bet
        For, if you kiss so often and no kindness,°   encouragement
        I have lost my speculation.° I'll allow you—   the money I bet

Rowland. Speak like a gamester now.

Tranio. It may be, two.

Rowland. Under a dozen, Tranio, there's no setting.°   *the bet is off*

    You shall have forty shillings; wink at small faults.   51

    Say I take twenty; come, by all that's honest,

    I do it but to vex her.

Tranio. I'll no by-blows.°   *side-blows, thus, no side bets*

    If you can love her, do. If you can hate her,

    Or any else that loves you—

Rowland. Prithee, Tranio—

Tranio. Why, farewell, twenty pound. 'Twill not undo me.

    You have my resolution.

Rowland. And your money   60

    Which, since you are so stubborn, if I forfeit,

    Make me a Jack-o'-Lent,[90] and break my shins

    For untagged points and counters.°   *laces without tags and tokens (worthless)*

        I'll go with you.

    But if thou get'st a penny by the bargain—

    A parting kiss is lawful?

Tranio. I allow it.

Rowland. Knock out my brains with apples. Yet a bargain.

Tranio. I tell you, I'll no bargains. Win and wear it.[91]

Rowland. Thou art the strangest fellow.

Tranio. That's all one.°   *all the same (doesn't matter)*

Rowland. Along, then. Twenty pound more, if thou dar'st,   71

    I give her not a good word.

Tranio. Not a penny. *Exeunt.*

[ACT 4, SCENE 5]

Enter Petruchio, Jaques, and Pedro.

Petruchio. Prithee, entreat her come. I will not trouble her

    Above° a word or two. *Exit Pedro.* Ere I endure   *more than*

    This life, and with a woman, and a vowed one°   *one committed*

---

90. A straw figure, or puppet, set up to be beaten and pelted with stones during Lent. It was burned on or before Easter.

91. "Win it and wear it" (proverb, Tilley W408).

To all the mischiefs she can lay upon me,
I'll go to plough° again and eat leek-porridge.   *work the land*
Begging's a pleasure to't,° not to be   *compared to it*
  numbered.°   *calculated*
No, there be other countries,° Jaques, for me.   *regions*
And other people, yea and other women:
If I have need, "here's money," "there's your ware,"°   *merchandise*
(Which is fair dealing). And the sun, they say,   10
Shines as warm there as here, and 'til I have lost
Either myself or her, I care not whether,°   *which*
Nor which first—
Jaques. Will your worship hear me?
Petruchio. And utterly outworn the memory°   *forgotten*
  Of such a curse as this, none of my nation
  Shall ever know me more.
Jaques. Out, alas, sir, what a strange way do you run?
Petruchio. Any way, so I outrun this rascal.°   *rogue (Maria)*
Jaques. Methinks now,   20
  If your good worship could but have the patience—
Petruchio. The patience, why the patience?
Jaques. Why, I'll tell you. Could you but have the patience—
Petruchio. Well, the patience.
Jaques. To laugh at all she does or, when she rails,° *rants*
  To have a drum beaten o'th' top o'th' house,
  To give the neighbors warning of her 'larum,°   *alarm, call to arms*
  As I do when my wife rebels—
Petruchio. Thy wife?   29
  Thy wife's a pigeon° to her, a mere slumber;   *sweetheart; simpleton*
  The dead of night's not stiller.°   *quieter*
Jaques. Nor an iron mill.
Petruchio. But thy wife is certain.°   *faithful*
Jaques. That's false doctrine.
  You never read of a certain° woman.   *wholly trustworthy*
Petruchio. Thou know'st her way.°   *ways; vagina*
Jaques. I should do, I am sure.
  I have ridden it night and day, this twenty year.
Petruchio. But mine is such a drench of
  balderdash,°   *drink of a jumbled mixture of liquors*
  Such a strange-carded° cunningness,°   *poorly prepared (as wool) / artfulness*
  the rainbow,
  When she° hangs bent in heaven, sheds not   *(the rainbow, goddess Iris)*
  her colors

    Quicker, and more, than this deceitful woman   42
    Weaves in her dyes of wickedness.

Enter Pedro.

    What says she?
Pedro. Nay, not a word, sir. But she pointed to° me,   *directed*
    As though she meant to follow. Pray, sir, bear it
    Easy° as you may. I need not teach your worship   *as easily as*
    The best man hath his crosses.° We are all mortal.   *trials, afflictions*
Petruchio. *[To Jaques]* What ails the fellow?
Pedro. And no doubt she may, sir.   50
Petruchio. What may she? Or what does she? Or what is she?
    Speak and be hanged.
Pedro. She's mad, sir.
Petruchio. Heaven continue it.
Pedro. Amen, if 't be his° pleasure.   *its (i.e., heaven's)*
Petruchio. How mad is she?
Pedro. As mad as heart can wish, sir. She has dressed herself
    (Saving your worship's reverence)[92] just i'th' cut°   *fashion; whore*
    Of one of those that multiply i'th' suburbs°   *(i.e., prostitutes)*
    For single money,° and as dirtily.°   *small change / foully*
    If any speak to her, first she whistles,   61
    And then begins her compass° *to draw a circle to indicate how much she wants*
        with her fingers,
    And points to what she would have.
Petruchio. What new way's this?
Pedro. There came in master Sophocles—
Petruchio. And what did master Sophocles, when he came in?
    Get my trunks ready, sirrah; I'll be gone straight.

Enter Sophocles.

Pedro. He's here to tell you. She's horn-mad,° Jaques.   *stark mad*
[Exeunt Pedro and Jaques.]
Sophocles. Call ye this a woman?
Petruchio. Yes, sir, she is a woman.   70
Sophocles. Sir, I doubt it.

---

92. "Begging your pardon, sir." The phrase is used when the speaker is about to say something offensive.

Petruchio. I had thought you had made experience.°   *a rendezvous with her*
Sophocles. Yes, I did so, and almost with my life.
Petruchio. You rid° too fast, sir.   *rode*
Sophocles. Pray, be not you mistaken. By this light,
    Your wife is chaste and honest as a virgin,
    For anything I know. 'Tis true, she gave me a ring.
Petruchio. For rutting.°   *copulating*
Sophocles. You are much deceived still.
    Believe me, I never kissed her since, and now,   80
    Coming in visitation like a friend,
    I think she is mad, sir. Suddenly she started°   *recoiled*
    And snatched the ring away and drew her knife out,
    To what intent I know not.
Petruchio. Is this certain?
Sophocles. As I am here, sir.
Petruchio. I believe you honest and, pray, continue so.
Sophocles. She comes.

Enter Maria.

Petruchio. Now, damsel,
    What will your beauty do, if I forsake you?   90
            [She makes signs.°]   *gestures*
    Do you deal by signs and tokens? As I guess, then,
    You'll walk abroad this summer and catch captains,
    Or hire° a piece of holy ground i'th' suburbs   *rent*
    And keep a nest of nuns?°   *open a brothel*
Sophocles. O do not stir° her! You see in what a case she is?   *agitate*
Petruchio. She is dogged,°   *obstinate, like a dog*
    And in a beastly case, I am sure. I'll make her,
    If she have any tongue,° yet tattle.° Sophocles,   *power of speech / speak*
    Prithee, observe this woman seriously
    And eye° her well, and, when thou hast done, but°   *observe / only*
       tell me
    (For thou hast understanding) in what case   101
    My sense was when I chose this thing.
Sophocles. I'll tell you, I have seen a sweeter—
Petruchio. A hundred times, cry oysters.°   *selling oysters*
    There's a poor beggar wench about Blackfriars
    Runs on her breech,° may be an empress   *who is incontinent*
      to° her.   *compared to*
Sophocles. Nay, now you are too bitter.

Petruchio. Ne'er a whit, sir.

I'll tell thee, woman, for now I have day° to see thee   *clear light*
And all my wits about me, and I speak   110
Not out of passion neither (leave your mumping);°   *grimacing, moping*
I know you're well enough. *[Aside]* Now would I give
A million but to vex her. *[To Maria]* When I chose thee
To make a bedfellow, I took° more trouble°   *took on / vexation*
Than twenty terms° can come to: such a cause   *court sessions*
Of such a title, and so everlasting
That Adam's genealogy° may be ended   *(i.e., humankind)*
Ere any law find thee.° I took a leprosy;   *your case would be resolved by law*
Nay, worse, the plague; nay, worse yet, a possession,
And had the devil with thee, if not more;   120
And yet worse, was a beast, and like a beast
Had my reward, a jade° to fling my fortunes   *worn-out horse*
For who that had but reason to distinguish
The light from darkness, wine from water, hunger
From full satiety,° and fox from fern-bush   *satisfaction*
That would have married thee?
Sophocles. She is not so ill.⁶   *had*
Petruchio. She's worse than I dare think of. She's so lewd
No court is strong enough to bear her cause.°   *consider her case*
She hath neither manners, honesty, behavior,   130
Wifehood, nor womanhood, nor any moral
Can force me think she had a mother.° No,   *(i.e., was human)*
I do believe her steadfastly and know her
To be a woman-wolf by
   transmigration.°   *the passage of a soul at death to another life form*
Her first form was a ferret's underground;
She kills the memories° of men. *[Aside]*
   Not yet?°   *ruins the reputations / She's not upset yet?*
Sophocles. Do you think she's sensible of this?
Petruchio. I care not.
Be what she will, the pleasure I take in her   139
Thus I blow off.° The care I took to love her,   *blow to the winds, disown*
Like this point,° I untie, and thus I loose it.   *lace that holds up hose*
The husband I am to her, thus I sever.
[To Maria] My vanity, farewell. Yet, for° you have been   *since*
So near me as to bear the name of wife,
My unquenched charity shall tell you thus much:
(Though you deserve it well) you shall not beg.

What I ordained your jointure,° honestly   *marriage settlement*
    You shall have settled on you, and half my house.°   *estate*
    The other half shall be employed in prayers—
    That meritorious charge I'll be at° also—   *undertake*
    Yet to confirm ye Christian. Your apparel,   151
    And what belongs to build up such a folly,
    Keep, I beseech you; it infects our uses.°   *undertakings*
    And now I am for travel.
Maria. Now I love you.
    And, now I see you are a man, I'll talk to you
    And I forget your bitterness.
Sophocles. [To Petruchio] How now, man?
Petruchio. O Pliny,[93] if thou wilt be ever famous,
    Make but this woman all thy wonders.   160
Maria. Sure, sir,
    You have hit upon a happy course, a blessèd,
    And what will make you virtuous.
Petruchio. [Aside] She'll ship me.°   *send me away*
Maria. A way of understanding I long wished for.
    And, now 'tis come, take heed you fly not back,° sir.   *retreat*
    Methinks you look a new man to me now,
    A man of excellence, and now I see
    Some great design set in you. You may think now,   169
    (And so may most that know me) 'twere my part°   *role*
    Weakly to weep° your loss, and to resist° you,   *mourn / argue with*
    Nay, hang about your neck and, like a dotard,°   *one who foolishly dotes*
    Urge my strong tie° upon you. But I love you,   *(as your wife)*
    And all the world shall know it, beyond
        woman,°   *more than any other woman could*
    And more prefer the honor of your country
    Which chiefly you are born for, and may perfect,
    The uses you may make of other nations,
    The ripening of your knowledge, conversation,
    The full ability and strength of judgment,
    Than any private love or wanton kisses.   180
    Go, worthy man, and bring home understanding.
Sophocles. [Aside] This were an excellent woman to breed
        schoolmen.°   *scholars*

93. Pliny the Elder was the first-century author of *Natural History,* a compendi-
ous encyclopedia of learning and art. It included many natural wonders.

Maria. For, if the merchant through unknown seas plough
        To get his wealth, then, dear sir, what must you
        To gather wisdom? Go, and go alone,
        Only your noble mind for your companion.
        And, if a woman may win credit with you,
        Go far, too far you cannot, still the farther
        The more experience finds you; and go sparing,°   *travel cheaply*
        One meal a week will serve you, and one suit,°   *set of outer garments*
        Through all your travels, for you'll find it certain,   191
        The poorer and the baser you appear,
        The more you look through still.°   *your true value is evident; see clearly*
Petruchio. [*To Sophocles*] Dost hear her?
Sophocles. Yes.
Petruchio. What would this woman do, if she were suffered,°   *allowed*
        Upon° a new religion?   *to promulgate*
Sophocles. Make us pagans. I wonder that she writes not.
Maria. [*To Petruchio*] Then, when time
        And fullness of occasion have new-made you   200
        And squared° you from a sot into a   *regulated*
          signor,°   *blockhead to a gentleman*
        Or, nearer,° from a jade into a   *more to the point*
          courser,°   *worthless horse into a racehorse*
        Come home an agèd man, as did Ulysses,[94]
        And I, your glad Penelope.
Petruchio. That° must have as many lovers as I languages, *who (i e., Penelope)*
        And what she does with one i'th' day, i'th' night
        Undo it with another.
Maria. Much that way, sir.
        For in your absence it must be my honor,
        That that° must make me spoken of hereafter,   *that which*
        To have temptations (and no little ones)   211
        Daily and hourly offered me (and strongly),
        Almost believed against me, to set off
        The faith and loyalty of her that loves you.
Petruchio. [*To Sophocles*] What should I do?

94. Odysseus (Ulysses in Latin) is a hero of antiquity in Homer's *Odyssey*. His wife Penelope remained faithful to him, putting off her many suitors with the famous ploy of saying she would make her choice when she completed the piece she was weaving. She worked on the task by day but unraveled what she had done by night.

Sophocles. *[To Petruchio]* Why, by my troth, I would travel.
  Did not you mean so?
Petruchio. *[To Sophocles]* Alas, no, nothing less,° man.   *anything but*
  I did it but to try° her. She's the devil   *test*
  And now I find it, for she drives me. I must go.⁹⁵   220
  [Calling] Are my trunks down there, and my horses ready?
Maria. Sir, for your house, and if you please to trust me
  With that you leave behind—
Petruchio. *[Calling]* Bring down the money.
Maria. As I am able, and to° my poor fortunes,   *to the extent of*
  I'll govern as a widow.° I shall long   *(as Homer's Penelope did)*
  To hear of your well-doing and your profit,
  And when I hear not from you once a quarter
  I'll wish you in the Indies or Cathay,°   *China*
  Those are the climes must make you.°   *bring profit to you*
Petruchio. *[Calling]* How's the wind?   231
  [Aside] She'll wish me out o'th' world anon.°   *immediately; soon*
Maria. For France
  'Tis very fair. Get you aboard tonight, sir,
  And lose no time. You know "the tide stays° no man."   *waits for*
  I have cold meats° ready for you.   *provisions for travel, leftovers*
Petruchio. Fare thee well.
  Thou hast fooled me out o'th' kingdom with a vengeance,
  And thou canst fool me in again.
Maria. Not I, sir.   240
  I love you better. Take your time and pleasure.
  I'll see you horsed.
Petruchio. I think thou wouldst see me hanged, too,
  Were I but half as willing.
Maria. Anything
  That you think well of, I dare look upon.
Petruchio. You'll bear° me to the land's end, Sophocles,   *accompany*
  And other of my friends, I hope?
Maria. Nev'r doubt, sir.
  You cannot want° companions for your good.   *lack*
  I am sure you'll kiss me ere I go. I have business,   251
  And stay long here I must not.
Petruchio. Get thee going
  For if thou tarriest but another dialogue,°   *wait to talk more*

---

95. Petruchio refers to the proverb, "He must needs go that the Devil drives" (Tilley D278).

I'll kick thee to thy chamber.
Maria. Fare you well, sir.
    And bear yourself, I do beseech you once more,
    Since you have undertaken doing wisely,   258
    Manly and worthily; 'tis for my credit.°   *honor*
    And for those flying fames° here of your follies,   *rumors*
    Your gambols,° and ill breeding of your youth,   *merriments*
    For° which I understand you take this travel,   *because of*
    Nothing should make me leave you else; I'll deal
    So like a wife that loves your reputation
    And the most large addition° of your credit,°   *mark of honor / reputation*
    That those° shall die. If you want lemon-waters,   *(follies of youth)*
    Or anything to take the edge o'th' sea off,°   *deter sea-sickness*
    Pray, speak, and be provided.
Petruchio. Now, the devil,
    That was your first good master, show'r his blessing   270
    Upon you all. Into whose custody—
Maria. I do commit° your reformation.   *pray for*
    And so I leave you to your *stilo novo.*°   *"new style"*
               Exit Maria.
Petruchio. I will go. Yet I will not. Once more, Sophocles,
    I'll put her to the test.
Sophocles. You had better go.
Petruchio. I will go, then. Let's seek my father° out   *father-in-law*
    And all my friends, to see me fair aboard.
    Then, women, if there be a storm at sea
    Worse than your tongues can make, and waves more broken   280
    Than your dissembling faiths are, let me feel
    Nothing but tempests, 'til they crack my
        keel.°   *main structural element (ship)*
              Exeunt.

ACT 5, SCENE 1

Enter Petronius and Byanca, with four papers.

Byanca. Now, whether I deserve that blame you gave me,
    Let all the world discern, sir.
Petronius. If this motion
    (I mean, this fair repentance of my daughter)

    Spring from your good persuasion, as it seems so,

    I must confess I have spoke too boldly° of you,   *harshly*

    And I repent.

Byanca. The first touch° was her own,   *touch of repentance*

    Taken no doubt from disobeying you;

    The second I put to her, when I told her   10

    How good and gentle yet, with free contrition,

    Again you might be purchased.° Loving woman,   *won back*

    She heard me, and, I thank her, thought me worthy

    Observing° in this point. Yet all my counsel   *heeding*

    And comfort in this case could not so heal her

    But that° grief got his share, too, and she sickened.   *except*

Petronius. I am sorry she's so ill, yet glad her sickness

    Has got so good a ground.°   *foundation*

Enter Moroso.

Byanca. Here comes Moroso.

Petronius. [*To Moroso*] O, you are very welcome.   20

    Now you shall know your happiness.

Moroso. I am glad on't.

    What makes° this lady here?   *prepares*

Byanca. A dish for you, sir,

    You'll thank me for hereafter.

Petronius. True, Moroso.

    Go, get you in, and see your mistress.

Byanca. [*To Moroso*] She is sick, sir, but you may kiss her

      whole.°   *back to health; hole*

Moroso. How.

Byanca. Comfort her.   30

Moroso. Why am I sent for, sir?

Petronius. Will you in and see?

Byanca. May be she needs confession.

Moroso. By St. Mary,

    She shall have absolution then, and penance;

    But not above her carriage.°   *what her conduct warrants; ability*

Petronius. Get you in, fool. *Exit Moroso.*

Enter Rowland and Tranio.

Byanca. Here comes the other, too.

Petronius. Now, Tranio—

[To Rowland] Good ev'n to you, too, and you're welcome.   40
Rowland. Thank you.
Petronius. I have a certain daughter—
Rowland. Would you had, sir.°   *(taking "certain" to mean "faithful")*
Petronius. No doubt you know her well.
Rowland. Nor never shall, sir.
    She is a woman, and the ways into her
    Are like the finding of a certain path
    After a deep-fall'n snow.
Petronius. Well, that's by the by° still.   *beside the point*
    This daughter that I tell you of is fall'n   50
    A little crop-sick° with the dangerous surfeit°   *stomach disorder / excess*
    She took of your affection.
Rowland. Mine, sir?
Petronius. Yes, sir,
    Or rather, as it seems, repenting.
    And there she lies within, debating on't.
Rowland. Well, sir?
Petronius. I think 'twere well you would see her.
Rowland. If you please, sir.
    I am not squeamish of° my visitation.   *I do not shrink from*
Petronius. But this I'll tell you: she is altered much.   61
    You'll find her now another Livia.
Rowland. I have enough o'th' old, sir.
Petronius. No more fool
    To look gay babies in your eyes,[96] young Rowland,
    And hang about your pretty neck—
Rowland. I am glad on't,
    And thank my fates I have 'scaped such execution.°   *destructive effect*
Petronius. And buss° you 'til you blush again.   *kiss*
Rowland. That's hard, sir.   70
    She must kiss shamefully ere I blush at it;
    I never was so boyish. Well, what follows?
Petronius. She's mine now, as I please to settle° her,   *bestow*
    At my command, and where I please to plant° her;   *place, establish*
    Only she would take a kind of farewell of you,
    And give you back a wand'ring vow or two

---

96. "Babies" are the "small image of oneself reflected in the pupil of another's eye" (*OED*). Thus Petronius is saying to Rowland that Livia is no longer foolish enough to gaze lovingly into Rowland's eyes.

You left in pawn;° and two or three slight oaths   *as a pledge*
She lent you, too, she looks for.
Rowland. She shall have 'em
With all my heart, sir; and, if you like it better,   80
A free release in writing.
Petronius. That's the matter.°   *matter at hand*
And you from her shall have another,° Rowland,   *a similar release*
And then turn tail to tail,° and peace be with   *turn back on one another*
    you.
Rowland. So be it. Your twenty pound sweats, Tranio.
Tranio. 'Twill not undo me, Rowland. Do your worst.
Rowland. [*To Petronius*] Come, shall we see her, sir?
Byanca. Whate'er she says
You must bear manly, Rowland, for her sickness
Has made her somewhat tettish.°   *peevish, irritable*
Rowland. Let her talk   91
'Til her tongue ache, I care not. By this hand,

Enter Livia, sick, carried in a chair by servants. Moroso by her.

Thou hast a handsome face, wench, and a body
Daintily mounted. [*Aside*] Now do I feel an hundred
Running directly from me, as° I pissed it.   *as if*
Byanca. Pray, bear her softly. The least hurry, sir,
Puts her to much impatience.
Petronius. How is't, daughter?
Livia. O very sick, very sick! Yet somewhat   99
Better, I hope, a little lightsomer°   *more light-hearted*
Because this good man° has forgiven me.   *(Moroso)*
[*To Byanca*] Pray, set me higher. O my head.
Byanca. [*To Livia*] Well done, wench.
Livia. Father, and all good people that shall hear me,
I have abused this man perniciously.
Was never old man humbled so. I have scorned him
And called him nasty names. I have spit at him,
Flung candles' ends in's beard, and called him
    "harrow,"°   *heavy farm implement with iron teeth*
That must be drawn° to all he does;   *(as a harrow is drawn)*
    condemned° him,   *disdained*
For methought then he was a beastly fellow   110
(O God, my side) a very beastly fellow.

And gave it out his cassock was a barge-
cloth° *rough canvas used to cover a barge*
Pawned to his predecessor by a
sculler,° *laborer who propels a barge with oars (sculls)*
The man yet living. I gave him purging comfits,° *candied laxatives*
At a great christening once,
That spoiled his camlet° breeches, and one night *expensive, exotic fabric*
I strewed the stairs with peas, as he passed down,
And the good gentleman (woe worth me° for't) *I deserve woe*
Ev'n with his reverend head, this head of wisdom, 119
Told° two-and-twenty stairs, good and true, *counted*
Missed not a step and, as we say, verbatim° *precisely*
Fell to the bottom, broke his casting-bottle,° *(for sprinkling perfumes)*
Lost a fair toadstone° of some eighteen *stone supposedly produced by a toad*
shillings,
Jumbled his joints together, had two stools,° *bowel movements*
And was translated.° All this villainy *carried from himself*
Did I; I, Livia, I alone, untaught.
Moroso. And I, unasked, forgive it.
Livia. Where's Byanca?
Byanca. Here, cousin.
Livia. Give me drink. 130
Byanca. There.
Livia. Who's that?
Moroso. Rowland.
Livia. *[To Rowland]* O my dissembler, you and I must part.
Come nearer, sir.
Rowland. I am sorry for your sickness.
Livia. Be sorry for yourself, sir. You have wronged me,
But I forgive you. Are the papers ready?
Byanca. I have 'em here. Will't please you view 'em?
Petronius. Yes. 140
Livia. Show 'em the young man, too. I know he's willing
To shift his sails,° too. 'Tis for his more *change his course*
advancement.
Alas, we might have beggared° one another. *impoverished*
We are young both, and a world of children
Might have been left behind to curse our follies.
We had been undone, Byanca, had we married,
Undone for ever. I confess I loved him,
I care not who shall know it, most entirely;
And once, upon my conscience, he loved me.

But farewell that. We must be wiser, cousin.   150
Love must not leave us to the world.° Have you done?   *unprovided for*
Rowland. Yes, and am ready to subscribe.°   *sign*
Livia. Pray, stay then.
 Give me the papers and let me peruse 'em,
 And so much time as may afford a tear
 At our last parting.
Byanca. [To the men] Pray, retire, and leave her.
 I'll call you presently.
Petronius. Come, gentlemen.   159
 The shower must fall.°   *there will have to be weeping*
Rowland. Would I had never seen her. *Exeunt all but Byanca and Livia.*
Byanca. Thou hast done bravely,° wench.   *excellently*
Livia. Pray heaven it prove so.
Byanca. There are the other papers. When they come,
 Begin you first, and let the rest subscribe
 Hard° by your side. Give 'em as little light   *close*
 As drapers° do their wares.   *cloth dealers*
Livia. Didst mark Moroso,
 In what an agony he was, and how he cried most
 When I abused him most?   170
Byanca. That was but reason.°   *only right*
Livia. O what a stinking thief is this!
 Though I was but to counterfeit,° he made me   *pretending*
 Directly sick indeed. Thames Street[97] to him
 Is a mere pomander.
Byanca. Let him be hanged.
Livia. Amen.
Byanca. And lie you still, and once more to our business.
Livia. Call 'em in.
 Now if there be a power that pities lovers,   180
 Help now, and hear my prayers. *[Byanca calls.]*

   Enter Petronius, Rowland, Tranio, Moroso.

Petronius. [To Byanca] Is she ready?

97. In *The Scornful Lady,* Fletcher describes Thames Street as "stinking of pitch
[tar] and poor john [dried, salted fish]" (2.3.95). Thus Livia is complaining that
Moroso's body odors "make smelly Thames Street like an aromatic scent-ball
(pomander) in comparison."

Byanca. She has done her lamentations. Pray, go to her.

Livia. Rowland, come near me. And before you
      seal,°   *sign and affix your seal*
  Give me your hand. Take it again. Now kiss me.
  This is the last acquaintance we must have.
  I wish you ever happy. There's the paper.

Rowland. Pray, stay a little.

Petronius. Let me never live more,
  But I do begin to pity this young fellow.   190
  How heartily he weeps!

Byanca. [*To Rowland*] There's pen and ink, sir.

Livia. [*To Rowland*] Ev'n here, I pray you. 'Tis a little emblem
  How near you have been to me.

Rowland. [*Signing*] There.

Byanca. [*To Petronius and Moroso*] Your hands, too, as witnesses.

Petronius. By any means. [*To Moroso*] To th' book,° son.   *official document*

Moroso. With all my heart. [*Petronius and Moroso sign the first deed.*]

Byanca. [*To Rowland*] You must deliver° it.   *affirm*

Rowland. There, Livia, and a better love light on thee. I can no
    more.   200

Byanca. [*To Petronius and Moroso*] To this you must be witness, too.

Petronius. We will. [*Petronius and Moroso sign the second deed.*]

Byanca. Do you deliver it now.

Livia. Pray, set me up.
  There, Rowland, all thy old love back,° and may   *returned*
  A new to come exceed mine, and be happy.
  I must no more.

Rowland. Farewell.

Livia. A long farewell. *Exit Rowland.*

Byanca. Leave her, by any means, 'til this wild passion   210
  Be off her head. Draw all the curtains close.
  A day hence you may see her. 'Twill be better.
  She is now for little company.

Petronius. Pray, tend her.
  I must to horse straight. [*To Moroso*] You must needs along, too,
  To see my son° aboard. Were but his wife   *son-in-law (Petruchio)*
  As fit for pity as this wench, I were happy.

Byanca. Time must do that, too. Fare ye well. [*To Moroso*]
    Tomorrow
  You shall receive a wife to quit° your sorrow.   *pay you back for*
                            Exeunt.

[ACT 5], SCENE 2

Enter Jaques, Pedro, and porters with chest and hampers.

Jaques. Bring 'em away, sirs.

Pedro. Must the great trunks go, too?

Jaques. Yes, and the hampers. Nay, be speedy, masters.
     He'll be at sea before us else.

Pedro. O Jaques, what a most blessèd turn° hast thou!   *change of luck*

Jaques. I hope so.

Pedro. To have the sea between thee and this woman.
     Nothing can drown her tongue but a storm.

Jaques. By your leave,
     We'll get us up to Paris with all speed;   10
     For, on my soul, as far as Amiens
     She'll carry blank.⁹⁸ *[To porters]* Away to Lyon
         quay°   *wharf on the Thames*
     And ship 'em presently. We'll follow ye. *[Exeunt porters.]*

Pedro. Now could I wish her in that trunk.

Jaques. God shield,° man, I had rather have a bear in't.   *forbid*

Pedro. Yes, I'll tell ye,
     For, in the passage, if a tempest take ye,
     As many do, and you lie beating° for it,   *are striving against the storm*
     Then, if it pleased the fates, I would have the master,
     Out of a powerful providence, to cry   20
     "Lighten the ship of all hands, or we perish,"
     Then this° for one, as best spared, should by   *(the trunk with Maria)*
         all means
     Overboard presently.°   *be thrown overboard immediately*

Jaques. O'° that condition,   *on*
     So° we were certain to be rid of her,   *so long as*
     I would wish her with us. But believe me, Pedro,
     She would spoil the fishing on this coast forever,
     For none would keep her company but dog-fish,°   *small sharks*
     As currish as herself, or porpoises,

---

98. "As far away as Amiens she will be able to hit us." "Blank" is the term for
the white at the center of a target. This is why Jaques wants to travel "with all
speed."

    Made to all fatal uses. The two Fish Streets,⁹⁹ does not apply   30

Made to all fatal uses. The two Fish Streets,[99]   30
Were she but once arrived among the whitings,
Would sing a woeful *miserere*, Pedro,
And mourn in poor john,° 'til her memory   *dried, salted fish*
Were cast ashore again with a strong sea-breach.
She would make god Neptune° and his   *god of the sea*
     fire-fork,°   *trident*
And all his demigods and goddesses,
As weary of the Flemish channel,°   *channel between England and Belgium*
     Pedro,
As ever boy was of the school.° 'Tis certain,   *as weary as boys are of school*
If she but met him fair,° and were well   *Neptune in an equitable fight*
     angered,
She would break his godhead.   40
Pedro.   O her tongue, her tongue.
Jaques. Rather, her many tongues.
Pedro.   Or rather, strange tongues.
Jaques. Her lying tongue.
Pedro.   Her lisping tongue.
Jaques. Her long tongue.
Pedro.   Her lawless tongue.
Jaques. Her loud tongue.
Pedro.   And her liquorish°—   *lustful, tempting*
Jaques. Many other tongues, and many stranger tongues   50
     Than ever Babel¹⁰⁰ had to tell his ruins,
     Were women raised° withal; but never a true one.   *created*

Enter Sophocles.

Sophocles. Home with your stuff again; the journey's ended.°   *cancelled*
Jaques. What does your worship mean?
Sophocles. Your master, O Petruchio, O poor fellows.

99. In London Old and New Fish Streets were known for their taverns serving fish dinners. "Whitings" are a favorite food fish, but Maria would spoil the fishing and have fish dealers singing Psalm 51 that begins, *"Miserere mei Deus"* ("Have mercy upon me, O God"). They would be forced to eat "poor john" (dried, salted fish) until her memory were carried away by a violent breaker ("sea-breach").

100. As told in Genesis (11:1–9), the inhabitants of Babel decided to build a tower up to heaven, and God reacted by giving them diverse languages ("tongues") so that they could no longer communicate.

Pedro. O Jaques, Jaques.

Sophocles. O your master's dead.
> His body coming back. His wife, his devil,
> The grief of°—her—   *because of*

Jaques. Has killed him?   60

Sophocles. Killed him, killed him.

Pedro. Is there no law to hang her.

Sophocles. Get ye in
> And let her know her misery. I dare not,
> For fear impatience seize me, see her more.
> I must away again. Bid her for wifehood,
> For honesty, if she have any in her
> Ev'n to avoid the shame that follows her,
> Cry if she can. Your weeping cannot mend it.
> The body will be here within this hour, so tell her,   70
> And all his friends to curse her. Farewell, fellows. *Exit Sophocles.*

Pedro. O Jaques, Jaques.

Jaques. O my worthy master.

Pedro. O my most beastly mistress, hang her.

Jaques. Split her.°   *tear her apart*

Pedro. Drown her directly.

Jaques. Starve her.

Pedro. Stink upon her.

Jaques. Stone her to death. May all she eat be
> eggs,°   *thought to be an aphrodisiac*
> 'Til she run kicking-mad° for men.   *furious*

Pedro. And he,   81
> That man that gives her remedy,° pray heav'n   *satisfies her lust*
> He may ev'n *ipso facto*° lose his longings.   *"by that very fact"*

Jaques. Let's go discharge ourselves.° And he that   *fulfill our obligations*
> serves her,
> Or speaks a good word of her from this hour,
> A Sedgley° curse light on him, which is, Pedro,   *(town in Staffordshire)*
> "The fiend ride through him booted and spurred, with a scythe
> at's back." *Exeunt.*

[ACT 5], SCENE 3

Enter Rowland [with a paper] and Tranio stealing behind him.

Rowland. What a dull ass was I to let her go thus?
Upon my life, she loves me still. Well, paper,
Thou only monument of what I have had,
Thou all the love now left me, and now lost,
Let me yet kiss her hand,° yet take my leave   *(i.e., handwriting)*
Of what I must leave ever. Farewell, Livia,
O bitter words, I'll read ye once again,
And then forever study° to forget ye.   *strive*
                    [He reads.]
How's this? Let me look better on't. A
     contract?°   *(i.e., a marriage contract)*
—A contract, sealed and ratified.   10
Her father's hand set to it, and Moroso's.
I do not dream, sure. Let me read again. *[He reads.]*
The same still. 'Tis a contract!
Tranio. 'Tis so, Rowland,
And, by the virtue of the same, you pay me
An hundred pound tomorrow.
Rowland. Art sure, Tranio,
We are both alive now?
Tranio. Wonder not; ye have lost.
Rowland. If this be true, I grant it.   20
Tranio. 'Tis most certain.
There's a ring for you, too. You know it. *[Tranio gives Rowland
     a ring]*
Rowland. Yes.
Tranio. When shall I have my money?
Rowland. Stay° ye, stay ye. When shall I marry her?   *wait*
Tranio. Tonight.
Rowland. Take heed now
You do not trifle me. If you do,
You'll find more payment° than your money comes to.   *punishment*
Come, swear, I know I am a man, and find   30
I may deceive myself. Swear faithfully,
Swear me directly, am I Rowland?
Tranio. Yes.
Rowland. Am I awake?

Tranio. Ye are.
Rowland. Am I in health?
Tranio. As far as I conceive.
Rowland. Was I with Livia?
Tranio. You were, and had this contract.
Rowland. And shall I enjoy her?   40
Tranio. Yes, if ye dare.
Rowland. Swear to all these.
Tranio. I will.
Rowland. As thou art honest, as thou hast a conscience,
    As that may wring° thee if thou li'st: all these   *distress*
    To be no vision, but a truth, and serious.
Tranio. Then by my honesty and faith and conscience,
    All this is certain.
Rowland. Let's remove our places. Swear it again.
Tranio. I swear, 'tis true.   50
Rowland. I have lost° then, and heaven knows I am glad on't.   *(his bet)*
    Let's go, and tell me all, and tell me how,
    For yet I am a pagan° in it.   *ignorant (as one who doesn't know of religion)*
Tranio. I have a priest, too,
    And all shall come as even as two testers.°   *coins worth six pence*
                  Exeunt.

[ACT 5], SCENE 4

Enter Petronius, Sophocles, Moroso, and Petruchio
borne in a coffin [carried by servants].

Petronius. Set down the body, and one call her out.

Enter Maria in black and Jaques.

    You are welcome to the last cast° of your   *stroke, throw of the dice*
        fortunes.
    There lies your husband, there your loving husband;
    There he that was Petruchio, too good for ye.
    Your stubborn and unworthy way has killed him
    Ere he could reach the sea. If ye can weep,
    Now ye have cause, begin, and after death

Do something yet to th' world, to° think ye honest.   *to let them think*
  [Maria weeps.]
So many tears had saved him, shed in time.
And as they are (so° a good mind° go with 'em)   *as long as / thought*
Yet they may move compassion.   11
Maria. Pray ye all, hear me
  And judge me as I am, not as you covet,°   *desire (to think)*
  For that would make me yet more miserable.
  'Tis true, I have cause to grieve, a mighty cause,
  And truly and unfeignedly I weep it.
Sophocles. I see there's some good nature yet left in her.
Maria. But what's the cause? Mistake me not. Not this man,
  As he is dead, I weep for; heaven defend° it,   *forbid*
  I never was so childish, but his life.   20
  His poor unmanly wretched foolish life,
  Is that my full° eyes pity. There's my mourning.   *tearful*
Petronius. Dost thou not shame?°   *Aren't you ashamed?*
Maria. I do, and even to water,°   *weep*
  To think what this man was, to think how simple,°   *foolish*
  How far below a man, how far from reason
  From common understanding and all gentry,°   *qualities of a gentleman*
  While he was living here, he walked amongst us.
  He had a happy turn°—he died. I'll tell ye,   *stroke of good fortune*
  These are the wants° I weep for, not his person.   *losses*
  The memory of this man, had he lived   31
  But two years longer, had begot more follies
  Than wealthy autumn flies.° But let him   *abundant autumn begets flies*
    rest.
  He was a fool, and farewell he: not pitied,
  I mean, in way of life or action,
  By any understanding man that's honest,
  But only in's posterity, which I,
  Out of the fear his ruins° might outlive him   *the results of his poor behavior*
  In some bad issue,° like a careful woman,   *children*
  Like one indeed born only to preserve him,   40
  Denied him means to raise. *Petruchio rises out of the coffin.*
Petruchio. Unbutton me.°   *(suggesting he is stifling)*
  I vow, I die indeed else. O Maria,
  O my unhappiness, my misery.
Petronius. *[To Maria]* Go to him, whore. I swear, if he perish,
  I'll see thee hanged myself.
Petruchio. Why, why, Maria.

Maria. I have done my worst, and have my end.° Forgive me.   *am finished*
    From this hour make me what you please. I have tamed ye,
    And now am vowed your servant. Look not strangely,°   *perplexedly*
    Nor fear what I say to you. Dare you kiss me?   51
    Thus I begin my new love. *[They kiss.]*
Petruchio. Once again!
Maria. With all my heart, sir. *[They kiss.]*
Petruchio. Once again, Maria! *[They kiss.]*
    O gentlemen, I know not where I am.
Sophocles. Get ye to bed then; there you'll quickly know, sir.
Petruchio. [To Maria] Never no more your old tricks?
Maria. Never, sir.
Petruchio. You shall not need, for, as I have a faith,°   *belief*
    No cause shall give occasion.   61
Maria. As I am honest°   *chaste*
    And as I am a maid° yet, all my life   *virgin*
    From this hour, since ye make so free profession,°   *promise, vow*
    I dedicate in service to your pleasure.
Sophocles. Ay, marry, this goes roundly off.°   *has a fair conclusion*
Petruchio. Go, Jaques,
    Get all the best meat° may be bought for money,   *food*
    And let the hogsheads blood.° I am born   *open (as a vein) the beer kegs*
    again.
                        [Exit Jaques.]
    Well, little England, when I see a husband   70
    Of any other nation stern or jealous,
    I'll wish him but a woman of thy breeding,
    And if he have not butter to his bread
    'Til his teeth bleed,[101] I'll never trust my travel.

        Enter Rowland, Livia, Byanca, and Tranio, as from marriage.

Petronius. What have we here?
Rowland. Another morris,° sir, that you must pipe to.   *country dance*
Tranio. [To Petronius] A poor married couple desire an
    offering,° sir.   *peace; dowry*
Byanca. [To Petronius] Never frown at it.
    You cannot mend it now. There's your own hand,°   *signature*

101. In the early modern period it was thought that teeth bled, blackened, and
fell out from too much sugar, represented here by bread and butter.

And yours, Moroso, to confirm the bargain. *[She shows them*
   papers.]
Petronius. My hand?   81
Moroso. Or mine?
Byanca. You'll find it so.
Petronius. A trick, I swear, a trick.
Byanca. Yes, sir, we tricked ye.
Livia. Father.
Petronius. Hast thou lain with him? Speak!
Livia. Yes, truly, sir.
Petronius. And hast thou done the deed, boy?
Rowland. I have done, sir,   90
  That that will serve the turn,° I think.   *(i.e., consummated the marriage)*
Petruchio. A match, then!
  I'll be the maker-up° of this. Moroso,   *finisher*
  There's now no remedy, you see. Be willing,
  For, be or be not, he must have the wench.
Moroso. Since I am overreached,° let's in to dinner,   *out-smarted*
  And, if I can, I'll drink't away.
Tranio. That's well said.
Petronius. *[To Rowland]* Well, sirrah, you have played a trick.
  Look to't,   99
  And let me be a grandsire within's
    twelvemonth°   *grandfather within a year*
  Or, by this hand, I'll curtail half your fortunes.°   *cut half the dowry*
Rowland. There shall not want° my labor, sir; your money.   *lack*
  [To Tranio] Here's one° has undertaken.°   *(Livia) / agreed to pay the money*
Tranio. Well, I'll trust her,
  And glad I have so good a pawn.°   *guarantee (Livia?)*
Rowland. I'll watch ye.
Petruchio. Let's in, and drink of all hands,° and be jovial.   *drinks for everyone*
  I have my colt again, and now she carries.
  And gentlemen, whoever marries next,   109
  Let him be sure he keep him to his text.°   *follow the rules*
                     Exeunt.

EPILOGUE

The tamer's tamed, but so, as nor the men
Can find one just cause to complain of, when
They fitly do consider,° in their lives   *consider that*
They should not reign as tyrants o'er their wives.
Nor can the women from this precedent
Insult or triumph,° it being aptly meant   *glory or boast*
To teach both sexes due equality
And, as they stand bound, to love mutually.
If this effect, arising from a cause
Well laid and grounded, may deserve applause,   10
We something more than hope our honest ends
Will keep the men, and women, too, our friends.

F I N I S.